D1194689

mental retardation ·
the law ·
guardianship

the report of the project to examine
the legal aspects of guardianship
protection as it affects the welfare
of the mentally retarded – the project was
supported by Grant 566-32-2
National Welfare Grant
Department of National Health and Welfare

NATIONAL INSTITUTE ON
MENTAL RETARDATION

Sponsored by Canadian Association for the Mentally Retarded

The *guardianship and the law*
project of the National Institute
on Mental Retardation *sponsored by*
the Canadian Association for the Mentally Retarded

Director
Barry B. Swadron LL.B. LL.M. *of the Ontario and Prince Edward Island Bars*

Advisory Council
Donald E. Zarfas M.D. C.M. D.PSYCH. C.R.C.P.(C) F.A.A.M.D. *Chairman*
William A. Kirk M.A.
Siegfried J. Koegler M.D. D.C.H.(Eng.) C.R.C.P.(C)
His Honour Judge Garth H. F. Moore
G. Allan Roeher B.A. B.S.W. M.A. PH.D.
W. Moira Skelton B.A. M.S.W.
Anna Stevenson LL.B.

Consultants
J. Desmond Morton Q.C. M.A. LL.B. *of the Irish and Ontario Bars*
N. David Starkman LL.B. *of the Ontario Bar*

Research Associates
Patricia J. Peters B.A. LL.B.
Donald R. Sullivan B.A. LL.B.

mental retardation -

the law -

guardianship

Barry B. Swadron LL.B. LL.M.
and Donald R. Sullivan B.A. LL.B.

published by National Institute on Mental Retardation

through Leonard Crainford, Toronto

mental retardation ,

the law ,

guardianship

© Copyright all rights reserved

published by the National Institute on Mental Retardation
through
Leonard Crainford Toronto

ISBN 0-9690438-3-X
Library of Congress Catalogue Card number 72-79669

designed by Leslie Smart
printed by Macdonald-Downie Limited

text set in Times New Roman
titles in Clarendon

Distributed by National Institute on Mental Retardation
            York University Campus
            4700 Keele Street Downsview Toronto Canada

to the memory of

my dear father

GEORGE NATHAN SWADRON

a good friend

this book is dedicated

mental retardation ·
the law ·
guardianship

introduction

Foreword

mental retardation · the law · guardianship is based upon a study which represents the type of project activity undertaken by the National Institute on Mental Retardation. It brings together available knowledge and experience in the field of mental retardation as a foundation for action and implementation.

The General Assembly of the United Nations recently approved a declaration of general and special rights for mentally retarded persons, a document prepared and approved by the International League of Societies for the Mentally Handicapped. This declaration, referred to many times in this book, reflects a progressive philosophy and a more enlightened attitude toward a group of the populace which has been viewed in a negative and inferior light for centuries.

The declaration parallels unprecedented world-wide action which seeks to provide services at the community level in contrast to the disposition of the problem by hiding the individual at home or transferring him to a large and remote institution.

Our ability to provide all necessary help in keeping retarded people in their home communities is only possible through the provision of necessary protection where and when needed. Their human rights and their privileges must not be restricted. We must convert the words of the declaration of the United Nations and the International League of Societies for the Mentally Handicapped into realistic action. The bridge between the words and the action is *guardianship*.

Not all persons classified as mentally retarded or handicapped need guardianship in the legal sense. All need a friend who cares. Some can cope with the existing legal, economic and social systems. Others could do so with a one-to-one helping relationship using existing provisions. Some need very special protection against possible deprivation, injury, abuse and injustice by society.

This book is designed to provide the necessary information and guidelines, by way of example, for parents, legal and social counsellors, agencies and governments to develop new or to adapt existing laws, services and practices to accommodate the needs of the mentally handicapped without deprivation of legitimate opportunities and human rights accorded other members of society.

It is both a reference book and a proposed master plan. It will help the individual legal and social counsellor to plan and to advise realistically on behalf of his client; it will keep the legislator up to date on statutory provisions; it will assist the financial counsellor or estate advisor to make correct decisions; and will enable the program planner to develop a personal guardianship service which will accommodate the total life needs of the individual.

The National Institute on Mental Retardation is planning program models for personal guardianship. The results of these efforts will complement this study.

G. ALLAN ROEHER
Director
National Institute on Mental Retardation

introduction

The rights of the mentally retarded are receiving increasing recognition. On October 24, 1968, the International League of Societies for the Mentally Handicapped pronounced the Declaration of General and Special Rights of the Mentally Retarded. The entire Declaration is reproduced as *Appendix A* to this volume.

At that time – and it is not too many years ago – when many of the mentally retarded were committed to mental institutions there to stay lengthy periods and often for life, the indications for protection were not so evident as they are today. The needs of the retardate were seen as no more than for food, shelter, clothing and basic care. For these needs, the superintendent of the institution was looked upon as the "guardian". Those of the retarded who lived at home were sheltered within the safety of their families or managed to struggle in communities, some of which were more understanding than others. Life was not so complex as it is now.

With the movement towards community programs, institutionalization is rapidly being relegated to a lesser role in the overall system of caring for the retarded. Of those who were once considered sure candidates for admission to institutions for the retarded, fewer and fewer are being so placed. Even with respect to those who are admitted to "mental hospital schools" or "training schools for the retarded", the likelihood is that such will be no more than a relatively minor episode in their "treatment plan".

Emphasis on community programs – considered by most, if not all, as an inherent good – has carried with it a situation which finds increasing numbers of disabled persons being maintained in the community, some of them chronically disabled. The complexities of life in this day and age tend to make their community existence more pronounced than it was in years gone by.

> "In modern times, with the spread of literacy, normal adults are able to understand and exercise their rights of choice more fully. Young people now choose their occupations or professions, their spouses, and the locations of their homes more independently of the traditions of their particular families. All of these changes make more conspicuous persons who cannot learn to read or who cannot understand fully the free decisions which other people make on their own behalf. Thus, a mild or even moderate degree of mental retardation which might have passed unnoticed in a simpler social system or in societies in which the 'extended family' is larger and more comprehensive, to-day presents a handicap to which the principle of complementation must be applied. This is particularly so as we promote a greater degree of integration of the retarded into normal community life."[1]

There is ample evidence that the protection of the retarded in the community is less than adequate. Crises arise from time to time with which they cannot cope, nor can it reasonably be expected that they could. As matters now stand, failure to cope sometimes allows no alternative but institutionalization.

The more fortunate of the retarded will have parents who help them along. A parent is a natural guardian to his or her child. Yet, the parents will not always be available. It is reported that the mortality rate is being reduced in some countries among infants and children with profound and severe mental retardation, with the consequence that greater numbers of them are outliving their parents.[2]

A parent is quick to recognize that he will eventually die and chances are good that the retarded son or daughter will survive him. "What will happen to my retarded son or daughter when I die?" is a question that was, and still is, posed with such frequency that it actually had a direct bearing upon the creation of the Project which led to the writing of this book. The real concern of a parent of a

References for Introduction are on page 9.

1

retarded person is demonstrated in the following account which appeared in a Toronto daily newspaper.[3]

"X-ray pioneer shoots son, wife, self in mercy killings
MONTCLAIR, N.J. (UPI) – Police yesterday said a physician who pioneered the x-ray treatment for cancer shot himself to death Sunday after killing his wife and mongoloid son in what a suicide note called mercy killings.

Dr. J. Thompson Stevens, 79, found dead in his bed, explained in the note that his wife was being treated for throat cancer and he was being treated for emphysema and that he felt both would die soon.

The note said his 49-year-old mongoloid son would have no surviving member of the family to care for him."

While few cases are so dramatic, the worry of the parent has an understandable reality which naturally intensifies as he grows older and, at the same time, less likely able to care for his retarded issue.

In fact, the changing picture is reflected in a name change of the organization which sponsored this Project. The Canadian Association for Retarded Children was formed on January 31, 1958. On April 26, 1969, it became the Canadian Association for the Mentally Retarded. "The primary reason for changing the name was a feeling on the part of the membership that the name implied that retarded remained 'eternal children'. As the Association moved out of operating schools, its focus shifted to sheltered workshops and residences reflecting the fact that the children of the membership had become adults. There was a concomitant growth of interest in the subject of guardianship reflecting their growing acceptance of the inevitable need for someone else to care for their retarded offspring."[4]

This work is the result of a Project established to study a concept of "guardianship" as a vehicle to protect the retarded in contemporary society.

Resulting from extensive thought and deliberation, the following is an excerpt from the statement of the "Purpose and Significance of the Project".

"In the light of the movement away from institutionalization of the retarded and the generally changing complexion of services provided for them, the problem of the adequacy of current laws emerges as a critical issue. It should be determined whether or not current laws offer an orderly system of personal and estate supervision as it would be required with more and more of the retarded living in the community.

The project will attempt to design and recommend a system of guardianship to suit the needs of the mentally retarded which will take into account the protection of both their personal well-being and their estates. Pertinent laws and practices thereunder in all Canadian provinces will be examined.

Should current laws be capable of accommodating an appropriate scheme of guardianship, the project will outline how such a scheme could best fit into the present context of the law and propose any necessary amendments. In the alternative that a sound scheme cannot properly operate under current laws, principles for new legislation will be formulated on a basis that will be universally adaptable to any of the provinces in Canada.

Issues which would have to be settled and resolved include: the criteria for, and nature of, guardianship; the manner and forum of decision of the need for guardianship; procedures for determination; and the identity, powers and duties respectively of the guardian and the ward.

Particular attention will be directed to developments in other jurisdictions, especially the United Kingdom and the United States, with respect to new laws and plans embracing guardianship."

The word "guardianship" has lent itself to various meanings both in common usage and in legal terminology. Taken in its broad sense, "guardianship" conveys the concept of providing protection, in one form or another, to maintain one's well-being. In terms of law, "guardianship" has been described as a "legally recognized relationship between a specified competent adult and another specified person, the 'ward' who, because of his tender age or because of some significant degree of mental disability, judicially verified, is considered to lack legal capacity to exercise fully some or all of the rights pertaining to adults generally in the country of which he is a citizen. The guardian is specifically charged with protecting the ward's interests and, for certain purposes, exercising essential rights on his behalf."[5]

The goal of new programs for the retarded is to achieve as normal a life as possible for the retarded person. This is referred to as the "normalization" principle.

> "The normalization principle means 'making available to the mentally retarded, patterns and conditions of everyday life which are as close as possible to the norms and patterns of the mainstream of society,' whether they are mildly or profoundly retarded, or whether they live in their own homes or group homes. Normalization means sharing a normal rhythm of the day, a normal routine of the week, including work and leisure time and the opportunity to undergo the normal developmental experiences of the life cycle."[6]

> • • •

> "Some of the retarded adults themselves definitely want to play a new role in society, to create a new image of themselves in their own eyes, in the eyes of their parents and in the eyes of the general public. This struggle for respect and independence is always the normal way to obtain personal dignity and a sense of liberty and equality."[7]

One of the most difficult problems we have encountered was the seeming conflict between two vital concepts.

The first is the concept that the retarded should, wherever possible, be treated in the same fashion as their normal counterparts. Indeed, this idea reflects the goal for which those concerned with the retarded and programming for them are constantly striving. That a retardate should be able to identify with the normal in everyday endeavors is a principle which is surely incontrovertible.

To allow the retardate to cope and live reasonably in the midst of other members of society sometimes requires a certain degree of supervision or protection. Forms of supervision and protection can be and are often offered in a simple and informal manner. Other forms of supervision and protection, however, require more than informality. The "helping" individual or body must, in given situations, be in a position to act in a manner which will be recognized as being effective by all concerned. Yet, the legal status of a "helper" may be no different than that of a mere stranger. In such case, the absence of any special relationship in law may render the help meaningless. Projecting a sound system which would create a legal relationship between the "helper" and the individual to be helped necessarily involves the planning of legislation which would give a special legal status to each.

The concept of granting a special legal status to certain retardates would seem to be a reasonably desirable and proper object. All the while, this second concept tends to set these retardates apart from their normal brethren. Indeed, there is no stronger way to set a class of persons apart from others than by law.

There is merit to the argument that the creation of a special legal status for the purpose of conferring rights can also carry with it, as part of the package, a restriction of rights. Such a restriction may not always be welcomed.

"Eluded searchers for 10 days
Retarded boy found on U.S. mountain

CASPER, Wyo. (UPI) – Searchers today found alive 9-year-old Kevin Dye, a mentally retarded epileptic boy who had been missing for 10 days in the wilds of Wyoming.

'He is alive and appears well and we've sent in a stretcher to bring him out,' Natrona County Sheriff Bill Estes said.

Searchers, using tracking dogs over a 30-square-mile area of Casper Mountain, sighted the boy and ran to him, Ellis said.

Since the boy has been missing, he had been seen several times but ran away from searchers.

In the pre-dawn hours today, U.S. Army experts used infra-red telescopes to try and catch Kevin.

The boy had been on the run since July 18 when he wandered away from his parents on an outing.

Searchers found leaves stacked in the shapes of hearts and crescents, stones piled in parallel lines and a ping pong paddle.

Thousands of searchers – expert mountain climbers and rescue specialists using bloodhounds, helicopters and horses – had tried to catch the boy.

Kevin's mother, Mrs. Phillip Dye, said the leaves arranged in the shape of a heart, crescents and the stones lined up were familiar.

'His favorite designs are the parallel lines and crescents,' she said.

Kevin is the only one of the Dye's four children suffering from mental retardation.

'I can't imagine why he is out there, unless he likes his freedom,' the boy's father said. 'He normally lives in a pretty restricted environment.' "[8]

Therein lies the conflict.

Who are the "retarded"? What is "mental retardation"? How is it measured? The problem of defining retardation has long occupied everyone working in the field. It is crucial in every attempt to understand the needs of those so labelled and in designing programs to meet these needs. Many definitions, founded in varied measurement concepts, have been postulated. None seems yet to have gained universal support.

In the past, mental retardation was diagnosed almost solely upon the basis of intelligence tests designed to measure the ability to reason abstractly and to manipulate symbols.

More modern times have seen social adaptation taken into account as a factor additional to performance on intelligence tests. The American Psychiatric Association defines mental deficiency as:

". . . those cases presenting primarily a defect of intelligence existing since birth, without demonstrated organic brain disease or known pre-natal cause. . . . the degree of intelligence defect will be specified as *mild, moderate,* or *severe,* and the current IQ rating, with the name of the test used, will be added to the diagnosis. In general, *mild* refers to functional (vocational) impairment, as would be expected with IQs of approximately 70 to 85; *moderate* is used for functional impairment requiring special training and guidance, such as would be expected with IQs of about 50-70; *severe* refers to functional impairment requiring custodial or complete protective care as would be expected with IQs below 50. The degree of defect is estimated from other factors than merely psychological test scores, namely, consideration of cultural, physical and emotional determinants, as well as school, vocational and social effectiveness."

Departing from reliance upon performance on intelligence tests, the American

Association on Mental Deficiency couples social effectiveness and a broader view of intelligence.

> "Mental retardation refers to sub-average general intellectual functioning which originates during the developmental period and is associated with impairment in adaptive behavior."

We believe that the A.A.M.D. definition is the most appropriate for our purposes.

Where questions of treatment and habilitation arise, we note the school of thought which maintains that social adaptation is the crucial factor, and that performance on any psychological test should be a minor consideration. That argument proceeds on the concept that maladaptive behavior is the consequence of learning maladaptive behavior, and that appropriate behavior may be taught in the presence of even the most severe defect.

> "A physiological defect or a limitation in concept (intelligence) inferred from behavior (in a test situation) is usually given as an explanation for the difference between retarded and normal individuals' responses to the same situation. The behaviors rather than the concept should be the focus of investigation.
>
> It is right and proper to ask if there are patterns of learning that have led to a limited behavioral repertoire. On the basis of such an analysis, testable programs may be developed to determine whether new experiences may lead to the generation of the serviceable behavior not previously learned. The focus of interest is shifted from a search for 'intelligence' to a search for the conditions of 'intelligent behavior'."[9]

The Project was commenced in August, 1967.

In order to derive the benefit of a multi-disciplinary approach, the Project Director established an Advisory Council composed of a number of professionals in various fields. The following is a listing by profession, of the members of the Advisory Council:

D. E. Zarfas, M.D., C.M., D.PSYCH., C.R.C.P.(C), F.A.A.M.D.
Chairman, *psychiatrist*

W. R. Kirk, M.A.
psychologist

S. J. Koegler, M.D., D.C.H. (England), C.R.C.P. (C)
paediatrician

His Honour Judge G. H. F. Moore
County Court Judge

G. A. Roeher, B.A., B.S.W., M.A., PH.D.
rehabilitation specialist

Miss W. M. Skelton, B.A., M.S.W.
social worker

Mrs. A. Stevenson, LL.B.
lawyer

The Advisory Council met on numerous occasions over the years. Their counsel and wisdom has been superb. Special thanks are acknowledged to Dr. Don Zarfas, the Chairman – internationally renowned – whose personal sacrifices were evident throughout.

Howard E. Richardson, Jr., Assistant Director of the National Institute on Mental Retardation, has consistently been a stalwart source of advice and support.

Professor J. Desmond Morton, Q.C., M.A., LL.B., now of the Faculty of Law, University of Toronto, a member of the Irish and Ontario Bars, was appointed as a Consultant to the Project. His guidance, so kindly made available at every stage, has been of inestimable value. His keen approach was always to keep us on our toes. N. D. Starkman, LL.B, a Toronto lawyer, also was appointed a Consultant.

Materials and data were collected from numerous sources including statutes, regulations, judicial decisions, texts, journal articles, conference papers and the press.

Meetings were held with individuals and groups including professionals in the field and parents of the retarded, not only to obtain their ideas but to test our proposals with them.

Facilities of various types for the retarded were visited.

One of the mainstays of the Project was a survey of Canadian practitioners, conducted to learn of problems at the "grass roots" level.

An estimated 10,000 lawyers in Canada were sent individual letters. The form of the English and French versions are respectively reproduced as *Appendices B and C*.

Every member of the Canadian Association of Social Workers, estimated at over 3,000, was also circulated an individual letter, the form of which is reproduced as *Appendix D*.

The response from members of these two professions was overwhelming. A great deal of subsequent correspondence with these communicants was found to be necessary and desirable. Much was learned from them.

The Project Director visited a number of Canadian Provinces and States of the United States. These were selected carefully to obtain the greatest exposure to relevant programs which were either in operation or in embryo.

At the Symposium of the International League of Societies for the Mentally Handicapped, on "Legislative Aspects of Mental Retardation" held in Stockholm in 1967, the question of guardianship was briefly studied. The matter of guardianship was discussed again in the same year at Montpellier, France during a symposium of the First Congress of the International Association for the Scientific Study of Mental Deficiency.

In May, 1969, the same League convened a Symposium entitled "Guardianship of the Mentally Retarded". This International Symposium, held in San Sebastian, Spain, boasted representation from some twenty-four countries. The Project Director was fortunate to be selected as the delegate from Canada and, while there, was honored to be appointed a Member of the Drafting Committee on Procedures.

The purpose of the San Sebastian Symposium was to make a complete study of the problem of guardianship of the mentally retarded from the juridical, familial and social points of view.

In preliminary documentation preceding the Symposium in San Sebastian, it was noted that the word "guardianship" does not have the same meaning in all countries and in all legislation. Nonetheless, the problems of "guardianship" were considered to be common. The Symposium was intended to give all concerned the opportunity to exchange experiences and ideas, to work towards correct and effective solutions, and to find the juridical base which will best safeguard the rights of the mentally retarded while giving them the necessary protection.

The San Sebastian meeting was ably chaired by Padré José Equía. In his introductory speech to the Symposium, he made the following significant remarks.

"Within the problem of Mental Deficiency it is important to organise services and special Institutions but no less essential are the prospects open in the fields of prevention and rehabilitation. But it is my belief that for the mentally deficient persons alive today, and who will survive us, it is a vital question to rely on social-legal instruments that guarantee their rights and protect their persons. In every part of the world, parents are unanimously and urgently pleading for an immediate and concrete answer to the painful problem of their orphan children's future.

In spite of this uncertain panorama, I have reasons to feel optimistic. The competent studies made on this matter, the international concern shared by different voluntary and official organs, the Stockholm and Montpellier Symposia which have enabled us to have clear ideas on how to look into the question, and the presence here of qualified representatives from 24 countries, are many arguments in support of my confidence. I am certain that, apart from all ethnic, ideological or linquistic differences amongst us, we shall be able to create some principles of universal value in which guardianship will be framed, the kind of guardianship we are all looking forward to so much."

Needless to say, the assembly at San Sebastian represented a concentration of knowledge and experience in the field which had never been so great. Indeed, the thoughts expressed, views held and conclusions reached in San Sebastian have been fully considered and taken into account in writing this volume.

In conjunction with his attendance at the San Sebastian Symposium, the Project Director took the opportunity of visiting a number of European countries to examine at first hand the practical situation in matters under investigation.

England was chosen because of the common tendency of legislation in Canadian provinces to parallel that enacted by Westminster. There was also a particular interest to be explored in respect of the provisions relating to guardianship as contained in the *Mental Health Act, 1959.*

France was placed upon the itinerary because of a desire to look into a system of guardianship as it might be contained under a *Civil Code.* This was seen as important because of the significant number of Canadians also living subject to a *Civil Code.*

Belgium is the country of headquarters for the International League of Societies for the Mentally Handicapped and, as such, was an appropriate place to visit. In addition, the existence of para-governmental agencies providing services in Belgium was considered a matter worthy of note.

Denmark was felt an important country in which to seek consultation in that some insight could be gained into the all-important Scandinavian experience. Laws and social services in Scandinavia are, in many respects, considered to be more advanced than those in other countries and were viewed as essential of fairly intensive study.

Through the courtesy and assistance of the Minister of National Health and Welfare and the Minister of External Affairs, meetings and visits to facilities were arranged by the Canadian Embassies in each of these countries. A wealth of information and data was obtained from the European study tour and these have found their way into this document.

References to laws and practices in foreign countries appear in various portions of the text. These were sometimes obtained from the source. Frequently, reliance had to be placed upon textbooks, journal articles and other documents including correspondence. Certain of these materials were dated. Some had already been subject to the interpretation of others. In the result, we cannot vouch for the currency of all of the foreign systems mentioned, nor for their absolute accuracy. We have proceeded on the basis that there is value in the description of a concept not known to the Canadian scene.

Even with respect to Canadian legislative materials, problems may arise. The extent of statutory coverage and what is happening in practice may bear very little, if indeed any, relationship one to the other. Not infrequently, excellent programs are executed through a sound and competent administration working with a minimum, and perhaps a total absence of legislative tools. What might be considered exemplary legislation could, on the other hand, on the practical side represent an extremely poor program: for example, through lack of funds or staffing problems.

Detailed laws which exact standards so high – making them nearly impossible to achieve – may result in services being spread at such a remarkably thin level as to be negligible in value. Bare enabling legislation, without prescribing particulars, may permit a flexibility which allows the administrative authorities to do the best they are able without unduly structuring their efforts. A satisfactory balance should be achieved.

One of our greatest problems found in the collection of data was difficulty in finding statutory regulations. Unlike statutory enactments, they are not centrally published and consolidated in any systematic way. Regulations made under the authority of a statute generally have the same force of law as does the statute itself. The contents of the regulations are, therefore, equally and sometimes more significant than the terms of the legislation. Being in an era which has been referred to as one of "government by regulation", the uncertainty of knowing whether the search for regulations has been fail-safe, tends to place the conscientious legal investigator in a posture less secure than he might have hoped.

The hardship with respect to regulations is not to infer the existence of an entirely rosy picture in regard to the identification of pertinent legislative provisions, although the situation in this instance is somewhat more comfortable. Unless one actually works with the statutory programs constantly in a given jurdisdiction, he would – in all honesty – be bound to concede that his opinions are at best based upon what he has found and may be subject to correction in the light of what he has failed or neglected to find. Many of the areas under investigation could be described as "legal jungles" with legislative amendments coming "fast and furious" in a manner that to trace them meaningfully is no easy task. Readers of this document must, in all fairness, recognize these limitations.

Many fields of the law are embraced in this book and a number of issues considered are legally technical. The intention being to reach both those learned in the law and those lay to it, seldom was it a simple task to draw the line in respect of what should be included. While the state of the law on certain points is set forth in such a manner that the reader can know what the legal posture is in a question confronting him, caution should be taken generally in relying upon what is contained herein. In many instances, each case turns on its particular merits. The factual circumstances of any given situation frequently vary from another. There can be no substitute for competent legal advice and, where indicated, such guidance should always be sought. The need to seek legal advice is reinforced by the fact that laws dealing with the subject matter discussed in the chapters which follow are, to a great extent, rapidly being modified. Modification of laws is only to be expected in topics as these wherein further knowledge and techniques are coming at an accelerated pace.

In the final Chapter, entitled "Guardians and Guardianship", we propose a scheme which would legislate a framework within which individual "wards" would receive the support and protective services they require. This is guardianship in its special legal sense and there is a definite need for it.

There are other means of providing support and protection to the retarded – "guardianship" in the general or broad sense. The format of this volume is geared to making these means known so that the benefits will accrue to the retarded on a collective or individual basis. We have set forth the laws and practices thereunder in many substantive fields as they apply to the retarded. While this has been done primarily to assess the existing situation, it has been done also with a view to collecting the information to make it available as a resource document for those interested in a particular retarded person or the mentally retarded in general. Families and friends of, and those working with, the retarded on a day-to-day basis, should be knowledgeable about these matters. If there is to be a scheme of guardianship in the special legal sense, guardians will have to be endowed with this knowledge as well.

Many areas examined disclose a need for amendment of laws or modifications in practice. Whenever a law is amended or a practice is modified in the proper direction, it will benefit the retarded as a group. We have, accordingly, made numerous recommendations which are directed to those in a position either to press for change or to effect it.

Barry B. Swadron
Project Director

Many people were of invaluable assistance in the preparation of this book and the research and investigations upon which it is based. At the risk of omitting some, we are pleased to acknowledge our gratitude to the following

Grace Aikman, Dick Allen, Gloria Bullen, John Crawford, Fagie Fox, William D. Gray, Cyril Greenland, Dottie Hewson, Bob Hodgson, Jennifer James, Larry Kent, Jack McKnight, Phil Roos, Doug Rutherford and members of the staffs of the Canadian Association for the Mentally Retarded and the National Institute on Mental Retardation.

References

1 INTERNATIONAL LEAGUE OF SOCIETIES FOR THE MENTALLY HANDICAPPED, CONCLUSIONS: SYMPOSIUM ON GUARDIANSHIP OF THE MENTALLY RETARDED 10 (1969) (hereinafter cited as SYMPOSIUM).

2 *Ibid.*

3 *Toronto Daily Star*, September 23, 1969, page 4.

4 Excerpt from a letter to the Project Director from Dr. G. Allan Roeher, Director of the National Institute on Mental Retardation, dated August 5, 1971.

5 SYMPOSIUM 9.

6 Nirje, Towards Independence, a paper prepared for the 11th World Congress of the International Society for Rehabilitation of the Disabled (Dublin, Ireland, 1969), at p. 3.

7 *Ibid.*, at p. 8.

8 *Toronto Daily Star*, July 28, 1971, page 1.

9 ULLMAN and KRASNER, A PSYCHOLOGICAL APPROACH TO ABNORMAL BEHAVIOR 566 (1969).

living
and
doing

living and doing

Introduction

There are a number of human endeavors considered in this chapter: residential settings; contracts; driving; voting; responsibility in tort; making a will; crime and corrections; and being a party to a civil action. We have attempted to deal with what seemed to us the essential activities: others are found in the ensuing chapters of this book. Yet others might also have been included: this is life, not only for the retarded, but for all people.

ARTICLE VII of the Declaration of general and special rights of the mentally retarded[1] provides

> "Some mentally retarded persons may be unable, due to the severity of their handicap, to exercise for themselves all of their rights in a meaningful way. For others, modification of some or all of these rights is appropriate. The procedure used for modification or denial of rights must contain proper legal safeguards against every form of abuse, must be based on an evaluation of the social capability of the mentally retarded person by qualified experts and must be subject to periodic reviews and to the right of appeal to higher authorities."

PRINCIPLE XXVI of the Canadian Mental Health Association's "Law and Mental Disorder"[2] reads

> "Denial or restriction of any given liberty, right or privilege by reason of mental disorder should be only by specific decision upon appropriate criteria, with provision for review and access to the courts."

The following is an excerpt from the Report of the Task Force on Law of the President's Panel on Mental Retardation.[3]

> "The retardate may . . . be excluded from a number of activities, or precluded from the exercise of what would be his rights if he were not retarded. This can happen without any formal challenge, or identification of retardation. But it does not render the procedure contrary to his interest, or to the public interest, provided the statutory or administrative requirements are reasonably related to the performance of the regulated activity. It is, however, important to avoid indiscriminate disqualification from a particular activity because of a finding of 'incompetence' under a statute regulating other activities of a different type."

In the three authoritative statements recited above, there is a recurring message. That message reflects the now incontrovertible proposition that should destroy for all time the once held doctrine of "universal incompetence".

Years ago, and not too many at that, it was a common conviction that a man was either "competent" or "incompetent" – for all purposes. To some extent, this was true in law. It is no longer. Still, many people – including so-called "experts" – seem to be living in the past and, we are sorry to report, this includes lawyers.

Because a person is found "incompetent" or "incapable" to do a particular thing, or, in a certain respect, it does not necessarily mean that he is incapable or incompetent to do something else, or, in another respect. We must look at each individual and each activity and determine every case on its own merits at the time. The sooner this is recognized, the better.

Exclusions or limitations of rights and opportunities should always be construed restrictively, and we recommend that all laws and practices thereunder conform to this principle.

Residential settings

ARTICLE IV of the Declaration of general and special rights of the mentally retarded reads as follows.

References for Living and doing are on pages 49 to 52.

"The mentally retarded person has a right to live with his own family or with foster parents; to participate in all aspects of community life, and to be provided with appropriate leisure time activities. If care in an institution becomes necessary it should be in surroundings and under circumstances as close to normal living as possible."[4]

As community resources develop for the mentally retarded, fewer are being placed in the traditional institutions for them and more are being discharged from these institutions to the community. Nonetheless, institutionalization of the retarded is still a very real occurrence and a critical phase in the life of many retardates.

Whether admission will be awarded or discharge will be arranged depends upon many factors. These factors include the needs of the individual; the programs offered at the particular facility and in the community; and the policy of the administration of the facility as prescribed locally or on a central basis. Local conditions such as the availability of accommodation and circumstances of ability to pay maintenance charges, where applicable, may also appear as factors. By and large, these matters are not so much regulated, as accommodated, by the law.

The law enters the picture more to regulate procedures in respect of institutionalization.[5] Where no compulsion is involved, these legal procedures may be no more complicated than that for placement in a general hospital for a physical illness, although this is not always the case. Where compulsion is involved, the law is often more exacting and it tends to prescribe criteria, rights and liabilities in a definitive fashion.

According to the constitution governing Canada, the power to make laws in respect of the establishment, maintenance and management of "hospitals, asylums, charities" and certain other institutions in and for a province is exclusively within the jurisdiction of each province.[6] Likewise is the power to make laws regarding "property and civil rights" in a province.[7] The combination of these powers confers upon each province plenary authority to pass legislation concerning institutions for the mentally retarded and mentally ill and the pertinent procedures involved. Accordingly, every province has its own statute or statutes dealing with mental hospitalization. The title of the principal Act in most provinces is the "Mental Health Act".[8]

Laws dealing with mental hospitalization in Canada have been radically changed in the last decade. Entirely new laws in Nova Scotia were enacted partly in 1960 and partly in 1965; Saskatchewan in 1961; Alberta and British Columbia in 1964; Manitoba in 1965; Ontario in 1967; Prince Edward Island in 1968; and New Brunswick in 1969. Further refinements have been made to the laws in some of these provinces since the time of the respective new legislative schemes. The laws in this field varying from one province to another, as they do, and there having been many recent amendments, one can determine what is the situation in a given province only by reference to the relevant statutes.[9]

At one time, there was a clear dichotomy in many Canadian laws: regulating the institutionalization of the mentally retarded on the one hand, and the mentally ill on the other.

A number of provinces had separate statutes dealing with each category. For example, in Manitoba, *The Mental Diseases Act*[10] dealt with the hospitalization of the mentally ill, while *The Mental Deficiency Act*[11] was its counterpart in the cases of "idiots, imbeciles, morons and moral deviates". These two Acts were repealed and replaced by one statute entitled *The Mental Health Act* in 1965.[12] Although the categories of the retarded and mentally ill are dealt with under one legislative roof, there is still a separate portion of the Act dealing exclusively with "mental retardates".

Alberta is another province wherein separate statutes dealt with these matters: in this instance the Acts were known respectively as *The Mental Diseases Act*[13] and *The Mental Defectives Act*.[14] *The Mental Health Act* of 1964 in Alberta[15] superseded both of the earlier statutes and placed the two categories on precisely the same footing. The new statute makes reference to the term "mentally disordered person", which is defined as a "person who is suffering from mental illness, mental retardation or any other disorder or disability of the mind."[16] Neither "mental illness" nor "mental retardation" is defined.

The Province of Ontario historically did not have separate statutes dealing with the mentally ill and the mentally retarded. Nonetheless, before that province's new mental health legislative scheme was enacted, there were distinctions drawn between the mentally ill and the retarded. Under *The Mental Hospitals Act*,[17] a "mentally defective person" was defined as a "person in whom there is a condition of arrested or incomplete development of mind, whether arising from inherent causes or induced by disease or injury, and who requires care, supervision and control for his own protection or welfare or the protection of others."[18] A "mentally ill person" was defined as a "person, other than a mental defective, who is suffering from such a disorder of the mind that he requires care, supervision and control for his own protection or welfare, or for the protection of others."[19] An example wherein a distinction was drawn is reflected in the provisions relating to voluntary admission. Whereas the mentally ill person could be so admitted, there was a statutory restriction prohibiting the mentally defective person from utilizing such a procedure.[20] By virtue of *The Mental Health Act, 1967*, the mentally ill and the mentally retarded are treated on an equal basis with respect to informal admission.[21] Indeed, there is no difference between the procedures to be followed in the case of either category. Moreover, not only are "mental illness" and "mental retardation" not defined: these terms are not even mentioned. The new generic term employed is "mental disorder", which is defined simply as "any disease or disability of the mind".[22] Ontario has, in this way, achieved absolute legislative unification in its new *Mental Health Act*.

There are some who would argue that since programming for the mentally retarded and for the mentally ill differ significantly, legislative unification is inappropriate. The test, it is submitted, does not relate to program, but rather to matters covered by statute. If it is found that the essentials to be dealt with by legislation can apply equally to the retarded as to the mentally ill, there is no reason why the two categories cannot be combined for legislative purposes. The trend towards such unification is a marked one, and given well-drafted legislative provisions, such unification would appear compatible with different programs respectively for the mentally retarded and the mentally ill.

It is planned here to review certain statutory procedures involved with institutionalization. In view of the diversity of these procedures amongst the various jurisdictions in Canada, it is practicable to examine closely the system in only one jurisdiction. *The Mental Health Act, 1967* in Ontario has been selected in this connection since it is a recent statute and is considered generally to be one of the most forward-looking Acts in the field. Moreover, it is serving as a model for other provinces.

As mentioned above, there is no distinction in the Ontario statute between the mentally retarded and the mentally ill. The Act defines a "psychiatric facility" as a facility for the observation, care and treatment of persons suffering from mental

15

disorder. This definition embraces a wide variety of facilities, many of which serve the retarded.

The admission of an individual to a psychiatric facility may be refused where the immediate needs in the case of the proposed patient are such that hospitalization is not urgent or necessary.

Basically, there are two procedures for admission to a psychiatric facility. The person may be admitted as an informal patient or as an involuntary patient.

Any person who is believed to be in need of the observation, care and treatment provided in a psychiatric facility may be admitted as an informal patient upon the recommendation of a physician. The physician who makes the recommendation may be a member of the staff of the psychiatric facility involved. The concept of informal admission is wider than the traditional "voluntary admission". In the case of the retarded, many of them could not be said to have the requisite intelligence to be volunteers nor, indeed, to appreciate the significance of institutionalization.

The value of the informal admission is clear when it is employed with respect to the retarded who, in former years, would have out of necessity been "certified" patients. It would have appeared, if the statistical data were related to the provisions of the legislation, that all of those "certificated" retardates represented persons detained "against their will". This was an unfortunate situation, since very few retardates who require institutionalization need be held on an involuntary basis.

The law in Ontario endeavors insofar as a law can to restrict the numbers of individuals who are hospitalized on an involuntary basis. The criteria are clearly set forth in the legislation. In order for a retarded person to be a proper candidate for involuntary admission, his retardation must be of a nature or degree so that he requires hospitalization in the interests of his own safety or the safety of others. It is an individual physician who determines these questions.

This physician must state why the retardate is not suitable for admission as an informal patient. Where a physician (who must personally examine the individual) is of the opinion that involuntary admission is indicated, he completes a form known as a "Physician's Application for Involuntary Admission". The application must be completed within seven days after the examination and serves as authority to convey the person to a facility as well as authority to the officials of that facility to detain him for a period of up to one month. Such an application becomes invalid if admission is not awarded within fourteen days.

Although they are intended for infrequent use, there are emergency procedures embodied in the Act to assist in arranging the examination of a person with a view to determining whether he requires institutionalization. Once these procedures are followed, any admission awarded would be on either an informal or an involuntary basis, whichever is indicated.

Where a retardate is detained as an involuntary patient for a period of one month and further detention is indicated, the procedure involves his attending physician, after personal examination, completing a "certificate of renewal". Such certificates of renewal are also based upon the safety risk concept and are to be completed by the attending physician at graduated intervals, so long as the retardate requires involuntary institutionalization.

An involuntary patient whose authorized period of detention has expired becomes an informal patient. It is also possible for an attending physician to change the status of an involuntary patient to an informal one. Conversely, an informal patient may be converted to an involuntary one through the action of a physician.

During institutionalization leaves of absence may be granted. The officer-in-charge of a psychiatric facility may, upon the advice of the attending physician, place a patient on leave of absence for a designated period of not more than three months, if the intention is that the patient shall return thereto. A leave of absence is not to be confused with the older concepts of "probation" or "conditional discharge", neither of which are available under the Ontario statute. Leaves of absence are appropriate where it is clear that the retardate will be returning to the facility: as for example, where his family or other persons are merely taking him on vacation.

The statute makes provision for the transfer of a patient from one psychiatric facility to another; and from a psychiatric facility to a general hospital where indicated because of a physical ailment. These are accomplished by local arrangement.

Discharge from a psychiatric facility is, by statute, to be granted when the patient is no longer in need of the observation, care and treatment provided there. In the case of an informal patient, there is no statutory restriction concerning his discharge. An involuntary patient's discharge would, of course, depend upon his degree of retardation and whatever element of safety risk to himself or others is involved.

Review boards to determine the issue of involuntary detention are established under the Act. An involuntary patient, or anyone on his behalf, may apply in writing to the chairman of the review board to inquire into whether the patient suffers from mental disorder of a nature or degree so as to require hospitalization in the interests of his own safety or the safety of others.

An application to a review board may be made each time a certificate of renewal is issued in his case, that is at prescribed intervals. When an application is made, the review board must conduct such inquiry as it considers necessary to reach a decision and may hold a hearing. Where a hearing is held, the patient may attend unless the chairman otherwise directs, and where he does not attend he may have a person appear as his representative. Upon the conclusion of an inquiry, the board chairman prepares a written decision and must send a copy to the applicant and to the officer-in-charge of the psychiatric facility. When the officer-in-charge receives a copy of the decision, he must take whatever steps are necessary to give effect to it.

When a person is institutionalized, many other rights may be affected. Some, such as the rights of communication and visitation, relate to the institutionalization itself.[23] These rights should be universally recognized and jealously protected.

At one time, very few years ago, persons admitted to a mental hospital on a compulsory basis were deemed in law to be incompetent to manage their affairs, and, generally, a public official assumed management on their behalf. This is, on the whole, no longer so. Today, most legislation requires each individual case to be determined on its own merits – a much more sensible course. We consider this matter in detail later under the topic dealing with property management by statutory committee.

Various additional rights, some of which are to be dealt with in this chapter, may be placed in issue because of the institutionalization. For example, the capacity of a patient in a mental hospital to make a contract or a will is questioned. While the fact of hospitalization is a matter to be taken into account, it should not be conclusive in denying any right.[24]

Progressive thinking in the mental retardation field is directed to "normalization" and care in the community, leading hopefully to a successful integration of the retardate into social life. The function of care, then, is training in self-suffi-ciency rather than mere custodial isolation. The greater the extent to which life in the training and care period parallels authentic social interaction, the greater is the ability of the retardate to cope when he takes his independent place in the community.

The physical structure of the residential facility is important emotionally and in furtherance of the goal of approximating community reality. Discussing re-tarded children, one authoritative source cites the following quotation.[25]

> "The realization that mentally retarded people have need of affection, approval, and dignified treatment prompted the current gradual change of institutional set-tings. Instead of huge, sterile barracks with endless rows of beds and little else, a homelike setting is advocated, planned around smaller units that include living rooms, playrooms, separate kitchens and dining rooms, and attractive bedrooms. The homelike atmosphere is underscored by the careful choice of personnel for such units or cottages. Their emotional stability and motivation guarantee their effectiveness as substitute parents. Dealing with a relatively small stable group of children and adults helps the retarded child, especially in his social maturation, in the areas of impulse control and the development of meaningful human relation-ships. The small group concept is extended to classrooms, workshops, and recrea-tional facilities. Children are grouped according to age, degree of retardation, and type of handicap. Only such grouping permits the tailoring of the program to fit the needs of the individual child."

The principles expressed would appear to apply equally to the retarded of all ages.

Specific residential care settings seem to be of six basic types.[26]

The large hospital schools. Training is the prime function of these schools, but it is often made impossible by conditions of overcrowding and understaffing. The available staff has no alternative but effectively to confine its activities to custodial supervision. These institutions sometimes have two thousand or more residents, with space and training facilities for hardly that many.

Regional centers. A facility smaller than the large schools seems to offer the best opportunity to provide high levels of care, treatment and training. Many such centers have admission restrictions of age and range of handicap thereby keeping resident populations manageable and offering specialized services. Centers of 300 to 500 beds have become the internationally accepted optimum size, balancing population and services against the *per diem* cost.[27]

Satellite residences. Normally limited to a 75 to 150 bed range, this size facility offers a high quality service but is regarded as uneconomic if it is operated as an independent unit.[28] In this size institution, adaptation of the number, variety and ranks of staff is difficult. Economic feasibility is attainable if the facility is oper-ated privately on a commercial basis, or as a satellite unit of a larger facility. As a satellite, a facility of this size is able to meet the need for specialized programs within the framework of services of the "parent" institution.

Community residences. These are units of eight to twelve beds, and commonly a service of a local association for the mentally retarded. While helping to meet the great need for residential settings that remain very close to normal community life, these units are not economical. If they are dependent solely upon the ability of the local associations to raise funds, the small "homes" are an impossible dream.

In some jurisdictions, public funds are made available. *The Homes for Retarded Persons Act, 1966*[29] enacted by Ontario is an example. That Act provides[30] that an approved corporation shall receive in public funds an amount equal to 80% of the cost of providing residential accommodation in an approved home for persons who are not wards of the Crown or of a children's aid society. The Regulations made pursuant to the Act specify standards of operation which must be met by any home applying for and receiving the grants made available by the Act.

These small group homes, operating in the community, seem likely to provide the closest approximation of what are said to be the ideal conditions. It should be noted that the small home setting will be of benefit only to those persons able to function, or to learn to function, in a manner not far removed from social norms. Further, such homes cannot provide necessary care or personnel to persons suffering from serious physical ailments.

Boarding homes. Serving as "half-way homes" for selected residents, these facilities are the final step in the progression from large institutions to integration in the community. Commonly housing three to six persons, boarding homes suffer from budgetary limitations, and the need for competent staff to search out and evaluate potential homes and "house parents". The same staff need is posed by problems of supervision.

Boarding home facilities of high quality are difficult to find. Their best utilization makes it essential that they receive only residents whose "readiness" for return to the community is at an advanced level.

Foster homes. Residential placements must be available for the retardate who is functioning in the community. Providing usually one or two beds, foster homes are generally the responsibility at present of agencies working under child welfare legislation. It may be possible to extend this program to include persons who are not in the care of these agencies, and do not require an institutional setting.

It would, of course, be most desirable if every province could provide the full spectrum of facilities outlined. The needs of retardates at each level, and those progressing from one to another, might then be met.

The emergence of these new facilities will, more and more, raise questions of law. Certainly, the respective powers, rights, duties, obligations, liabilities and responsibilities of the resident and those to whom he is entrusted must be clarified. Patterns of residential care do not appear sufficiently crystallized as yet to know with any certainty what is the comprehensive legal position. We recommend that where any legislation is enacted dealing with residential care of the retarded, consideration be given to defining, where possible, the status in law of the residents and those charged with their care.

Contracts

Concern has often been expressed regarding persons with mental handicaps becoming involved in foolish or unfair contracts. The concern is founded in the belief that the weak-minded are particularly vulnerable to unscrupulous businessmen, high-pressure salesmen and exaggerated advertising claims.

The case files of lawyers and social workers abound in examples of imprudent contracts entered into at a severe cost which cannot be later avoided. The first natural reaction of many when hearing of a case such as that of an almost-illiterate person being pressured into a time-payment purchase of an encyclopaedia is to demand special protective legislation. The error should not be made, however, of attempting to deal in a vacuum with this problem.

The essence of our economic system is the contract. All facets of commercial life have been founded upon the concept of "a bargain for a bargain": two persons agreeing to trade goods, to sell and buy goods, or to provide a service for payment. The history of our society has been primarily one of free enterprise, with state intervention in private arrangements being, until recently, considered objectionable. The assumption must be that official thinking believed everyone equal in bargaining power, or, and more likely, was indifferent to the effects of obvious differences in economic and business skill and strength.

The older principles of the common law, and some local custom, still retain great force in contract law. A primary principle of this law is that a contract, once made, must be performed by both parties.

A contract is essentially a promise made by one party in return for a promise made by another. When both have promised, each is bound. Thus, a housewife who promises to pay for a set of encyclopaedias and a company which promises to deliver it, can each be sued by the other for any default. There is no changing of mind permissible after a contract is made.

It must be recognized that this "sanctity of the contract" is essential to the carrying on of business. A storekeeper, for example, cannot be expected to maintain inventory, hire staff, rent premises and deliver his goods on a contract of sale if a buyer can change his mind and send the goods back, or keep them and refuse to fulfil his promise to pay for them. Nor can a workman be expected to go to a factory every day, work eight hours, and on payday be told by his employer that the company has changed its mind and will not pay for the work done. Everyone must be able to depend on the enforcement of his contract by the courts of law. Our economic system would otherwise collapse.

To suggest that some special class – such as the retarded – should arbitrarily be able to wipe out contracts after the other party has performed his part of the bargain is to invite chaos. Few would feel inclined to deal with these handicapped persons. No one can say with certainty who the retarded are, nor which of them are incapable of dealing in ordinary commercial matters. It is not only the retarded who make foolish bargains or administer their money improvidently.

Long has it been a rule of the common law that the courts will not make a bargain for the parties. Before a contract is made and binding, each party must give or promise to give something to the other. The courts have not been concerned that the two parties may receive unequal benefits.[31] In fact, unequal benefit – or profit – is the basic rationale of free enterprise. A court will not investigate to see if one party gives more than he gets: he merely has to get something. The law feels that only the parties themselves really know the value of some specific service or product to them.

When a retardate binds himself by a contract, his rights become mingled with those of the other party which must be protected as well. Accordingly, the only real way for a mentally handicapped person to escape obligations he took upon himself is to prove either (a) that actually there was no contract, or (b) that there was a contract, but it was induced by fraud, misrepresentation or undue influence.

In the normal contract situation, the required formalities of an offer being accepted, consideration passing between the parties, signatures, and other "technicalities" will be met. The transaction will take on the binding nature of a contract unless it can be proved that one of the parties did not intend to make that contract.

As noted earlier, the courts refuse to interfere in the "free choice" of parties who make a contract to arrange the terms of it themselves. The courts do insist, however, that the "free choice" be more than a mere illusion: the mind of each party must be competent to understand the transaction and free from control by any other person.

A retardate may be so deficient mentally that he lacks the necessary competence to contract. The test of capacity is that he comprehend the nature of the agreement into which he enters and its consequences.[32] The matter does not rest here, however.

Because other people have to be protected as well, a retardate may make an outrageously foolish contract and the courts will not release him from it unless the other party knew of his disability and took advantage of it. The protection is in the law, of course, for the benefit of "honest" businessmen and citizens who deal with the handicapped unaware of their disability. Nonetheless, where a sharp commercial operator had no reason to think a retardate showed any traits other that that stupidity and gullibility common to much of the consuming public, even very hard dealing will be upheld by the common law.

Actual knowledge of the handicap on the part of the person dealing with a retardate is not necessary to prove. If that other party has such facts as to put him on inquiry and he then does nothing, he will be held to have shown such wilful disregard of the facts that the court will treat him as if he had notice.[33] Thus, a businessman would be deemed to have been aware of a mental handicap if his customer behaved in such a manner that an ordinarily reasonable person would suspect something was wrong. It should be noted that the burden of proving that a retardate was incapacitated, and that the other party was aware of the incapacity, lies on the person seeking to avoid the contract.[34]

Even if it is proved that a retardate was incapable of contracting and such was known to someone dealing with him, the retardate may be bound if the contract was for "necessaries".

For example, under *The Sale of Goods Act*[35] in Alberta, section 4 reads, in part, as follows.

> "Where necessaries are sold and delivered to an infant or minor or to a person who by reason of mental incapacity or drunkenness is incompetent to contract, he must pay a reasonable price therefor."

Similar legislative provisions appear in all of the other common law provinces.[36]

"Necessaries" are defined in the Alberta statute to mean goods suitable to the condition in life of the infant or minor or other person and to his actual requirements at the time of the sale and delivery.[37]

The retardate must pay for these "necessaries" whatever his condition at their purchase or the knowledge of the other party. One legal writer maintains that the individual in this situation is liable for the full contract price agreed upon, not merely for a reasonable price.[38]

If the incapacity defence fails, there is one further argument available. Should the contract have been induced by lies about price, quality or the meaning of the contract, the agreement is valid, but can be struck down later as fraudulent or based on misrepresentation. This remedy is available to everyone.

It is questionable what proportion of contracts in which retardates imprudently become bound are induced by fraud or misrepresentation. The common law has not considered the sale of unnecessary items objectionable, and even where price or interest rates are very high, the agreements have been upheld as made by "free choice".[39]

There has been some legislative intervention. A long-standing example is that dealing with the charging of extremely high interest rates on loans. Ontario, in 1912, enacted such legislation,[40] but that in the other provinces is of very recent origin. The Ontario legislation,[41] like that in most of the other provinces, deals only with the making of loans by private persons or by loan institutions such as banks or finance companies. The relevant Ontario provision allows the court to strike out interest charges agreed upon and substitute its version of a fair rate, as may be seen from the following.

"Where, in respect of money lent, the court finds that having regard to the risk and to all the circumstances, the cost of the loan is excessive and that the transaction is harsh and unconscionable, the court may,

(a) re-open the transaction and take an account between the creditor and the debtor;

(b) notwithstanding any statement or settlement of account or any agreement purporting to close previous dealings and create a new obligation, re-open any account already taken and relieve the debtor from payment of any sum in excess of the sum adjudged by the court to be fairly due in respect of the principal and the cost of the loan;

(c) order the creditor to repay any such excess if the same has been paid or allowed on account by the debtor;

(d) set aside either wholly or in part or revise or alter any security given or agreement made in respect of the money lent, and, if the creditor has parted with the security, order him to indemnify the debtor."[42]

There seems no reason why this protection should not be extended to cover the cost of credit in credit sales, where items are brought on time payments. Certain of the provinces have made this advance.[43]

Consumer protection laws have been enacted in various provinces. The main thrust of this legislation is commonly directed at itinerant sellers and the sale of goods on credit terms.

In those jurisdictions with legislation on the point, registration and licensing is required of itinerant sellers. Such sellers are those dealing other than in a fixed place of business. The provisions embrace the activities, therefore, of those selling door-to-door or in any other manner involving an unsolicited approach to the consumer.

Because of the high-pressure tactics often used in such situations, a consumer may cancel a contract made with an itinerant seller by giving the seller notice of cancellation within a time specified in the Acts. This time period is short, being for example, two days in Ontario,[44] four in Manitoba[45] and Saskatchewan,[46] and ten in Newfoundland.[47] British Columbia may be pioneering, for its statute[48] as amended[49] has no time limit for cancellation of a contract made in the dwelling place of a consumer.

The right to cancel is limited to those contracts under which the consumer has not yet paid all of the money agreed, or has not yet received the goods for which he contracted. Such contracts are termed "executory".

The second function of the consumer protection laws is illustrated by sections 16 and 21 of the Ontario enactment. Every executory contract must be in writing and contain all relevant information about the sale: the names and addresses of the parties, the price of the goods and method of payment, a description of the goods, the terms on which credit is extended, the cost of the credit, and the warranties applicable. Unless these requirements are met, and each party receives a copy of the document, the contract is not binding. In a credit sale the cost of the credit in interest and carrying charges must be detailed in percentages and dollars.

The rationale underlying the consumer protection Acts is that some consumers are being exploited, and that the appropriate protection is afforded by providing the consumer with all information pertinent to the contract. It is assumed that armed with this information, and secure in the absence of hidden tricks or technicalities, the reasonable consumer is capable of making intelligent choices in the face of the blandishments of the salesman.

The problem for the retardate is that he is not a reasonably intelligent consumer. He needs help beyond the tools of self-sufficiency endowed by these Acts. The solution to his contractual vulnerability would lie in the power of some authority to ensure that "fairness" means more, when a retardate is contracting, than mere absence of hidden information. There is not at the present time in Canadian law the opportunity to exercise such a power of relief.

Probably the most far-reaching effort in this field is that of the highly controversial section 2-302 of the *Uniform Commercial Code*,[50] which has been adopted in a number of states in the USA. That section, profoundly influential in leading recent thinking, reads as follows.

> "(1) If the court as a matter of law finds the contract or any clause of the contract to have been unconscionable at the time it was made the court may refuse to enforce the contract, or it may enforce the remainder of the contract without the unconscionable clause, or it may so limit the application of any unconscionable clause as to avoid any unconscionable result.
>
> (2) When it is claimed or appears to the court that the contract or any clause thereof may be unconscionable the parties shall be afforded a reasonable opportunity to present evidence as to its commercial setting, purpose and effect to aid the court in making the determination."

In the Official Comment to section 2-302, it is noted that the courts are empowered to consider the quality of the bargain itself: in effect, to "make the bargain for the parties". There is no other instance of such a radical departure from traditional commercial practice.

Section 2-302 does not attempt to define "unconscionability", apparently in recognition of the hopelessness of setting down standards to cover all situations. The Comment contains the statement, however, that the "basic test is whether, in the light of the general commercial background and the commercial needs of the particular trade or case, the clauses involved are so one-sided as to be unconscionable under the circumstances existing at the time of the making of the contract". The section means, in effect, that a court is to look at a particular contract in a particular case, decide if it is fair, and if it is not, either change it or throw it out. This is probably the only viable alternative to maintaining the present "hands-off" principle in Canada. Legislation cannot itself set the standards: it can do no more than tell a judge to impose his concept of fairness upon a case.

Protection of the weak in Canadian commercial law is rudimentary in comparison to that afforded in the *Uniform Commercial Code*.

Even if safeguards were to exist to relieve the handicapped from the burdens of imprudent contracts, they would at best be a salve applied after the burden was assumed. The problems and turmoil of litigation, and the fact that knowledge of the legal remedies would be necessary before the retardate would seek them, suggest that a first line solution should be sought which would serve as a preventive measure.

Consequently, we recommend that steps be taken to educate and counsel the mentally handicapped at the "grass roots" level in respect of the making of contracts and their implications in modern society.

It is our further recommendation that the provinces seriously consider the adoption in their statutes of a provision similar to section 2-302 of the *Uniform Commercial Code*. The implementation of such a law would endow not only the mentally handicapped, but also the general population, with what appears to be a much needed protective mechanism of a remedial nature.

Driving

The opportunity to drive is necessarily incidental to the fulfilment of many social roles. To deny this opportunity to the retarded may constitute "an unjust infringement" of their liberty and represents "a serious psychological obstacle to . . . mental, social and vocational adjustment".[51]

The provinces have legislation which makes fitness to drive a condition of holding a licence. The statutes vary greatly in the degree to which they specify standards of fitness, and the proof required for a finding of non-fitness. The relevant statutory provisions are as follows.

LEGISLATIVE RESTRICTIONS RELATING TO DRIVING IN CANADA

Alberta
Highway Traffic Act, R.S.A. 1970, c. 169.
The Minister may refuse to issue an operator's licence to a person unless he is satisfied by examination or otherwise of the physical and other competency of the applicant to drive a motor vehicle, without endangering the safety of the general public. (s. 6).

British Columbia
Motor-vehicle Act, R.S.B.C. 1960, c. 253.
Applicant for licence must submit himself to such examination as to his fitness and ability to drive or operate motor-vehicles as may be prescribed by the Superintendent of Motor-vehicles – also holder of licence. (s. 18).
Upon proof to the satisfaction of the Superintendent of the existence of unfitness to drive, he may cancel or suspend licence. (s. 78).

Manitoba
Highway Traffic Act, R.S.M. 1970, c. H60.
The Registrar shall not issue a driver's licence to a person who is a mentally disordered person within the meaning of *The Mental Health Act*. (s. 23). The Registrar may require an applicant or holder of a licence to undergo a medical examination and produce a certificate of a medical practitioner that the holder or applicant is not suffering from any disability that would render him a source of danger. (s. 26).

New Brunswick
Motor Vehicle Act, 1955, S.N.B. 1955, c. 13.
The Registrar of Motor Vehicles may refuse to grant a licence to any person who has previously been adjudged to be afflicted with or suffering from any mental disability or disease and who has not at the time of the application been restored to competency by the methods provided by law; or to any person when the Registrar has good reason to believe that such person by reason of physical or mental disability would not be able to operate a motor vehicle with safety upon the highways. (s. 72).

Newfoundland
Highway Traffic Act, S.N. 1962, c. 82.
The Registrar of Motor Vehicles may before or after a licence is issued require the person to undergo a medical examination and produce a certificate to determine whether that person is physically and mentally competent to operate a motor vehicle. The Registrar shall not issue a licence to a person whose record, in the opinion of the Registrar, makes him unsuitable to hold a licence, and in forming that opinion, the Registrar may consider the physical and mental condition or history of the applicant. (ss. 49, 52). A person shall not drive if he suffers from a disease or physical or mental disability which might cause his driving to be a source of danger to other persons. (s. 130).

Nova Scotia

Motor Vehicle Act, R.S.N.S. 1967, c. 191.

The Department of Highways and Public Works shall not issue a driver's licence when in the opinion of the Department the person is afflicted with or suffering from such physical or mental disability or disease as will serve to prevent him from exercising reasonable and ordinary control over a motor vehicle. (s. 60). When the Registrar has reason to believe that the holder of a licence is incompetent to drive a motor vehicle or is afflicted with mental or physical infirmities or disabilities rendering it unsafe for him to drive, he may require an examination and report. (s. 251).

Ontario

Highway Traffic Act, R.S.O. 1960, c. 172.

No driver's licence shall be issued to a person afflicted with or suffering from any mental disability or disease or to a person where the Minister of Transport has good cause to believe that such person by reason of physical or mental disability would not be able to operate a motor vehicle safely. (R.R.O. 1960, Reg. 227, s. 18, as amended by O. Reg. 373/66).

Prince Edward Island

Highway Traffic Act, 1964, S.P.E.I. 1964, c. 14.

The Registrar of Motor Vehicles may, before or after issuing a licence, require the person to undergo a medical examination and produce a certificate thereof in such form as the Registrar may prescribe, to determine whether that person is physically and mentally competent to operate a motor vehicle. The Registrar shall not issue a licence to a person whose record, in the opinion of the Registrar, makes him unsuitable to hold a licence and in forming that opinion he may consider the physical or mental condition or history of the applicant. (ss. 69, 72).

Quebec

Highway Code, R.S.Q. 1964, c. 231.

The competency of drivers and chauffeurs shall be established by means of examinations undergone before persons authorized for such purpose by the Minister of Transport and Communications and in accordance with the provisions of the regulations. (s. 19, and see O/C 418, dated Feb. 14, 1961).

Saskatchewan

Vehicles Act, R.S.S. 1965, c. 377.

The Highway Traffic Board shall not issue a licence or permit to any person who is known to the Board to be afflicted with or suffering from such physical or mental disability or disease as might prevent him from exercising reasonable and ordinary control over a motor-vehicle while operating it upon a public highway. The Board may suspend or revoke a licence where satisfied that the holder is afflicted or is suffering as above. (ss. 67, 92). The Board must keep a record of all persons who have been reported to the Board as having any of the above conditions. (s. 22).

It will be noted that the licensing authorities either clearly or implicitly have the power to refuse to issue or to revoke a licence in the case of a mentally unfit person. It is questionable whether these legislative schemes fulfil the purposes for which they are intended.

One of the purposes of the licensing provisions is, of course, to deny the privilege of operating a motor vehicle to some persons. Given the tremendous social problem of death and destruction on the roads, it is clear that there can be no right to drive. Public regulation is essential, and a driver's licence must be considered a privilege to be earned. There is a right involved, however: the right not be denied arbitrarily a privilege available to others. Denial should be firmly rooted only in real proof of danger to the public, an interest which must be protected.

Where certain licences are involved, as for instance, for an airline pilot, rigorous testing of an applicant – physical and mental – is conducted. On the other hand, an application to be licensed to drive a car is so commonplace, present systems of licensure cannot afford such luxurious testing methods. The usual procedure in Canada is merely to require successful completion of academic and practical driving examinations, and the provision of some personal information about the applicant.

Public licensing tests are often administered through a bureaucratic system where the examiners are, whatever their other qualifications, probably untrained in detecting mental handicap. At the time of application there may, under present conditions – despite pointed questions on standard forms – be very little effective screening actually occurring.

There are probably a great many people appalled at the notion that retarded persons are or may be licensed to drive. That feeling is, no doubt, founded in a belief that they lack the intelligence necessary properly to operate a motor vehicle, and consequently pose a clear threat to life and property. Some would support a blanket prohibition of licensing any retarded person and would hope that the licensing system achieved that object. Otherwise, they would argue that the tests should be made more stringent.

If we posit a retardate applying for a licence, the questions are can he complete the forms, learn the rules of the road, and gain sufficient dexterity in operation of a vehicle to pass the tests? If he can, he will be licensed, whatever his intelligence. The crucial issue then becomes whether retardates cause more accidents than drivers of "normal" intelligence.

Evidence suggests that there is a real relationship between high accident rates and certain emotional states. The evidence also suggests that it is not intellectual limitations, but rather social and emotional adjustments, that are the determining factors in accident rates. Discussing his own studies and those of other researchers, one expert[52] reports a definite correlation between accidents and parental disharmony, marital problems, financial and career stresses, sexual identity anxieties and suicidal tendencies. Another expert[53] notes that the major traffic hazards are the alcohol- and drug-dependent persons, and the aggressive acting-out character disorders.

It would appear that there is no need for any campaign to prevent retardates from securing driving licences. The existence of retardation is not relevant to a finding of fitness to drive and we recommend that the licensing authorities so recognize. What is important is inability to learn to drive safely. That inability exists in a sizeable proportion of the population and does not merely include the retarded.

Perhaps our licensing procedures are not screening out enough applicants. Nevertheless, at present there is no evidence to support depriving the retarded of licences to drive if they are able to pass the tests.

No one has identified retarded drivers as representing a greater accident risk. It could be that they are fit drivers. In the alternative, it may be the case that few of them are driving because they either have no interest in doing so or fail to meet the licensing requirements.

Maybe driving tests should be made more rigid, the case of every driver in an accident be considered by a board of experts, and every driver be re-examined periodically. The implementation of any such programs should apply to the whole community generally. There seems no reason for the application of any special rules – of either a privileged or a discriminatory nature – to the retarded.

In some jurisdictions it has been the practice for the licensing authorities to suspend or revoke a licence systematically upon hospitalization or adjudication of incompetency. Often there may be no proof of disability related to driver fitness. Such automatic practices, not facing the proper issues, are a denial of natural justice. Justice requires that there be no suspension or revocation on the ground of mental unfitness without a complete consideration of the particular case by an appropriate tribunal. (Some provinces have established by statute – or otherwise – medical advisory boards which may be helpful in this respect.) The matter could reach the attention of the licensing authorities and be placed before the tribunal in a number of ways. Selective reporting on either a mandatory[54] or voluntary basis may be indicated.

We have been unable to discover any statistical data relating to retardates who wish to drive, their success rate in obtaining licences, and their driving performance records in comparison to the driver population. These data are, of course, vital to a proper assessment of the significance of these matters in practical terms, and we recommend that such a study be undertaken.

Voting

The basic right and duty of a citizen in a democracy is the exercise of the franchise. Disenfranchisement can be equated only to second-class citizenship and such a drastic step should be a measure of the most extraordinary nature.

> "Yet the right of a citizen to vote is not the only consideration involved. Society has also an interest worthy of protection: namely, the right to bar persons from voting who are for some reason incapable of making the rational decisions which exercise of the franchise requires. Yet, if the goal of our system is the establishment of efficient government through implementation of the collective opinion of as many citizens as possible, the stringency of the rule of exclusion employed must be determined in light of the policy favoring as broad an electoral base as possible."[55]

The Canadian political system is federal in nature. There are, therefore, separate elections for Parliament and each of the provincial legislative assemblies. Canada and each province have legislation regulating the electoral process within their respective jurisdictions. A prime ingredient of such legislation is the definition of the class of persons entitled to be registered as voters. Differences in definition result in the odd situation that a given person may be entitled to vote in a national election, but not in a provincial election. The same may be true in reverse. Moreover, some of the Acts are unclear in meaning.

The history of voting rights has been one of ever-broadening franchise. There was a time, of course, when there were no "voters". Through later periods the vote was extended to landowners of increasingly smaller estates until finally any financial status requirement was abolished. In this century, the sexual bar was removed. The principle now operating is one of universal suffrage, with only certain persons excepted. These exceptions are specified in the Canadian and provincial election statutes. Inmates of penal and mental institutions, and those found incompetent, are generally denied the right to vote.

The following represents the statutory posture concerning the mental element across Canada.

LEGISLATIVE PROHIBITIONS RELATING TO VOTING IN CANADA

Alberta
Election Act, R.S.A. 1970, c. 117, s. 16.
The following persons are disqualified to be registered as electors and shall not vote:

. . . a person who is a patient in a mental hospital or school for mental defectives, [but this] does not apply to a person who is not mentally incompetent and who is in a hospital as a voluntary patient under . . . *The Mental Health Act.*

British Columbia
Provincial Elections Act, R.S.B.C. 1960, c. 306.
No specific exclusion appearing.

Manitoba
Elections Act, R.S.M. 1970, c. E30, s. 16.
The following persons are disqualified from voting . . . Persons who are patients in mental hospitals or institutions for mental retardates.

New Brunswick
Elections Act, S.N.B. 1967, c. 9, s. 43.
The following persons are disqualified from voting and shall not vote . . . every person who is restrained of his liberty of movement, or deprived of the management of his property by reason of mental disease or infirmity.

Newfoundland
Election Act, S.N. 1954, c. 79, s. 4.
The following persons are disqualified from voting . . . every person lawfully committed to an institution for the treatment of mental illness.

Nova Scotia
Elections Act, R.S.N.S. 1967, c. 83, s. 26.
The following persons shall not be entitled to be registered as electors . . . a person who is legally restrained of his liberty of movement or deprived of the management of his property by reason of mental illness.

Ontario
Election Act, 1968-69, S.O. 1968-69, c. 33, s. 11.
Persons who are . . . patients in mental hospitals, or who have been transferred from mental hospitals to homes for special care as mentally incompetent are disqualified from voting.

Prince Edward Island
Election Act, S.P.E.I. 1963, c. 11, s. 22.
The following persons shall not be entitled to be registered as electors . . . a person who is legally restrained of his liberty of movement or deprived of his property by reason of mental illness.

Quebec
Election Act, R.S.Q. 1964, c. 7, s. 48.
The following shall not be entered on an electoral list nor shall they vote . . . insane persons confined in a hospital for the mentally ill and interdicted persons.

Saskatchewan
Elections Act, R.S.S. 1965, c. 4, s. 30.
Persons disqualified from registration and voting . . . Any person . . . who on polling day is in a school for mentally retarded persons or is a patient in a mental hospital . . . is a patient in a psychiatric centre or psychiatric ward . . . is mentally incompetent . . . is a person whose affairs are being administered by the Administrator of Estates.

Canada
Canada Elections Act, S.C. 1960, c. 39, s. 14.
The following persons are disqualified from voting at an election and incapable of being registered as electors and shall not vote nor be so registered . . . every person who is restrained of his liberty of movement or deprived of the management of his property by reason of mental disease. . . .

A full discussion of the ludicrous effects of such statutory provisions has already been published, and the reader is referred to that source.[56] For example, it should be noted that the adult retardate living at home, who might be more intellectually deficient than his institutionalized counterpart (who cannot vote), is not excluded from voting.

The exclusions are apparently based upon the assumption that proper and intelligent citizenship is impossible because of mental disorder in the stated contexts.

The important question is whether it is justifiable to deny the vote to the mentally handicapped at all. The matter does not appear to have been the subject of judicial consideration, and some may think that it has little practical consequence. It may well be that most retardates would not vote even when afforded the opportunity. On the other hand, there is no indication that the votes of retardates would be cast in a manner any more reprehensible than that of many persons not prohibited.

> "Can a test be devised to determine whether a person has sufficient understanding to vote? An informal survey of Canadian psychiatrists discloses that opinion is divided on this question. While the majority of those surveyed are of opinion that an appropriate test could be devised, the Committee is reluctant to formulate one and apprehensive of advocating its use, should one be designed.
>
> What would be the operative criteria upon which such a test could be constructed? Some might say that a person has sufficient understanding to vote only if he is able to discriminate among the candidates, has a knowledge of the election process, and has an appreciation of the democratic system. Whether or not these are valid criteria, there is no doubt that the existence of mental disorder could render a person less competent, or incompetent, in these respects. Would we not be on dangerous ground, however, by suggesting the adoption of such a test? Many persons who are not considered mentally incompetent, in fact totally lack the outlined ability, knowledge and appreciation. No one questions their right to exercise their franchise. What of those who vote for a candidate because he has a 'nice sounding name' or a 'neatly groomed moustache?' What of those who, hearing the constant expression of 'Vote as you please, but please vote', feel duty bound to do so, and pick a name 'out of a hat'? Do we examine their mental processes to determine their competency to vote? Is it not possible that a person who is less competent, because of mental disorder, to exercise his franchise in the way in which it is intended, is still more competent in that regard than some of his 'normal' counterparts? The fact must be faced and accepted that these are the peculiarities of the democratic system and are part and parcel of it."[57]

Unless a prohibitive measure concerning the right to vote is demonstrated to be necessary, the right to dignity and first-class citizenship should not be impugned.

In the final analysis, we recommend that the mentally handicapped should in no case be prohibited from voting so long as they are otherwise qualified and are able to satisfy election officials of the same by compliance with any formalities that the law may require.

Responsibility in tort

Injury to the person, property or interests of another may be done in a variety of ways. Physical assault, trespass to or destruction of property, defamation, and interference with business all come within the law of torts. "Tort" is the legal term for a "civil wrong". Whether or not the criminal law takes an interest in the damage done, the person injured has the right to seek financial compensation.

For our purposes, two alternative states of mind are material to the commission of a tort. One may do the injury deliberately, or negligently by acting without due care. Usually one is not liable for an injury if it occurred by unavoidable accident.

There must be some form of intention that the harm should occur. That intention is clear when a conscious and deliberate choice is made to injure another or his property. Intention to commit the tort is also assumed when it is the result of negligence: driving carelessly on the highway means that one ignores the possibility of accident, presumably does not care about potential injury, and in making the deliberate choice to drive carelessly, is deemed to intend the consequences of that behavior.

It is clear then that the mental state is an extremely important element of a suit for damages in tort.

We have considered the potential result when the person causing the damage or injury has a mental disability, such as retardation. It is difficult to find reported decisions in tort dealing with the retarded, although "insanity" has often been considered in the courts.[58] In *Morriss v. Marsden*,[59] the defendant for no explicable reason had attacked the plaintiff with a hammer. The defendant was found to be a certifiable lunatic with a diagnosis of catatonic schizophrenia. The court stressed that the assault must have been an intended act: ". . . *i.e.* a voluntary act, the mind prompting and directing the act . . . must be averred and proved."[60] The defendant was found to know the nature and quality of his act – that it would cause injury – which was the reason for its commission. Whether he knew the act was wrong or not was immaterial.

A similar decision was reached in *Phillips v. Soloway*,[61] where an insane man attacked the plaintiff with a knife and cut out his eyeball. Intention to commit the act being found, and injury proved, it was held to make no difference whether the defendant was or was not capable of knowing that his act was wrong.

The same rules would, we believe, apply in the case of retardation. If a retardate damaged property, as for example, by breaking a window with a rock, compensation would be directed if he knew that the rock would break the window, and made the choice to throw it in any event. In any case in which it could be shown that a retardate is aware of the consequences of his act, he is liable in tort for any damages caused by it. If his mental disability precluded his understanding of the consequences of an act, then he could not be said to have formed the intention to cause or risk those consequences. Where overt conduct does not show the nature of one's foresight, the standard applied is the foresight that a reasonable man in the community would show. The retardate may or may not fall below that standard in any particular situation. Foresight of consequences is based upon understanding and experience, and its actual level presents an extremely difficult problem of assessment.

In the United States, the Restatement of the Law of Torts provides a concise declaration of the law on this point.

> "Unless the actor is a child, his insanity or other mental deficiency does not relieve the actor from liability for conduct which does not conform to the standard of a reasonable man under like circumstances."[62]

Where a retardate causes damage to an individual, but because of his disability is found not liable in tort, another person may sometimes be held liable instead.

A parent may be liable for the tort of his child committed with his knowledge and acquiescence. In the case of *Thibodeau v. Cheff*,[63] a retarded sixteen-year-old, addicted to smoking and the use of matches, set fire to a neighbor's haystack. His father was held liable in damages since he had known of the likelihood of danger arising to property from the boy's habit and had failed to take steps to avert disaster by removing the object of danger or by corporal restraint of the boy.

A parent is not legally responsible for the tort of his child merely because of the family relationship. The parent is not liable unless he has become a party to the wrongdoing as, for example, by directing or sanctioning it. Liability arises where the parent "allows" the tort to happen by suggesting its commission or ignoring its likelihood.

A section of the Restatement of the Law of Torts reads

> "One who takes charge of a third person whom he knows or should know to be likely to cause bodily harm to others if not controlled is under a duty to exercise reasonable care to control the third person to prevent him from doing such harm."[64]

Liability of another for the tort of a mentally retarded person may be excluded by legislation. Examples may be found in enactments dealing with mental hospitalization. One such statute is *The Mental Health Act*[65] of Prince Edward Island, the pertinent section of which reads: "No action lies against any psychiatric facility or any officer, employee or servant thereof for a tort of any patient."[66]

Conversely, legislation may impose liability where it would not otherwise exist. An illustration of this may be found in highway traffic laws which make the owner of a motor vehicle liable for loss or damage resulting from negligence of the driver (whether or not the owner was in the car). An exception to this absolute liability occurs where the car is taken without the consent of the owner.[67]

Making a will

Possibly the most common advice received from lawyers relates to the desirability of making a will. The will is an essential element in the planning of one's affairs. Quite apart from the fact that a valid last testament ensures that the property of an individual goes to those whom it is desired should have it, the legal and financial consequences in the absence of a will are often serious.

When a person dies, his assets devolve upon his personal representative. It is the personal representative of the deceased who administers the estate and the distribution of the assets, subject to the supervision of the court.

The "executor" named in a will makes an application to the court for probate in order that the will can be declared officially to be the true last will and testament of the deceased.

Where the deceased died without a will, the application for administration of the estate is usually made by the next-of-kin. The court then appoints an "administrator" of the estate.

The documents that are issued by the court to the executor are called "Letters Probate": those to the administrator are known as "Letters of Administration".

The executor is required to follow the instructions in the will. The administrator is bound to follow the terms of the laws dealing with what happens to property when there is no will. In many cases where a person dies intestate, that is without a will, the property is "tied up" much longer than might otherwise have been necessary. Since legal fees and court costs are borne by the estate, these may consume a good part of it, leaving few – and sometimes no – assets to be distributed to the heirs-at-law. This situation, of course, provided the tragic scenario of Dickens' *Bleak House*.

It is sometimes said that "if you don't make a will, the state will make one for you". This "state-made will" is embodied in legislation which provides for the scheme of distribution to be followed where various family members survive the deceased person who dies intestate, setting out the share which each of these is to receive.[68] Often it may happen that the scheme devised by statute follows the desires of the deceased which would have been expressed in a will. If the deceased, however, had wanted to divide his property in a manner other than that set out in the governing Act, the absence of a will would frustrate his final wishes.[69]

Although the advantages of having a will are clear, not everyone is in a legal position to make one. The law requires that a person attempting to dispose of his property by will must have the mental capacity to do so. There is no hard and fast rule that determines capacity in this regard. The finding is made only by a judicial weighing of the facts in each individual case.

The probate procedure requires the executor to show that the testator signed the document presented, that it was properly witnessed, and that the testator had capacity at the time the will was executed by him. If the document appears rational, and there are no other facts to suggest otherwise, the testator is deemed to have had that capacity.

An objection to the testator's capacity will normally come from someone who is dissatisfied with the scheme of distribution set out in the will in the hope of setting aside the document on the ground that the testator was not able to deal sensibly with his property. If the argument of lack of capacity succeeds, the will then is refuted, and the estate is dealt with in the same manner as if no will were made. Otherwise the will is granted probate.

If the issue of testamentary capacity is raised, a full inquiry is made before the court. The burden of proving incapacity is upon the party who alleges it, that is the party objecting to the validity of the will. Evidence is produced in an attempt to show that the testator failed to meet the tests which the courts have devised to assist in the difficult decision about the mental state of the deceased at the time the will was executed.

The tests which the court will apply have been summarized[70] as follows.

Did the testator understand the nature of the act he was about to perform; that is, did he fully comprehend that he was making a testamentary disposition?

Did the testator have such a memory and comprehension as to be able to appreciate the nature and extent of his estate?

Did the testator comprehend and appreciate the claims of persons who normally should have been the objects of his bounty?

Did the testator have such judgment as allowed him to make a disposition of his property with understanding and reason?

Some retarded persons may well be able to meet the tests. Others may not be able to do so. If a retardate is not able to meet the tests, the effect is that he is deprived of the right to leave his property to whomever he chooses, and to determine how it will be shared. This may seem unfair, and an infringement of a right vitally associated with the right to own property and function in society with dignity. Without denying that some curtailment of liberty is involved, it may well be that the legal tests of capacity are justified as protection for those who succeed the retardate. If he is not able to deal wisely with his property, then the prevention of exploitation and foolishness must be balanced against an unfettered right to deal freely with property. Should his property be preserved by requiring that it be disposed of in accordance with the legal rules of distribution, or should the human dignity of a mentally handicapped person be considered of a higher value than property considerations?

Even if it is believed that the mentally handicapped person has testamentary capacity, there is no guarantee that the will will not be attacked. Indeed, every testator runs this risk. The will of a retardate is just that much more vulnerable.

The slightest suggestion of possible contention of the will should raise a serious doubt as to whether a will should be made by the retardate. Since the legal costs arising from contention – whether or not the attack on the will is successful – may be greater than the estate can or should withstand, the wisdom of making a will should receive considerable attention from the practical point of view. In other words, even where the retardate appears to have testamentary capacity, the possibility of his estate devolving upon an intestacy should not be ruled out. Each case must, of course, be judged on its merits.

Once it has been decided that the mentally handicapped person is going to have a will, it is often suggested that a psychiatric report be obtained on the subject of his capacity in that regard at the time. Some go so far as to advise that a psychiatrist be a witness to the will. The advisability of the psychiatric witness has been questioned since it is said to involve the implication that the testamentary capacity of the individual is "borderline", thus ultimately casting doubt on the validity of the will.[71] As can be seen, this is not an area in which one can rest assured.

Apart from the matter of testamentary capacity, there is another issue which may arise in these cases. Where "undue influence" is brought to bear upon an individual in connection with the preparation of his will, the will may be vitiated by a court.[72] Because the retarded are more susceptible to pressure than are others, the possibility of undue influence becomes a matter of real concern. The burden of proving undue influence is upon the person who alleges it.[73]

Viscount Haldane has given the following description of undue influence which will render a will void.

> "Undue influence in order to render a will void, must be an influence which can justly be described by a person looking at the matter judicially, to have caused the execution of a paper pretending to express a testator's mind, but which really does not express his mind, but something else which he did not really mean."[74]

In the case of *Lucier v. Lynch*,[75] a decision of the Court of Appeal for Ontario, the effect of the issue is considered.

> "The principle is, that wherever a will is prepared under circumstances which raise a well-grounded suspicion that it does not express the mind of the testator, the Court ought not to pronounce in favour of it unless that suspicion is removed."[76]

It is our recommendation that counselling be made available to retardates who have estates and wish to make wills, concerning the wisdom or otherwise of so doing, and that such counselling should, without exception, be based upon legal advice given in the particular case, bearing in mind the delicate issues involved.

The potential incapacity of a retardate raises an issue for his parents when they are making their wills. Can they reasonably leave property to their retarded son or daughter when he or she may not be able to pass it on in a manner that the parents would consider desirable? This problem is dealt with later in chapter four as a matter of estate planning.

Crime and corrections

There has in Canada, during the past decade, been a great deal of study in the criminal law and correctional fields. The more we learn, the clearer it gets how little we know. Nevertheless, it is possible to say that there have been advances through recent changes in the law and improvements in programs.

Crime and corrections being such vast topics in themselves, even without the complication of mental handicap, it is hard to do fairness here in a consideration of all of the significant issues. Consequently, the reader is referred to some of the contemporary major works.[77]

There is a belief among some that the mentally retarded are more prone to criminal conduct than others. This belief is based sometimes on statistical data, other times on impressions.

A number of factors must be taken into consideration. It may be that a retarded person is suspected of or charged with crime unfairly through fear or a lack of understanding of his behavior. Bad elements may take advantage of certain retarded who are normally harmless and counsel them to involvement in crime. Perhaps retarded who are actually involved in crime are more easily apprehended due to their limited intelligence. There is the risk that the suggestibility of some retardates will allow them to confess readily to acts they have not committed. The criminal process may be used – rather abused – to obtain some measure of attention or supervision for persons of restricted intelligence where other community programs simply do not provide the answers. Moreover, the retarded person is the one less likely than his more fortunate counterparts to be aware of his rights as an accused person, including the right to retain a lawyer or obtain assistance through a plan of legal aid, thereby taking advantage of what might seem natural and prove helpful to others. If for no reasons than the foregoing, one should be particularly wary of statistics tending to show or forming impressions that the retarded are more likely to commit crime than others.

> "When one examines the problems of delinquency as it is encountered in mental deficiency practice, one finds that the problem of low intelligence is only one, and not the most important, of the factors which determine the occurrence of this form of behaviour. Low intelligence does modify the patient's attitude to and performance of the delinquent act, but delinquency is determined more by personality structure and social environment than by intellectual endowments."[78]

It is most important that a mentally retarded person who is suspected or accused of crime be identified as being retarded at the earliest possible stage – the time of apprehension. Here, the police are involved. We are aware that at least some police forces receive special training and education to assist them in the identification and proper handling of the mentally handicapped. Apprehension of the retardate and his placement in a foreign situation might be harder on him than on a person of normal intelligence. He might be more susceptible to making an admission or signing a confession than others, and such admission or confession may be either untrue or in some way unfair.

We recommend that a review be made of the training and education of the police in identifying and handling mentally handicapped suspects and accused persons, to ensure that they are adequate.

There is no excuse for a retarded person appearing in criminal court without a lawyer. Where a court has reason to believe that an accused person has a mental handicap, it should be the duty of the court to ensure that he is legally represented. We recommend that the *Criminal Code* be amended to make it a statutory duty of the court to appoint a lawyer for an unrepresented accused person under such circumstances. With the establishment of recent legal aid plans in the various provinces, this should not present any difficulty whatsoever.

The procedure on preliminary inquiry in the *Criminal Code* provides that a justice may remand an accused, by written order, to such custody as the justice directs for observation for a period not exceeding thirty days. Such an order may be made where, in the opinion of the justice, supported by the evidence of at least one duly qualified medical practitioner, there is reason to believe that the accused person is "mentally ill".[79] Similar provisions exist upon trial of an indictable offence[80] and upon trial of a summary conviction offence.[81]

The remand for observation mechanism is an important one and could be essential in the identification of a retardate. For some reason, however, the term used in all three provisions of the *Code* is "mentally ill". It is possible that a wide construction of "mentally ill" in the context would include mental retardation, but in such a vital matter there should be no room for doubt. It is therefore recommended that the sections in the *Code* authorizing remands for observation be amended to ensure that mental retardation is included within their scope. These sections could also be improved by allowing the remand for up to sixty days (additional time may sometimes be required by the "observing" authorities), and enabling the court to order the remand in the absence of the supporting evidence of a physician (in compelling circumstances, where a physician is not available).[82]

According to the *Criminal Code*, a court, judge or magistrate may, at any time before verdict, where it appears that there is sufficient reason to doubt that the accused is, on account of insanity, capable of conducting his defence, direct that an issue be tried whether the accused is then, on account of insanity, unfit to stand his trial.[83]

Recent amendments to the *Code* have incorporated into the law significant changes in respect of the issue of fitness to stand trial. These changes are of particular importance in cases where retarded persons are accused of crime.

A Guest Editorial[84] which appeared in the *Canadian Bar Journal* for April, 1966, explored certain of these problems in depth. Because the Standing Committee on Justice and Legal Affairs of the House of Commons relied heavily upon this Editorial in arriving at a unanimous opinion for amendment, it is reprinted below.

"The matter of the fitness of an accused person to stand his trial is one which may be raised by the defence, the prosecution, or by the court itself. In order to be fit in this respect, the accused must have the capacity to understand the nature and object of the proceedings against him, to comprehend his own condition in reference to such proceedings, and to make a rational defence.

Where it appears that there is sufficient reason to doubt that an accused is, on account of insanity, capable of conducting his defence, the court may direct that the fitness issue be tried. A finding of unfitness to stand trial results in a suspension of criminal proceedings, and the custody of the accused, probably in a mental hospital, under warrant of the Lieutenant-Governor of the province. Subsequent trial of the accused is not precluded, and he may be returned to court for that purpose at a later date.

It would be a dark day for the administration of criminal justice, were we knowingly to convict a person who, due to mental disorder, is handicapped in answering a criminal charge. Yet, while we are not convicting this individual, neither are we acquitting him. The possibility of his innocence cannot be excluded. Indeed, his innocence is presumed.

The practice in Canada is to resolve the fitness question as soon as the court is satisfied that the matter is placed in doubt. This has meant that the special issue is sometimes determined as a preliminary one at the outset of the trial. Where the accused is found unfit to stand trial under such circumstances, not only is there absent an opportunity to present a defence, but the prosecution has not had to test its case. The main issue at trial – innocence or guilt – is left completely untouched. Detention for an indeterminate time, perhaps for life, follows as a matter of law.

It might be argued that the individual has no real cause for complaint inasmuch as he should be held in a mental hospital in any event. Some, and perhaps most, persons who have been found unfit to stand trial are, admittedly, proper candidates for mental hospitalization. It is erroneous, however, to state that all of them are. It is recognized that many mentally disordered living in the community do not need to be institutionalized. If they were charged with crime, some of them undoubtedly would be found unfit to stand trial. The fact is that unfitness to stand trial is not an illness which requires hospitalization, but rather a legal concept which has relation only to the criminal trial process. Were it not for the criminal charge, some persons who are now confined in mental hospitals as unfit to stand trial, would otherwise be in the community.

Once the mental condition of the individual found unfit to stand trial appears to be such that he is probably fit in that respect, he may be returned to court to be tried. Not all of these persons will have this opportunity. Some may never sufficiently recover from their illness. Others may suffer from an irreversible condition. Where the accused has a certain degree of mental deficiency, for example, he is, and always will be, unfit to stand trial, and accordingly is under the law liable to be detained for the rest of his life. He is, on the basis of a criminal charge alone, damned – a victim of the system by which we determine guilt or innocence. To state the potential injustice at its highest, it is possible under the law for an innocent person who does not require mental hospitalization to be detained in a mental hospital for the rest of his life. As shocking as it may sound, there may be no way to prevent it from happening. It is possible, however, to minimize the risk of occurrence.

While we would not allow the conviction of a person unfit to stand trial, there is no reason why he should not be given the chance to be acquitted. It is possible to obtain an acquittal without the benefit of assistance from the accused. Such acquittals are won every day in court. The prosecution may fail to establish its case, making it unnecessary for a defence to be called. Defence counsel may have in his battery a strong defence of alibi to which witnesses are available to testify. Under the present Canadian law relating to fitness to stand trial, such matters are not brought to light, there being no clear authority which would allow development of the main issue.

There was, in the United Kingdom, a conflict of authority as to whether a trial of the special issue could be postponed, and the problem came before the Criminal Law Revision Committee for consideration. The Committee's Third Report, presented to Parliament in September, 1963, contained a recommendation of their majority that postponement of the trial of the special issue be allowed. That recommendation was accepted and passed into law as part of the *Criminal Procedure (Insanity) Act,* 1964. Section 4 of the statute authorizes the court to postpone consideration of the fitness question, if of opinion, 'having regard to the nature of the supposed disability . . . that it is expedient so to do and in the interests of the accused, ...' The issue may be postponed until any time up to the opening of the case for the defence.

Those concerned with the administration of criminal law in Canada would be well advised to consider carefully this recent amendment. Although there is room for debate respecting certain of the procedural details, there should be no argument against the principle upon which the amendment is based. A Canadian criminal court should have the power to postpone, where indicated, a trial of the special issue, and this power should be expressed by amendment to the *Criminal Code.*

It would be a step in the direction of justice."

And, indeed, the *Criminal Code* was amended.[85] Under the new provisions, where the issue of fitness to stand trial arises before the close of the case for the prosecution, the court, judge or magistrate may postpone directing the trial of the issue up until any time up to the opening of the case for the defence.[86] In a case where the issue has been postponed and the accused is acquitted at the close of the case for the prosecution, the issue of fitness to stand trial is not to be tried: the individual is entitled to his freedom.[87]

In addition to the added flexibility of the law which allows the issue of fitness to stand trial to be postponed, a number of additional rights in relation to the fitness issue have been conferred. The most important of these rights is that if there appears sufficient reason to doubt the fitness of an accused to stand trial, the court, judge or magistrate is required, if the accused is not represented by counsel, to assign counsel to act on his behalf.[88] Legal representation where the issue of fitness to stand trial arises is absolutely crucial.

A person who is found unfit to stand trial may appeal to the Court of Appeal against that verdict on certain grounds of appeal under certain conditions.[89] The Attorney General or counsel instructed by him for the purpose may appeal to the Court of Appeal against the verdict that an accused is unfit to stand trial, on any ground of appeal that involves a question of law alone.[90] Until the recent amendments, there was no appeal whatsoever from a finding of unfitness to stand trial.

New powers of a Court of Appeal include that to set aside a conviction and find the appellant unfit to stand trial and order that he be kept in safe custody to await the pleasure of the Lieutenant Governor.[91] Where a Court of Appeal allows an appeal against a verdict that the accused is unfit to stand trial, it is required, subject to what is stated in the next sentence, to order a new trial.[92] Where the verdict that the accused is unfit to stand trial was returned after the close of the prosecution's case, the Court of Appeal may, even though the verdict may have been proper, if it is of the opinion that the accused should have been acquitted at the close of the case for the prosecution, allow the appeal, set aside the verdict and direct a judgment or a verdict of acquittal to be entered.[93]

Under certain circumstances, a person who is found unfit to stand trial and against whom that verdict is affirmed by the Court of Appeal may appeal to the Supreme Court of Canada.[94]

If a person is found unfit to stand trial, the court is required to order "that the accused be kept in custody until the pleasure of the Lieutenant Governor of the province is known" and any plea that has been pleaded is to be set aside.[95] The Lieutenant Governor of the province may then make an order for the safe custody of the accused "in the place and in the manner" that he may direct.[96] Such custody is considered at a later point herein.

It should be noted that an individual who has been found unfit to stand trial has been found neither guilty nor innocent. He is still liable to be tried on the charge against him.[97]

It is not an uncommon occurrence for the criminal process to be "suspended" on what many would see as "humanitarian" grounds. The typical example is found in the case of a person who is charged with crime and who appears to have a mental handicap. He is, thereupon, sent for observation to a mental hospital, the staff of which confirms the handicap and reports that they have an appropriate program of treatment or training for him. While the court or the Crown Attorney has the power to insist on the return of the individual for trial, they do not always do so. Through various mechanisms – either formal or informal – the judge or the prosecuting authority might relate a message to the effect that the institution should do what it can for the person. Whether or not he will be required in court at a later date on the charge is not always clear: indeed, it might be clear that that decision is not being made at the time. All the while, the individual might be fit to stand trial and, therefore, ostensibly he should be tried according to the terms of the criminal law. He might spend months, and sometimes years, in the institution.

Where the charge is a minor one, it seems appropriate to "withdraw" the charge and channel the accused person through what could be termed "mental health procedures". Often nothing is gained by prosecuting cases of this nature. The charge, however, is not always "withdrawn". To subject the person to trial on a minor offence after he has undergone his course of treatment or training is a humiliating experience and could easily undo the good that has been done. Moreover, he will have been denied the right to a "speedy trial". We recommend, therefore, that consideration be given, in the case of a minor charge, to placing a mentally handicapped accused person in a program of rehabilitation rather than in the criminal process, but only where a decision is then taken to withdraw the charge for all time.

Where the charge is a serious one, it is doubtful that the passage of time will exclude the criminal process. Should the charge be grave enough that the institutional authorities might be concerned that the person is potentially dangerous (simply in view of the charge), the charge should be tried at once. Even where a number of years has elapsed and the criminal proceedings are "stayed" (a decision is taken not to proceed), the staff of the institution might be hesitant to release the person since the very fact of the gravity of the charge – which, by the way, has not been proved – indicates that precautions should be taken. Had there been a trial, the person might have been acquitted. He, also, can complain of undue delay in his trial. Consequently, it is recommended that nothing short of a court finding of unfitness to stand trial should stand in the way of a criminal trial on a serious charge.

Still on the question of fitness to stand trial, it is felt that the recent amendment to the law concerning postponement does not go far enough. As mentioned, postponement of the trial of the fitness issue is permissible up until any time up to the opening of the case for the defence. No reason is seen why defence counsel should be denied the opportunity of himself calling evidence before the court proceeds on the issue of fitness. It may very well be that there is a good defence of self-defence or alibi which can best or only be established in that way. Our recommendation follows that the *Criminal Code* be amended to allow the court to postpone the fitness issue even later than the present law permits.

On occasion, persons undergoing preliminary inquiry may be clearly unfit to stand trial because of mental handicap. A court at this stage has, under the current law, no power to make a finding on the fitness question. It has been said that an accused who is "unfit" should not have to undergo a preliminary hearing. Not only must he do so, but to wait until his trial proper might result in a severely handicapped person languishing in prison for a lengthy period of time. The recommendation is put forward that the *Criminal Code* be amended to permit the advancement of the determination of the fitness issue in a proper case to the stage of preliminary hearing.

Under Canadian criminal law either a person is criminally responsible or he is not. Criminal responsibility is determined according to a modified version of the test laid down in *M'Naghten's Case*,[98] and reference is made to section 16 of the *Criminal Code*.[99]

> "(1) No person shall be convicted of an offence in respect of an act or omission on his part while he was insane.
>
> (2) For the purposes of this section a person is insane when he is in a state of natural imbecility or has disease of the mind to an extent that renders him in-

capable of appreciating the nature and quality of an act or omission or of knowing that an act or omission is wrong.

(3) A person who has specific delusions, but is in other respects sane, shall not be acquitted on the ground of insanity unless the delusions caused him to believe in the existence of a state of things that, if it existed, would have justified or excused his act or omission.

(4) Every one shall, until the contrary is proved, be presumed to be and to have been sane."

Consequently, every accused person is presumed by law to be and to have been sane. Where an accused is retarded to an extent that renders him incapable of appreciating the nature and quality of an act or omission or of knowing that an act or omission is wrong, he will not be convicted, but is entitled to an acquittal on the ground of insanity.

There is a great deal of case law interpreting Section 16 of the *Code* which is available elsewhere[100] and it will not be recited here.

A number of other tests of criminal responsibility have been developed and these, as well, will not be recited here.[101]

ARTICLE VI of the Declaration of general and special rights of the mentally retarded[102] provides, in part, that the "mentally retarded person . . . . [i]f accused, . . . has a right to a fair trial with full recognition being given to his degree of responsibility." On its face, the Canadian criminal law – with its either responsible or not responsible posture – does not, on the question of guilt or innocence, take into account "degrees of responsibility".[103] Then, again, neither does the criminal law in most Anglo-American jurisdictions.

In England, the concept of "diminished responsibility" was introduced by statute in 1957, but it is of extremely limited application, being available as a defence only on a charge of murder. An accused person who successfully pleads diminished responsibility is still convicted, but of the lesser offence of manslaughter. The wording of the relevant provisions[104] is noteworthy.

"(1) Where a person kills or is a party to the killing of another, he shall not be convicted of murder if he was suffering from such abnormality of mind (whether arising from a condition of arrested or retarded development of mind or any inherent causes or induced by disease or injury) as substantially impaired his mental responsibility for his acts and omissions in doing or being a party to the killing.

(2) On a charge of murder, it shall be for the defence to prove that the person charged is by virtue of this section not liable to be convicted of murder.

(3) A person who but for this section would be liable, whether as principal or as accessory, to be convicted of murder shall be liable instead to be convicted of manslaughter.

(4) The fact that one party to a killing is by virtue of this section not liable to be convicted of murder shall not affect the question whether the killing amounted to murder in the case of any other party to it."

There is a suggestion that, even in the absence of a statutory defence, something akin to diminished responsibility might be available as a defence.[105]

Although we view the possibility of incorporating the concept of "diminished" or "partial" responsibility in Canadian criminal law as a major issue to consider, we cannot begin to do so. The topic is overwhelming: to treat it lightly is to do it injustice.

We do recommend, however, that the full area of criminal responsibility in Canada be fully reassessed and, in particular, to determine whether the concept of diminished responsibility should be a part of it. This is the feeling of the Ouimet Committee.

> "We are of the view that section 16 of the *Criminal Code* could now reasonably stand a full and complete reassessment . . . . Any extensive reconsideration relating to the issue of responsibility would, of course, be bound to take cognizance of the concept of 'diminished responsibility'."[106]

The *Criminal Code*,[107] as recently amended, allows a person acquitted on account of insanity to appeal to the court of appeal against that special verdict under certain conditions.[108] This opportunity of appeal did not exist before.

Where the accused is acquitted on account of insanity, the court is required to order that "he be kept in strict custody in the place and in the manner" that the court directs "until the pleasure of the Lieutenant-Governor of the province is known."[109] The Lieutenant Governor may then make an order for the safe custody of the accused "in the place and in the manner" that he may direct.[110] A discussion of such custody is considered in the ensuing pages.

An interesting concept has been put forward in connection with the trial of mentally retarded persons. This concept would see accused persons dealt with according to their mental, rather than chronological age. The *Juvenile Delinquents Act*,[111] a federal statute, for the purposes of the Act, defines a "child" as "any boy or girl apparently or actually under the age of sixteen years, ..."[112]

A Bill[113] introduced into the House of Commons in 1965 would have amended the definition so that it would read "any boy or girl apparently or actually under the age of sixteen years and any male or female person mentally under that age, ..."[114]

The "Explanatory Note" printed with the Bill describes its purpose as follows.

> "The passage of the *Juvenile Delinquents Act* marked our recognition that a juvenile charged with an offence against our criminal laws should not – as well for the good of the community as for his own good – be exposed to the usual public and trial process of the criminal courts: and, if adjudged an offender, can not comprehend and benefit by and therefore should not undergo the penal punishment of an adult offender.
>
> Since the passage of the Act, scientific technologies enable us to define the mental age of a person in terms of an equivalent chronological age. The purpose of this Bill is simply to update the law in accord with these scientific advances and so apply the Act to those mentally retarded persons who have a mental age within the age limits protected by the Act."

Postponing, for the moment, discussion of this Bill, it would be even more interesting to speculate what would be the effect were the mental age concept introduced into the *Criminal Code*[115] itself. A person who is under the age of seven cannot be convicted under the *Code*.[116] A person over seven but under the age of fourteen cannot be so convicted "unless he was competent to know the nature and consequences of his conduct and to appreciate that it was wrong".[117] Those who are knowledgeable about the range of mental age within the retarded class will see that such an amendment to the *Code* would have a significant impact.

Turning now to a consideration of the Bill as introduced to amend the *Juvenile Delinquents Act*, we do not endorse it. From a practical point of view, the lack of precision involved and the controversy invited in determining mental age represents major difficulties. The measurement of mental age, while ascertained through a mathematical formula, is based upon an exercise about which there certainly could not be said to be universal agreement. Quite apart from that, however, it seems to us that a retarded adult should, if for no other reason than pursuing the doctrine of "normalization", be tried in adult court just as any other adult. In this section on crime and corrections, it can be seen that the current criminal law does take account of, and has safety valves for, the mentally retarded. Admittedly, improvement and refinement are indicated both in the law and its application, but beyond this we should not go.[118]

Persons detained under the order of the Lieutenant Governor in Canadian provinces are commonly referred to as the "criminally insane". Such detention stems originally from England where persons in this category were said to be held at the Pleasure of His Majesty.[119]

Individuals held under such an order comprise three main groups as follows:

(a) Those found by a court to be unfit to stand trial on account of insanity.

(b) Those found by a court not to have been criminally responsible at the time of the offence charged and, as a result, not guilty on account of insanity.

(c) Those found to be mentally disordered while in a prison or correctional institution, either before or after trial.

Until recently, it was generally thought that persons detained under an order of the Lieutenant Governor would never be released and that life-long custody was, to all intents and purposes, inevitable. It has always been doubtful whether a warrant or order of the Lieutenant Governor could be attacked in the courts. Indeed, the mere production of the documentation representing the Lieutenant Governor's order may be a good and sufficient answer to the writ of *habeas corpus*.

Such persons have been released in various provinces over the years but, until recently, the machinery employed for this purpose has, for the most part, been no more than *ad hoc*.

Saskatchewan did, in 1946, establish by Order-in-Council two boards to review the cases of persons detained pursuant to an order of the Lieutenant Governor and these boards still function, although there is some question about their regularity.

The first mandatory review of these persons in Canada by statute itself was provided in Ontario by *The Mental Health Act, 1967*.[120] That Act provides for the appointment of a body known as an advisory review board and, in fact, such a board was appointed in 1968. The board is composed of a Supreme Court Judge as chairman, two psychiatrists, a lawyer and a layman and it has jurisdiction to consider the case of every patient in a psychiatric facility who is held pursuant to a warrant of the Lieutenant Governor. According to the statute, the case of every such patient must be considered by the advisory review board once in every year, commencing with the year next after the year in which the warrant was issued. Reviews by this board do not depend upon application: each case is reviewed on an automatic basis. Moreover, there is provision for the case of an individual to be reviewed before he is otherwise eligible or more frequently than once in each calendar year upon the written request of the Minister of Health. The advisory review board is required to conduct such inquiry as it considers necessary to reach a decision and may hold a hearing (which in the discretion of the board may be held in private) for the purpose of receiving oral testimony. Where a hearing is held, the patient may attend unless the chairman otherwise directs and, where the patient does not attend, he may have a person appear as his representative. The patient or his representative may call witnesses and make submissions and, with the permission of the chairman, may cross-examine witnesses. The officer-in-charge of a psychiatric facility must, for the purpose of an inquiry, furnish the chairman with such information and reports as the chairman requests. An advisory review board or any member of it is, by statute, entitled to interview a patient or other person in private. In order for there to be a quorum, all five members of the advisory review board must consider the case. Four out of five members are required to make a recommendation of the board. Considering the composition of the advisory review board, it can be seen that no recommendation can be made unless at least one legal member or one psychiatric member sides with the majority. Upon the conclusion of an inquiry, the chairman of the advisory review board is required to prepare a written report of the recommendations of the board and transmit a copy to the Provincial Cabinet. It can be gathered from the name of the board that it acts only in an advisory capacity to Cabinet. However, experience thus far indicates that Cabinet relies heavily upon the recommendations of the advisory review board. Indeed, during the calendar year 1968, slightly over 100 cases were considered by the board and, without exception, Cabinet decreed that every one of the recommendations of the board be accepted.

Recent mental health legislation in the provinces of Prince Edward Island [121] and New Brunswick[122] contains similar provisions for the review of patients detained pursuant to an order of the Lieutenant Governor.

Three provinces, therefore, have now seen fit to provide for such review bodies in their own legislation.

By amendment to the *Criminal Code* in 1969,[123] the Lieutenant Governor of a province is empowered to appoint a board to review the case of persons held by virtue of an order of the Lieutenant Governor. Such a board is to consist of not less than three and not more than five members, at least two of whom are duly qualified psychiatrists and at least one of whom is a lawyer. Three members, at least one of whom is a psychiatrist and one a lawyer, constitute a quorum. Such a board is, according to the *Code*, required to review each case not later than six months after the making of the order of the Lieutenant Governor and at least once during every six months following the date the case was previously reviewed so long as that person remains in custody under the order. A board appointed under the *Code* is required forthwith after each review to report to the Lieutenant Governor setting out fully the results of the review. In addition to the periodic reviews stated, the board must review any case when requested to do so by the Lieutenant Governor and report to him.

The above-noted provisions in the *Criminal Code* are, as can be seen, different from the provisions in provincial legislation already enacted in the three provinces mentioned. In either case, the board would be appointed provincially. There may be a constitutional issue involved and, consequently, there is some question as to whether it should be Parliament or the provinces enacting legislation of this nature. Because of the technicalities involved, it is not intended in this volume to consider the constitutional question. Nonetheless, what is clear is that there is now statutory provision dealing with the review of individuals held by order of the Lieutenant Governor. Since the detention under such an order can, in many instances, be considered to be "preventive" and that strikes at the very heart of civil rights, it can be said that there is no excuse in any province for failing to establish an appropriate review body to consider periodically these cases on a real and extensive basis. We recommend that each province examine its practices relating to review of persons detained upon the order of the Lieutenant Governor to ensure that they are effective and fair.

There is every indication that bold, new approaches are indicated in selected cases even before they reach the review level.

It could be that a retarded person found unfit to stand trial does not require institutionalization. Depending upon the nature of the offence charged, the history of the accused and other pertinent factors, it should be open for the Lieutenant Governor to make an order not involving institutionalization which now follows as a matter of course. Accordingly, we recommend that release from custody following a finding of unfitness to stand trial be considered a possibility in appropriate instances. Were such a recommendation followed, the individual would still be subject to undergo trial if and when he should become "fit" in that respect. This, however, does not stand in the way of our recommendation. He would merely be a person out of custody who is awaiting trial.

Likewise, in the case of persons found not guilty on account of insanity. We see no reason why, in an appropriate case, such an individual should not be released from custody under the initial order of the Lieutenant Governor. It is our recommendation, therefore, that following an acquittal by reason of insanity, release from custody be viewed as a potential disposition. A person so released would no longer be liable to further proceedings under the criminal law: he will have had his "day in court".

The last two recommendations (concerning release from custody under the initial order of the Lieutenant Governor) are not clearly authorized under the *Criminal Code* as it now reads and it may be necessary to amend the pertinent section.[124]

Some attention should be given to the conditions under which those held pursuant to an order of the Lieutenant Governor are held. It is estimated that there are 1,000, more or less, of them across Canada.[125] Each province looks after its own. The number each province has ranges from a few to a few hundred. The physical accommodation, conditions of custody, and the programs made available to these detainees vary greatly from one province to the next. Needless to say, it is difficult to maintain appropriate programs for so few people. While some provinces have seen fit to mingle these persons with others, thereby enabling the former to reap the benefits of existing programs, other provinces have not. In the end result, there are a number of people – although not many, relatively speaking – whose lot could, if the proper officials put their minds to it, improve readily by leaps and bounds. A certain proportion of these are retarded, but we have no statistical data to present. We recommend that each province take a hard look at the accommodation, custody and programs for persons detained under the order of the Lieutenant Governor with a view to improving their chances of rehabilitation.

Once an accused person is convicted, the problem becomes one of disposition. The alternatives available to a judge are imprisonment, suspended sentence and probation, or a fine. A variety of considerations apply to the sentencing decision: these include the age of the prisoner, the manner in which the offence was committed, the background and personality of the prisoner, his criminal record, his prospects for rehabilitation, and the interests of the public.

Evidence of a mental handicap may have been part of the trial, depending upon the nature of the defence made. Some lawyers have been reluctant to put forward the issue of mental disability because the potential consequent incarceration in mental hospital could be for a longer period than any sentence of imprisonment that might have been imposed. This has become less prevalent in those provinces with review boards authorized to recommend or order release of mental patients. Accused persons appearing without counsel may also not have the mental issue properly put before the court.

Whether the mental handicap has been raised at trial or not, it certainly should be fully explored in a pre-sentence report – these are now prepared in relatively few instances – and any arguments directed to sentence. Psychiatric and psychological assessments should be part of this report to the judge, in addition to the sociological consideration of the prisoner's environment and history, where mental capacity may be impaired. The difficulty of providing such assessments in many jurisdictions is recognized, but it is essential that a judge be fully apprized of the condition of any person before him for sentence. We recommend that a court be bound to order a pre-sentence report in the case of every person convicted with respect to whom mental handicap is known or suspected.

If it is determined that a prisoner is to some extent retarded, and if the condition may have been a cause of his conduct, then the condition should be the determining factor in his treatment.

> "For such persons, imprisonment for the sake of punishment is never appropriate. . . . The mentally retarded offender, whether dangerous or not, requires rehabilitation addressed to the sources of his deviant behaviour."[126]

For some retardates, prison may be the proper rehabilitative environment. For most others, prison will certainly not be the proper place of disposition.

A massive amount of literature has been dedicated to the study of poor conditions in prisons, with feeble resources, poorly trained staff, brutality, and criminal influences receiving much attention. It is not proposed to duplicate those arguments here, but rather merely to note that full recognition must be given to the many deplorable facets of prison life.

The following is an excerpt from an article reporting the results of a nationwide survey of adult and juvenile penal and correctional institutions in the United States.

> "Our findings on the survey and the case study lead us to the conclusion that the mentally retarded offender is doubly disadvantaged. He is, because of his mental condition, disadvantaged in terms of adapting to the requirements of life in society. Offending, he becomes disadvantaged in terms of his rejection by various agencies in the society. For example, mental hospitals are not enthusiastic about receiving mentally retarded offenders since they are not seen as being mentally ill. Institutions for the retarded have historically been insistent on the removal of delinquent and criminal elements from their populations. Prisons, the destination of many retardates who offend, are unable to offer programs for these individuals but are also powerless to exclude them."[127]

Some penal institutions may make sincere efforts with respect to retarded inmates. Hampered by a lack of necessary staff and financial resources, and outdated concepts in many instances, the efforts are often no more than marginally successful. One authority ably points to the social consequences.

> "In 1906 a physician at the Indiana State Prison recommended that 'defective' inmates be separated from the others for special treatment. The 'special treatment' he had in mind was close custodial care for the longest permissible period. In most prisons today, his recommendation is being scrupulously followed.
>
> It is neither ignorance of nor indifference to the special needs of these prisoners on the part of correctional authorities that has produced this situation. Rather, it results from the pathetically limited resources of most prison systems which simply cannot be stretched to provide meaningful programs for both 'normal' and retarded inmates.
>
> •　•　•
>
> But it is more than that. While the retarded prisoner is perhaps more easily apprehended and convicted, and is certainly confined for longer periods than offenders of normal intellectual capacity, he is eventually released. Thus it is no

less than the enlightened self-interest of society that should demand that the mentally retarded prisoner be recognized as such, and that his confinement be rehabilitative rather than merely custodial."[128]

Once retribution is rejected as a factor in sentencing retardates, then individual offenders may be treated according to their needs. A detailed examination of the relationship between the condition and the offensive behavior is essential in each case. A retardate may commit a criminal act for a variety of reasons. Punishment, retraining in social skills, psychiatric treatment or counselling and care on probation may be variously indicated for different offenders. It may be that the condition of the prisoner and the effect of that condition on his behavior should become the crucial elements in the sentencing decision.

The foregoing is not an attempt to deny that some offenders are a danger to society and must be isolated. Even then, however, the estimate of dangerousness should be founded in facts derived from extensive investigation, and not, as often happens, a mere presumption from the fact of mental handicap.[129]

It is facile to say that judges should know everything about a prisoner before sentence, and that they should impose sentence to secure the best rehabilitation, when facilities are not available to permit effective sophistication on the Bench.

If probation is ordered because a judge is aware of the futility of imprisonment, due to the heavy workload of probation staff there is, unfortunately, only meager return. While in the community on probation, the retardate will probably find inadequate opportunity for care and rehabilitation available in even the largest metropolitan centers. The need is desperate for programs of community residential care. The extremes of punitive, criminalizing imprisonment and earnest (but ineffective) probation service efforts gravely fail to meet society's needs.

While reasonable alternatives to imprisonment remain inadequate, or where imprisonment is indicated in a particular case, a further consideration arises. It may be that for justice to be done, the mental disability of a prisoner should be a factor leading to mitigation of sentence. If a prisoner was less able to appreciate the consequences of his behavior, or suffers from a handicap in meeting the demands of the law, then his punishment should be less severe than that imposed upon others not so handicapped. The courts have not been consistent in either accepting or rejecting this principle. In *Regina v. Mitchell*,[130] a case of indecent assault, the Supreme Court of Ontario reduced the sentence from nine months imprisonment to two years probation on suspended sentence. However, in *Regina v. Watson and Watson*,[131] where retarded parents were convicted of manslaughter for maltreatment of their child, the Ontario Court of Appeal raised the sentence from two to five years. The Court stated that retarded people commit such offences more often than other persons, that the intellectually inadequate can be made aware of the criminality of such conduct, and that the higher sentence should be imposed to serve as public notice (to the retarded presumably) that such behavior will be punished. The trial judge had considered the mental deficiency a ground justifying the lower sentence.

When the program of a correctional institution fails to meet the needs of mentally handicapped prisoners, there should be means of tailoring special programs for them. Legislation in the correctional field is becoming more and more innovative and flexible. There is, for example, talk in Canada of allowing certain offenders to serve their sentences on weekends so as to minimize the risk of losing their jobs. There seems no reason why the handicapped cannot reap the benefits and be part of new schemes of this order. We recommend that laws be amended so that, in appropriate instances, mentally handicapped prisoners may be permitted

CRIME AND CORRECTIONS

to take advantage of community resources for them. One way of doing so would be by living in prison, but taking their training in the community. If programs of this type were established, then the officials of the community training services would be expected to make their facilities available for this purpose. It has been brought to our attention that workshops for the retarded have shown a reluctance to take convicted persons. This is, in our view, a reprehensible attitude and must be changed.

Sometimes it will be the case that the handicapped prisoner will require the treatment or training provided in, for example, a provincial psychiatric facility. Legislative provisions exist in both the federal and provincial spheres for transferring such a prisoner.[132] Often, however, undue delays are evident because of "red tape" in such procedures. They should be capable of being effected swiftly. We therefore recommend that laws providing authority for transfers of prisoners from correctional institutions to psychiatric facilities be amended, where indicated, so as to allow these transfers to take place without delay on the basis of local arrangements.

Another device which should here be considered is that of parole. It may be that a retarded prisoner could benefit by being placed on parole and serving the remainder of his sentence in the community. He could, in this manner, take advantage of the community resources for his rehabilitation – which are unavailable to him in prison – while under the supervision of his parole officer. This leads to our recommendation that community agencies for the handicapped make the existence of their services known to the parole authorities (both federal and provincial) encouraging the use of these services to facilitate parole in appropriate cases.

In England, a new approach in cases of defined mentally handicapped offenders was introduced by the *Mental Health Act, 1959*.[133] Under certain circumstances, a convicted offender may become the subject of a "hospital order" or a "guardianship order" in lieu of sentence. In addition to other requirements, the court must be of the opinion, "having regard to all the circumstances including the nature of the offence and the character and antecedents of the offender, and to the other available methods of dealing with him, that the most suitable method of disposing of the case is by means of [such an] order. . . ."[134] Moreover, a magistrate's court acting under this procedure has the power, if it thinks fit, to make such an order without convicting the individual where the court "is satisfied that the accused did the act or made the omission charged".[135] While these alternatives are a significant departure from current Canadian criminal law, we recommend that study be directed to the possibility of their incorporation into our jurisprudence.

A definite step forward in the attempt to ameliorate problems in this field has recently been taken in one metropolitan center by the Metropolitan Toronto Association for the Mentally Retarded. In mid-1970, a new committee – The Committee for Representation Through Understanding – was established. Its purpose is "to attract the attention of the various legal, judicial, and law enforcement bodies with respect to the treatment of suspected and convicted individuals who are mentally retarded."[136] An organizational meeting was held to which were invited representatives of various agencies and other interested persons. There the long term goal was stated as "to eventually have the law recognize that there is a difference, at least where the mentally retarded are concerned, between chronological age and mentally attained age."[137] Initially, the Metropolitan Toronto Association for the Mentally Retarded has offered to try and assist various law enforcement, custodial, and judicial bodies in their respective dealings with the mentally retarded. Members of all of these bodies have already indicated a willingness to co-operate in this program of the Association. There is no doubt but that an improvement of the overall system will be fostered by the efforts of this new Committee.

Specifically, it is hoped that this new Committee might, on a local basis, look into matters such as:

the level of police training in assisting them to recognize and identify the mentally retarded suspected of, or charged with crime;

the application of that training in practice by the police in dealing with the retarded;

the accessibility of lawyers to the retarded at the earliest possible stage in the criminal process;

the availability in law of legal aid to retarded accused persons;

the effectiveness in delivery of available legal aid to the retarded;

the conditions of pre-trial custody as they relate to the retarded;

the effective practical availability of bail to the retarded; and

the post-conviction stage as it relates to the retarded.

The situation in the matters listed above may range from exemplary to deplorable. Moreover, it will vary from one locality to another. Indications are that there should be similar studies undertaken in all localities.

We recommend that committees be established such as – The Committee for Representation Through Understanding – at the local level to study and urge improvement in the treatment of mentally retarded persons who find themselves in the criminal or correctional processes.

Being a party to a civil action

Rights and privileges are meaningless unless they are complemented by an ability to enforce them in law. The right to apply to a court and to sue for relief is essential.

The converse – the "right" to be sued – is perhaps not so readily enviable. The dignity and humanity of adulthood is dependent upon an acceptance of responsibility for one's behavior. If for any reason one's ability to accept that responsibility is denied, then maturity, dignity, and to some extent humanity are denied. Removal of liability to court action therefore is not a blessing. It is an act of degradation, and in a very real sense a refutation of independence and equality. The person wishing to sue should not be forgotten. If a prospective defendant is protected from suit, the right of the other party to enforce his interests is lost.

For persons afflicted with one mental disability or another, court proceedings are often incomprehensible. They are helpless to instruct counsel intelligently, to institute or defend legal action, and have little understanding of their rights or the remedies available to them.

In civil actions, various approaches are possible. Mentally handicapped persons could be treated like anyone else, which might see many absurd actions put before the courts and would make them helpless to defend themselves.

In the alternative, the mentally handicapped could be proscribed altogether as civil litigants. The result of such a proscription would be the denial to them of the opportunity to enforce and protect their rights, and the denial to others of relief for suffering or loss caused by the handicapped. It is obvious that a middle ground is the only just and sensible answer.

The provinces have sought this middle ground between equally unacceptable alternatives. The essence of the compromise reached is to introduce a third person to act for and with the handicapped party.

Persons of "unsound mind" are generally described in law as being either "so found" or "not so found". The difference between these two states is that, in the former, a "mental incompetency" hearing[138] has been held and incompetence was found. A "committee" (usually one person) for the incompetent person is always appointed at such a hearing. The term "not so found" means that no hearing has been held, but that if a hearing were held, a finding of incompetence would be made.[139] A hearing is, therefore, not a prerequisite to actual incompetence for litigation purposes.

Civil procedure rules may provide that after a writ of summons commencing an action is served, no further steps may be taken against a mentally handicapped defendant who has no "committee". The plaintiff may apply to the court and ask that a "guardian *ad litem*" (for the purposes of the litigation) be appointed for the defendant. The guardian *ad litem* then takes over and conducts the defence of the action. If the defendant has had a committee appointed by a court under mental incompetency proceedings, the committee defends the action.

Similar provisions govern the situation when it is the mentally handicapped person himself who wishes to sue. If he has been found mentally incompetent by a hearing, he will have a committee and the committee normally would bring the action.

A retardate who wishes to sue and has not had a committee appointed for him may sue only through a "next friend". A next friend is a person appointed by the court, upon application, to look after the interests of the handicapped individual and prosecute the action. Usually a parent or relative is appointed to act as next friend. The appointment is not made until the person to be appointed consents and agrees to act. A next friend may be responsible for the costs of the action if it is not won.[140]

Where a retardate is sued, his incompetence must be brought to the attention of the court by someone else. This is a problem. A plaintiff not being aware of the retardation may construe a lack of action taken in defence as a wilful ignoring of the claims against him. A plaintiff would then obtain default judgment. This problem, and the converse situation where a retardate has a claim that may go unpressed, demonstrates an obvious need.

One significant concern is that if a retardate is injured or victimized, a suit to recover damages is seriously compromised by his condition. A party must be able to explain to the court his injuries; the facts surrounding the incident; and to withstand cross-examination. Where, as often happens, the retardate is the only person in a position to know all the facts, his case may be hopeless and his right to relief unenforceable. Similar considerations apply to the defence of an action by a retardate. It is a very difficult matter. Perhaps justice would be served by relaxing the strict rules of evidence applied at trial in these cases, although sympathetic awareness by the judge or jury might achieve the same end.

The rules of practice in civil litigation are extremely complex to the layman. They vary from one province to another, and are peculiar to the context of the laws in the particular province. Whether or not these rules are fair as they relate to the handicapped is an issue which can be resolved only by legal experts familiar with the broad scope of the substantive law in a given province. We recommend the establishment of committees in each province to examine the rules of civil practice, with a view ultimately to their improvement, if and where indicated.

References

1 International League of Societies for the Mentally Handicapped, October 24, 1968. The entire declaration is reprinted as Appendix A.

2 CHALKE, SWADRON & GRIFFIN, THE LAW AND MENTAL DISORDER (PART TWO: CIVIL RIGHTS AND PRIVILEGES) 2 (1967).

3 THE PRESIDENT'S PANEL ON MENTAL RETARDATION, REPORT OF THE TASK FORCE ON LAW 21 (1963) (hereinafter cited as TASK FORCE).

4 *Ibid.*, reference 1.

5 Institutionalization is variously dealt with in hundreds of works. The reader is referred to some of the more significant which include: SWADRON, DETENTION OF THE MENTALLY DISORDERED (1964); CHALKE *et al.*, THE LAW AND MENTAL DISORDER (PART ONE: HOSPITALS AND PATIENT CARE) (1964); LINDMAN & MCINTYRE (eds.), THE MENTALLY DISABLED AND THE LAW (1961), Chapters 2 to 5; TASK FORCE, especially pp. 27-31; NEWMAN (ed.), INSTITUTIONALIZATION OF THE MENTALLY RETARDED (1967); ROBITSCHER, PURSUIT OF AGREEMENT: PSYCHIATRY & THE LAW (1966); and EDWARDS, MENTAL HEALTH SERVICES (3rd ed. 1961).

6 *British North America Act, 1867*, 30 & 31 Vict., c. 3, s. 92, head 7 (U.K.).

7 *Ibid.*, head 13.

8 The principal statutes, province by province, are: Alberta – *The Mental Health Act,* R.S.A. 1970, c. 231; British Columbia – *Mental Health Act, 1964*, S.B.C. 1964, c. 29; Manitoba – *The Mental Health Act*, R.S.M. 1970, c. M110; New Brunswick – *Mental Health Act*, S.N.B. 1969, c. 13; Newfoundland – *The Health and Public Welfare Act*, R.S.N. 1952, c. 51; Nova Scotia – *Nova Scotia Hospital Act*, R.S.N.S. 1967, c. 210, and *Municipal Mental Hospitals Act*, R.S.N.S. 1967, c. 202; Ontario – *The Mental Health Act, 1967*, S.O. 1967, c. 51; Prince Edward Island – *The Mental Health Act*, S.P.E.I. 1968, c. 37; Quebec – *Mental Patients Institutions Act*, R.S.Q. 1964, c. 166; and Saskatchewan – *The Mental Health Act*, R.S.S. 1965, c. 345. (The foregoing citations reflect either the general statutory revision or year of enactment of the particular statute. Subsequent amendments are not included.)

9 For a discussion of a potential scope for uniformity in laws of this nature, see Swadron, *Recent Mental Health Legislation*, 14 CANADA'S MENTAL HEALTH 10 (Sept.-Dec. 1966).

10 R.S.M. 1954, c. 161.

11 R.S.M. 1954, c. 160.

12 S.M. 1965, c. 48.

13 R.S.A. 1955, c. 200.

14 R.S.A. 1955, c. 199.

15 S.A. 1964, c. 54.

16 *Ibid.*, s. 2.

17 R.S.O. 1960, c. 236.

18 *Ibid.*, s. 1(k).

19 *Ibid.*, s. 1(l).

20 *Ibid.*, s. 20(3)(b).

21 S.O. 1967, c. 51, s. 7.

22 *Ibid.*, s. 1(f).

23 See, generally, CHALKE, SWADRON & GRIFFIN, THE LAW AND MENTAL DISORDER (PART TWO: CIVIL RIGHTS AND PRIVILEGES) (1967), and in particular, Chapter 2, entitled "Rights of Patients in Psychiatric Hospitals".

24 See ALLEN, FERSTER & WEIHOFEN, MENTAL IMPAIRMENT AND LEGAL INCOMPETENCY (1968), especially p. 46 *et seq.* dealing with hospitalization and incompetency.

25 Kirk, Guidelines for the Planning and Construction of Residences for the Ambulatory Mentally Retarded, Fall, 1969, at pp. 1 and 2, citing Freedman and Kaplan.

26 Interdepartmental Committee on Mental Retardation (Government of Ontario), Position Statement.

27 *Ibid.*, p. 7.

28 *Ibid.*, p. 8.

29 S.O. 1966, c. 65.

30 *Ibid.*, s. 8.

31 *MacLaughlan v. Soper* (1965), 50 M.P.R. 339 (P.E.I.), where an aged and infirm woman sold her land for one dollar, and the contract was upheld.

32 *Imperial Loan Co. v. Stone* (1892), 1 Q.B. 599.

33 *Grant v. Imperial Trust*, [1935] 3 D.L.R. 660.

34 *Wilson v. R.*, [1938] S.C.R. 317. See generally Coutts, *Contracts of Mental Incompetents*, SPECIAL LECTURES OF THE LAW SOCIETY OF UPPER CANADA 49 (1963).

35 R.S.A. 1970, c. 327.

36 In British Columbia, see *Sale of Goods Act*, R.S.B.C. 1960, c. 344, s. 9; in Manitoba, see *The Sale of Goods Act*, R.S.M. 1970, c. S10, s. 4; in New Brunswick, see *Sale of Goods Act*, R.S.N.B. 1952, c. 199, s. 3; in Newfoundland, see *The Sale of Goods Act*, R.S.N. 1952, c. 222, s. 3; in Nova Scotia, see *Sale of Goods Act*, R.S.N.S. 1967, c. 274,

s. 4; in Ontario, see *The Sale of Goods Act*, R.S.O. 1960, c. 358, s. 3; in Prince Edward Island, see *The Sale of Goods Act*, R.S.P.E.I. 1951, c. 144, s. 4; and in Saskatchewan, see *The Sale of Goods Act*, R.S.S. 1965, c. 388, s. 4.

37 *Ibid.,* footnote 35, s. 4(3).

38 Coutts, *op. cit.,* p. 68.

39 *W. W. Distributors & Co. Ltd. v. Thorsteinson* (1961), 26 D.L.R. (2d) 365 (Man. C. of A.).

40 See 2 Geo. V, c. 30.

41 *The Unconscionable Transactions Relief Act*, R.S.O. 1960, c. 410.

42 *Ibid.,* s. 2. In *Re Scott & Manor Inv. Ltd.,* [1961] O.W.N. 210 (Co. Ct.), it was decided that a fair test of reasonableness in a mortgage loan is whether the loan could have been secured at a lower cost.

43 See Ziegel, *Recent Legislative and Judicial Trends in Consumer Credit in Canada,* ASPECTS OF COMPARATIVE COMMERCIAL LAW 133 (1969). For example, in Manitoba, see *The Unconscionable Transactions Relief Act,* R.S.M. 1970, c. U20, s. 3; in Nova Scotia, see *Unconscionable Transactions Relief Act,* R.S.N.S. 1967, c. 319, s. 2.

44 *The Consumer Protection Act, 1966,* S.O. 1966, c. 23, s. 18 (1).

45 *The Consumer Protection Act,* R.S.M. 1970, c. C200, s. 61.

46 *The Direct Sellers Act Amendment Act, 1970,* S.S. 1970, c. 14, s. 2, adding s. 5A.

47 *The Direct Sellers Act,* S.N. 1966, c. 86, s. 23 (1).

48 *Consumer Protection Act,* S.B.C. 1967, c. 14, s. 7 (1).

49 S.B.C. 1969, c. 5, s. 5 amending s. 7 (1).

50 National Conference of Commissioners on Uniform State Laws, 1952.

51 ALLEN, FERSTER & WEIHOFEN, MENTAL IMPAIRMENT AND LEGAL INCOMPETENCY 344 (1968): see, generally, Chapter 7 entitled "Operation of a Motor Vehicle", pp. 344-53. See, also, LINDMAN & MCINTYRE (eds.), THE MENTALLY DISABLED AND THE LAW 268 (1961).

52 Dr. William A. Tillman, reported in transcript of proceedings of "Mental Disorders" (Workshop No. 3), contained in ONTARIO DEPARTMENT OF TRANSPORT, SEMINAR ON THE MEDICAL ASPECTS OF SAFE DRIVING 36-38 (1970).

53 Dr. R. Ian Hector, reported in transcript of proceedings of "Mental Disorders", *ibid.,* footnote 52.

54 For example, in Ontario, see s. 145 *a* of *The Highway Traffic Act,* R.S.O. 1960, c. 172, enacted by S.O. 1968, c. 50, s. 25 which reads as follows: "Every legally qualified medical practitioner shall report to the Registrar [of Motor Vehicles] the name, address and clinical condition of every person sixteen years of age or over attending upon the medical practitioner for medical services, who in the opinion of such medical practitioner is suffering from a condition that may make it dangerous for such person to operate a motor vehicle." This section also includes two protective clauses which are considered vital: the physician is given absolute statutory protection from suit for reporting under the section; and, the report is given "privileged" status in law. Reporting of this nature is viewed critically in CHALKE, SWADRON & GRIFFIN, THE LAW AND MENTAL DISORDER (PART TWO: CIVIL RIGHTS AND PRIVILEGES) 88-89 (1967): see, generally, Chapter Seven entitled "Operating a Motor Vehicle", pp. 76-92.

55 ALLEN, FERSTER & WEIHOFEN, MENTAL IMPAIRMENT AND LEGAL INCOMPETENCY 366 (1968): see, generally, Chapter 9 entitled "Capacity to Vote and Hold Public Office", pp. 364-69. See also LINDMAN & MCINTYRE (eds.), THE MENTALLY DISABLED AND THE LAW 268-69 (1961).

56 CHALKE, SWADRON & GRIFFIN, THE LAW AND MENTAL DISORDER (PART TWO: CIVIL RIGHTS AND PRIVILEGES) (1967): see Chapter Five entitled "Voting", pp. 52-63.

57 *Ibid.,* p. 61.

58 See generally Robins, *Liability in Tort of Mental Incompetents,* SPECIAL LECTURES OF THE LAW SOCIETY OF UPPER CANADA 77 (1963).

59 [1952] 1 All E.R. 925.

60 *Ibid.,* p. 926.

61 (1956), 6 D.L.R. (2d) 570 (Man. Q.B.).

62 AMERICAN LAW INSTITUTE, RESTATEMENT OF THE LAW: SECOND – 2 TORTS 16, section 283B (1965).

63 (1911), 24 O.L.R. 214.

64 *Ibid.,* footnote 62, p. 129, section 319.

65 S.P.E.I. 1968, c. 37.

66 *Ibid.,* s. 57.

67 See, for example, *The Highway Traffic Act* (Ontario), R.S.O. 1960, c. 172, s. 105(1).

68 See, for example, in Manitoba, *The Devolution of Estates Act,* R.S.M. 1970, c. D70, ss. 6 to 10; in Ontario, *The Devolution of Estates Act,* R.S.O. 1960, c. 106, s. 30. Not all provinces employ the same title for their statutes dealing with this matter: in Saskatchewan, the pertinent enactment is *The Intestate Succession Act,* R.S.S. 1965, c. 126.

69 It should be noted that even where there is a will, it may be varied by virtue of legislation dealing with dependants' relief. Such legislation affords relief where there has

been an omission of benefit to a family member who should have a claim on the bounty of the deceased and merit his support: see, for example, in Ontario, *The Dependants' Relief Act*, R.S.O. 1960, c. 104, s. 2.

70 Williston, *Testamentary Capacity*, SPECIAL LECTURES OF THE LAW SOCIETY OF UPPER CANADA 89, 96 (1963). See, generally, LINDMAN & MCINTYRE (eds.), THE MENTALLY DISABLED AND THE LAW 264-66 (1961).

71 See ROBITSCHER, PURSUIT OF AGREEMENT: PSYCHIATRY & THE LAW 52 (1966).

72 *Wingrove v. Wingrove* (1885), 11 P.D. 81.

73 *Craig v. Lamoureux*, [1920] A.C. 349 (P.C.).

74 *Ibid.*, p. 357.

75 [1947] 1 D.L.R. 830.

76 *Ibid.*, p. 837.

77 SWADRON, DETENTION OF THE MENTALLY DISORDERED (1964), Chapters 7 to 12 inclusive; CHALKE, SWADRON, MORTON & GRIFFIN, THE LAW AND MENTAL DISORDER (PART THREE: CRIMINAL PROCESS) (1969); THE CANADIAN COMMITTEE ON CORRECTIONS, REPORT (TOWARD UNITY: CRIMINAL JUSTICE AND CORRECTIONS) (1969) (popularly referred to as the "Ouimet Report"), Chapter 12, entitled "Mentally Disordered Persons under the Criminal Law"; LINDMAN & MCINTYRE (eds.), THE MENTALLY DISABLED AND THE LAW (1961), Chapter 11, entitled "Mental Disability and the Criminal Law"; and TASK FORCE 31-40.

78 Shapiro, *Delinquent and Disturbed Behaviour Within the Field of Mental Deficiency*, contained in DE REUCK & PORTER (eds.), THE MENTALLY ABNORMAL OFFENDER 76, 76 (1968).

79 S.C. 1953-54, c. 51, s. 451 (*c*) (i) (A).

80 *Ibid.*, s. 524 (1a), as amended by S.C. 1960-61, c. 43, s. 22.

81 *Ibid.*, s. 710 (5), as amended by S.C. 1960-61, c. 43, s. 42.

82 Some provinces, in their statutes, authorize remands for observation on a similar basis recommended herein for the *Code*. See, for example, *The Mental Health Act, 1967* (Ontario), S.O. 1967, c. 51, s. 15: "Where a judge or magistrate has reason to believe that a person in custody who appears before him charged with an offence suffers from mental disorder, the judge or magistrate may, by order, remand that person for admission as a patient to a psychiatric facility for a period of not more than two months." The term "mental disorder" is defined (see s. 1(*f*)) as "any disease or disability of the mind" which includes mental retardation. A constitutional issue is involved: see Swadron, *Remands for Psychiatric Examination in Ontario*, 6 CRIMINAL LAW QUARTERLY 102 (1963).

83 S.C. 1953-54, c. 51, s. 524 (1).

84 Swadron, *The Unfairness of Unfitness*, 9 CANADIAN BAR JOURNAL 76 (1966). This Editorial is reprinted here with the kind permission of the *Canadian Bar Journal*, in which it was first published.

85 See, generally, the *Criminal Law Amendment Act*, S.C. 1968-69, c. 38.

86 *Ibid.*, s. 47(1), substituting a new s. 524(2).

87 *Ibid.*, s. 47(2), substituting a new s. 524(5).

88 *Ibid.*, s. 47(1), adding a new s. 524 (1b).

89 *Ibid.*, s. 55(2), substituting a new s. 583(2).

90 *Ibid.*, s. 56, adding a new s. 584(3).

91 *Ibid.*, s. 60(1) (2), amending s. 592(1).

92 *Ibid.*, s. 60(3), substituting a new s. 592(6). In the United States, federal convictions may be attacked collaterally: see Swadron, *Collateral Attack of Federal Convictions on the Ground of Mental Incompetency*, 39 TEMPLE LAW QUARTERLY 117 (1966).

93 *Ibid.*, s. 60(3), adding a new s. 592(7).

94 *Ibid.*, s. 64, adding a new s. 597B.

95 *Criminal Code*, 1953-54, c. 51, s. 524 (4).

96 *Ibid.*, s. 526.

97 *Ibid.*, s. 524(6), as amended by S.C. 1968-69, c. 38, s. 47 (2).

98 (1843), 10 Cl. & F. 200, 8 E.R. 718.

99 S.C. 1953-54, c. 51.

100 See, for example, SWADRON, DETENTION OF THE MENTALLY DISORDERED (1964), especially Chapter 11 entitled "Criminal Responsibility". Perhaps more important than the issue of criminal responsibility is what happens to the individual afterwards: see Swadron, *Criminal Responsibility – A Secondary Problem*, 11 CHITTY'S LAW JOURNAL 274 (1963), and Swadron, *Criminal Responsibility – A Secondary Problem* (reprinted with Discussion) 9 CANADIAN PSYCHIATRIC ASSOCIATION JOURNAL 512 (1964).

101 Some of these tests are listed in SWADRON, *ibid.*, at pp. 391-93.

102 International League of Societies for the Mentally Handicapped, October 24, 1968. The entire declaration is reprinted as Appendix A.

103 "Degrees of responsibility" may be taken into account at the sentencing level which is discussed later.

104 *Homicide Act, 1957*, 5 & 6 Eliz. 2, c. 11, s. 2 (U.K.).

105 In *Regina v. Lenchitsky*, (1954) CRIMINAL LAW REVIEW 216, it was held by the English Court of Criminal Appeal that the jury were entitled to take into consideration the fact that the accused was a feeble-minded person in assisting them in coming to a conclusion as to whether or not he had an actual intent to kill or inflict grievous bodily harm.

106 THE CANADIAN COMMITTEE ON CORRECTIONS, REPORT (TOWARD UNITY: CRIMINAL JUSTICE AND CORRECTIONS) 222 (1969). See also, REPORT OF THE ROYAL COMMISSION, THE LAW OF INSANITY AS A DEFENCE IN CRIMINAL CASES (1956), especially at p. 38, wherein it is stated: "We feel that if the defence of diminished responsibility is to be recognized at all it should be recognized in all cases"; and the interesting questions raised and discussion in Scollin, *Diminished Responsibility*, (CANADIAN) BAR (ASSOCIATION) PAPERS 241 (1962).

107 S.C. 1953-54, c. 51.

108 *Ibid.*, s. 583(2)(*b*), substituted by S.C. 1968-69, c. 38, s. 55. See, also, s. 592 of the *Code*, as amended, in respect of the new powers of a court of appeal in this area.

109 *Ibid.*, s. 523(2).

110 *Ibid.*, s. 526.

111 R.S.C. 1952, c. 160.

112 *Ibid.*, s. 2(1)(*a*). There is provision for increasing the age to eighteen in any province by proclamation of the Governor in Council: see s. 2(2).

113 Bill C-7: first reading April 8, 1965.

114 *Ibid.*, s. 1.

115 S.C. 1953-54, c. 51.

116 *Ibid.*, s. 12.

117 *Ibid.*, s. 13.

118 In the United States, a "specially constituted court, empowered to assume wardship over any adult person shown to be substantially impaired in his intellectual capacity, who has committed an act which, if committed by an adult without such impairment, would constitute a felony or serious misdemeanour", has been suggested. See Allen, *Toward an Exceptional Offenders Court*, 4 MENTAL RETARDATION 3, 5 (Feb. 1966) (U.S.).

119 See *Criminal Lunatics Act* (1800), 39 & 40 Geo. 3, c. 94, s. 2 (U.K.).

120 S.O. 1967, c. 51, s. 31: see also ss. 28 to 30 inclusive.

121 *The Mental Health Act*, S.P.E.I. 1968, c. 37, s. 29.

122 *Mental Health Act*, S.N.B. 1969, c. 13, s. 34.

123 S. 527A, as enacted by S.C. 1968-69, c. 38, s. 48.

124 See s. 526 which provides that the Lieutenant Governor may make an order for the "safe custody" of the accused in the place and manner that he may direct.

125 THE CANADIAN COMMITTEE ON CORRECTIONS, REPORT (TOWARD UNITY: CRIMINAL JUSTICE AND CORRECTIONS) 230 (1969).

126 TASK FORCE 39.

127 Brown and Courtless, *The Mentally Retarded in Penal and Correctional Institutions*, 124 AMERICAN JOURNAL OF PSYCHIATRY 1164, 1168 (1968).

128 Allen, *The Retarded Offender: Unrecognized in Court and Untreated in Prison*, 32 FEDERAL PROBATION 22, 27 (September 1968).

129 For a discussion of the prognosis for future lawbreaking by retarded offenders see Power, *Subnormality and Crime – II*, 9 MEDICINE, SCIENCE AND THE LAW 162 (1969). See also Stürup, *Will This Man Be Dangerous?*, THE MENTALLY ABNORMAL OFFENDER 5 (1968).

130 [1965] 2 O.R. 632.

131 [1968] 1 O.R. 279.

132 See *Criminal Code*, S.C. 1953-54, c. 51, s. 527; *Penitentiary Act*, S.C. 1960-61, c. 53, s. 19; in Ontario, see *The Department of Correctional Services Act, 1968*, S.O. 1968, c. 27, s. 17(2).

133 7 & 8 Eliz. 2, c. 72.

134 *Ibid.*, s. 60(1). See, also, THE CANADIAN COMMITTEE ON CORRECTIONS, REPORT (TOWARD UNITY: CRIMINAL JUSTICE AND CORRECTIONS) (1969), especially at p. 236, where the Committee recommends an amendment to the *Criminal Code* by authorizing a court to issue a "hospital permit".

135 *Ibid.*, s. 60(2).

136 Letter, dated August 26, 1970, from Mr. Robert H. Bradshaw, Chairman, Committee for Representation Through Understanding, to the Project Director.

137 Letter, dated September 25, 1970, from Mr. Robert H. Bradshaw to the Project Director (see *ibid.*).

138 Mental incompetency proceedings are discussed at length later in this book.

139 *Manton v. Tompsett*, [1948] O.W.N. 457.

140 *Young v. Heron*, (1868) 14 G.R. 580.

work
and
working

work and working

Introduction

"The mentally retarded person has a right . . . to such education, training, habilitation and guidance as will enable him to develop his ability and potential to the fullest possible extent, no matter how severe his degree of disability. No mentally handicapped person should be deprived of such services by reason of the costs involved."[1]

"The mentally retarded person has a right to economic security and to a decent standard of living. He has a right to productive work or other meaningful occupation."[2]

A retarded person who has full economic security need not depend upon the financial resources of the state nor of anyone. As his earning ability grows stronger, so does his dependency diminish. One writer[3] considers this advantage and notes other significant, positive factors as well.

"1 A working retardate is generally a happier person. Work gives self-esteem and a feeling of accomplishment and worth.

2 Work lends adult status to a retardate, and thus adds to his dignity in the sight of others.

3 In our work-oriented society, positive attitudes will generally be expressed toward the worker, and negative ones toward the drone. Thus, the retardate's adjustment will be enhanced by the community attitudes he encounters.

4 The family of the working retardate is, generally, a better adjusted family. Since work tends to make the retardate more acceptable, it engenders positive attitudes in the family benefiting the retardate indirectly.

5 A retardate capable of working will be less likely to become an economic burden to his family or society.

6 A working retardate contributes to the economic welfare of society.

7 He earns an income that is likely to give him more of the material benefits enjoyed by the majority of our citizens.

8 Idleness can lead to nonadaptive or maladaptive behaviour."[4]

During periods of high unemployment, such as that seen in Canada at the present time, certain groups are more likely to suffer than others. It may be difficult to find ears sympathetic to the handicapped in such a competitive labor market. Nevertheless, it is inherently important for us to find ways and means of entry for the handicapped into the stream of employment.

There are, in Canada, numerous programs of financial support which offer assistance to the handicapped through the provision of benefits such as general welfare and disability allowances. The rationale behind habilitation efforts is to render unnecessary the reliance of the handicapped on these benefits. While financial support programs are inherently proper, their application in practice may have the effect of severely restricting or defeating altogether the ultimate goal of self-sufficiency. Without having here to analyze the operation of the schemes of financial support, it seems to be generally so that the allowance decreases by the amount of income earned. The reduction of benefits simply perpetuates stagnation at that level. Incentive to betterment is lost. So, also, may be the actual possibility of betterment. If there is to be a reduction in benefits, and we believe that there should be, the formula for determining this reduction should be such that it recognizes the need for something in the nature of a "boost" during the transitional

References for Work and working are on pages 75 to 76.

55

period. ("Welfare" is often given in the form of a "tax-free holiday" to new industrial ventures to give them impetus.) We recommend that there be "benefit reduction holidays" for the handicapped during the crucial period. The fruits of such an investment would be reaped not only by the immediate benefactors but also by society.

Vocational rehabilitation, qualification standards, mandatory employment laws, fair employment practices, workmen's compensation and unemployment insurance, all vital matters, are considered in the ensuing pages.

Vocational rehabilitation

Education and training are now recognized as essential to a successful role in society. Particularly is this true for the mentally handicapped, for they are the least able to develop to their full potential without assistance.

At first thought, the public school system would seem the logical *situs* of such training. That there are many problems involved in such an approach has not gone unnoticed.

> "The general principle that every child has the right to be educated has clearly been adopted by all provinces, and has been written into provincial statutes going back over many years. What is less clear is whether this right exists regardless of physical or mental disability in the child, and whether education is to be defined only in terms of a single one track school system that, in theory at least, admits all children. It is not clear whether the definition can somehow be stretched to cover individual differences, and to include the provision of compensatory, remedial, and special educational services for children who have special needs.
>
> Historically, in many countries including Canada, certain groups, such as the mentally retarded, have been excluded from the public educational system while services for other rather well defined groups such as the blind and the deaf have been secured only by specific acts of legislation. In all Canadian provinces the recent trend has been to bring special services, including schools for the retarded, under provincial legislation, though not always under the Public Schools Acts, and to make provisions for an increasing number of exceptional children within the public school system itself. Yet the guiding principle remains unclear, and at present we are left with many anomalies; provisions existing in some school districts but not in others; or available for certain categories of handicapped children, but not for others."[5]

Even where training programs for the retarded were provided by the public school system, the efforts had rarely been successful. In the past, the integration of retarded and normal children was usually an act of omission rather than commission. Failure to diagnose handicaps, scarcity of financial and personnel resources, and the lack of understanding of the need for special programs hardly helped the retardate to receive functional training in the schools. The fortunate few had an opportunity to benefit from workshop or on-the-job experience provided by local private groups.

Two developments occurred. When resources became available, many schools began vocational training for indicated members of their student body. In large centers, entire vocational schools were opened to serve a surrounding district. Perhaps of necessity, these schools often pitched their expectations of the social roles of their graduates at a low level.

It is essential that the retarded be educated to the peak of their ability. Provincial laws specify a "school-leaving age", making it mandatory that a student remain in attendance at school until he attains the prescribed age. These laws may be advantageous where there are appropriate resources which answer the educational needs of the individual. On the other hand, where the resources necessary for the individual are non-existent, school-leaving laws may be a marked disadvantage and do a great deal of harm to the student who would be better off elsewhere by, for example, commencing his actual vocational training. Provisions which subject a retardate to frustration and humiliation have no place in our statutes. Perhaps some should be allowed to leave school earlier; others later. We recommend that the school-leaving age be sufficiently flexible to accommodate the special requirements of the handicapped.

Governments have moved to make possible the development of vocational rehabilitation facilities outside the school system on an extensive scale.

The Vocational Rehabilitation of Disabled Persons Act[6] (Canada) was proclaimed in force on December 1, 1961. It was initially administered by the Department of Labour, but the administration was transferred to the Department of Manpower and Immigration effective October 1, 1966.

The Minister is empowered, with the approval of the Governor in Council, to enter into an agreement with any province, for up to six years, to provide for the payment of contributions to the province in respect of the costs incurred by the province in undertaking a "comprehensive program" for the vocational rehabilitation of the disabled.[7] "Vocational rehabilitation" is defined as any process of restoration, training and employment placement, including services related thereto, the object of which is to enable a person to become capable of pursuing regularly a substantially gainful occupation.[8] A "disabled person" is defined as a person who because of physical or mental impairment is incapable of pursuing regularly any substantially gainful occupation.[9]

The federal contribution represents 50 per cent of the costs, which are determined as prescribed in the agreement with the province.[10] The comprehensiveness of the program is a matter of agreement and includes such of the following services and processes as are specified in the agreement:[11]

"(*a*) assessment and counselling services for disabled persons;

(*b*) services and processes of restoration, training and employment placement designed to enable a disabled person to dispense with the necessity for institutional care or the necessity for the regular home service of an attendant;

(*c*) providing for utilizing the services of voluntary organizations that are carrying on activities in the province in the field of vocational rehabilitation of disabled persons;

(*d*) the training of persons as counsellors or administrators to carry out programs for the vocational rehabilitation of disabled persons;

(*e*) the co-ordination of all activities in the province relating to vocational rehabilitation of disabled persons; and

(*f*) such other services and processes of restoration, training and employment placement in respect of disabled persons as are specified in the agreement."

The Minister of Manpower and Immigration is empowered to co-ordinate federal activities in the field.[12] He may also undertake relevant research, and if appropriate such research may be conducted in cooperation with any province.[13] In addition, he may publish any research undertaken.[14]

On the provincial side, reference is made, for example, in Ontario to *The Vocational Rehabilitation Services Act, 1966*,[15] proclaimed in force on February 29, 1968. This Act is administered by the Department of Social and Family Services and at the functional level by the Director of the Vocational Rehabilitation Services Branch. A "disabled person" is defined in substantially the same terms as in the federal statute.[16]

The Minister of Social and Family Services, with approval of the Lieutenant Governor in Council, has the power to make agreements with the Government of Canada or with any person or organization for the purpose of providing vocational rehabilitation services to disabled persons or in respect of the provision of such service.[17] Provision is made for the Provincial Cabinet approving organizations providing such services to which capital grants may be paid.[18] Cabinet may also approve workshops for capital grants purposes.[19] (A "workshop" is defined as "a place where any manufacture or handiwork is carried on and that is operated for the purpose of providing useful and remunerative employment and work training or work assessment under actual or simulated working conditions for vocationally handicapped persons.")[20]

The Ontario statute, in an ambitious manner, provides that a rehabilitation program "shall be established" to provide:[21]

> "(a) goods or services to enable a disabled person to become capable of pursuing regularly a substantially gainful occupation;
>
> (b) services for the assessment of the individual, medical, social and psychological needs of a disabled person and for the formulation of the vocational rehabilitation services likely to be required to meet his needs;
>
> (c) rehabilitation counselling, including guidance and adjustment services, and assistance in obtaining, and succeeding in, a substantially gainful occupation;
>
> (d) for the payment of costs of assessment, training, pre-vocational training, work adjustment training, and personal adjustment training, including books and training materials;
>
> (e) for the payment to disabled persons of maintenance allowances and travelling allowances, including travelling allowances for a disabled person's guide or escort, to the extent necessary to enable the disabled person to derive the full benefit of vocational rehabilitation services provided under this Act;
>
> (f) medical, surgical or psychiatric treatment or procedures related or directed thereto that may be expected within a reasonable period of time to eliminate or favourably modify any chronic, cyclical or slowly-progressive impairment that renders a person disabled;
>
> (g) appliances designed to support or take the place of a part of the body or to increase the acuity of a sensory organ;
>
> (h) necessary initial occupational and business tools, equipment, supplies and licences;
>
> (i) for the payment of grants,
>   (i) to approved organizations for the establishment and expansion of workshops and for other capital purposes, and
>   (ii) to organizations for the operation of workshops and the provision of other vocational rehabilitation services;
>
> (j) for the training of persons as counsellors and administrators to carry out the rehabilitation programme;
>
> (k) for research relating to vocational rehabilitation services and for the payment of grants to persons or organizations for this purpose; and
>
> (l) for such other matters and services as are prescribed by the regulations."

The Director of the Vocational Rehabilitation Services Branch has, among his duties, to determine the eligibility of each applicant. The scope of the Director's powers and duties are listed in the statute as follows:[22]

"(a) make known the rehabilitation programme established under this Act to disabled persons and to any other interested person;

(b) receive applications for vocational rehabilitation services, determine the eligibility of each applicant and, where the applicant is eligible, determine the nature and extent of the vocational rehabilitation services necessary to meet his needs and direct their provision accordingly;

(c) carry out and administer the rehabilitation programme, established under this Act, and foster, coordinate and improve the programmes of organizations or agencies providing vocational rehabilitation services;

(d) enter into arrangements with such persons and organizations as may be necessary for the provision of services under this Act;

(e) compile statistics and reports relating to the provision of vocational rehabilitation services or the need for such services under this Act; and

(f) carry out such other duties as are assigned to him by this Act and the regulations."

So far as civil rights are concerned, legal process is available to an applicant or recipient, as the case may be, in the form of a hearing and review by a board of review of a decision, order or directive of the Director.[23]

There is extensive power to make regulations under the statute in Ontario which may embrace just about everything one could think of in relation to the program.[24] The actual regulation[25] is framed in what could be described as minute detail.

Matters dealt with by regulation include: the meaning of "substantially gainful occupation"; eligibility for maintenance allowance and formulae for determination thereof; eligibility for travel and accommodation assistance; eligibility for vocational rehabilitation services; establishment of a medical advisory board to advise the Director; criteria for suspension or cancellation of vocational rehabilitation services; and details concerning capital grants.

Whether the system described works well is difficult to assess. From the point of view of its structure, however, it would appear that this package is one of the most detailed encountered.

Consideration of rehabilitation programs involves an understanding of the nature of the phenomenon of retardation, its characteristics, and the manner in which it may most easily be overcome. Vast areas of psychological and social working concerns are involved to intricate depths. That there is not agreement among professionals in the field in issues of classification, understanding and treatment orientation further complicates matters. It is beyond our scope to analyze the various theories and current debates.

Nevertheless, we refer to one point of apparent controversy. The general view of retardation, at least among the lay public, seems to be that of a condition of inferior intelligence and sub-standard learning ability. In short, retardation is seen as an incomplete development of the mind.

The task of rehabilitation is commonly seen as teaching the retardate the full utilization of his limited capacity. Some authors maintain the general assumption that the retarded learn more slowly and retain less than normal people may be incorrect.[26] They argue that out of the assumption are created educational programs based upon a theory of lack of intelligence and a general or unitary condition: the retardate is inferior in all aspects of learning. The result is described as an educational program consisting of presentation of the same materials that are given to normal people, but in lesser amounts and at a slower rate. In disputing this basic assumption, it has been stated

"However, the research that is available on the abilities of retardates suggests something different: that the learning deficiency of mildly and moderately retarded persons is task-specific or related to only certain aspects of the learning situation. Some evidence even suggests that under certain conditions the learning and retention of retardates are quite adequate – comparable, in fact, to the normal."[27]

Another argues, in similar fashion, that the basing of programs for the retarded on their IQ or some other test places an inflexible ceiling on their development. Retardates may be capable of growth, or even do very well in one or two fields of endeavor. They require merely a chance to find or develop these abilities, in actual and challenging situations.

"We are not denying the existence of differences in levels of intelligence. We are insisting that these differences be determined concretely in a variety of situations at different points of time and under a system of expectations and rewards which would stimulate maximum exertions. We are insisting that intelligence is what intelligence does."[28]

One scheme which seems to proceed on the views just described is that of the Fonds National – a semi-autonomous organization – in Belgium. Under that scheme, handicapped persons enter into a special contract with employers for a ten- to fifteen-month training period. The handicapped individual works for the employer and the Fonds National pays his salary and social security. There is, therefore, no cost to the employer. The latest available information,[29] based upon three years of experience and 305 cases, discloses not one case of a person so placed leaving his employer's service at the completion of the training period.

Revenue for this program is derived from compulsory payments made through plans of automobile insurance and workmen's compensation. There is a surcharge of 1½ per cent on all automobile insurance and compensation premiums, which is paid directly to the Fonds National by the agency collecting the premiums.

However enlightened or extensive rehabilitation programs may be when designed, they are unlikely to accomplish a great deal without sufficient professional staff. The retardation treatment and training field is currently suffering a severe shortage of trained personnel, both professional and supportive. Some reasons for the staff shortage were suggested during a 1969 joint Canada–United States conference[30] convened at Banff to study the manpower problem.

"Since in current retardation services duties are demanding, facilities poor, the hours long, the salary low, promotions few and far between, and retirement provisions inadequate, a dearth of applications from qualified people is to be expected. Under *such conditions* there is a shortage, and indeed there should be."[31]

The main thrust of the Banff Conference was a discussion of means of increasing staff in the field through expanded training, research, building and financing programs. A somewhat different approach was taken by one prominent Canadian writer. Noting the exploding need for better services, he declared

"As long as there is a booming demand for medical and paramedical personnel to treat the more affluent and successful members of society it is unlikely that mental retardation – which has low status and prestige – will ever attract enough competent professionals. In this respect, the mentally retarded, together with the indigent, the aged, and the chronically sick, are twice cursed in our success-oriented economy: first for being disabled and second because they cannot respond adequately to the modern miracle cures."[32]

His thesis is founded upon the link between poverty and retardation,[33] and his proposed solution is two-fold. He would eradicate much of retardation by eradicating poverty and its concomitants of low intellectual stimulation, poor schooling and poor health. Institutions are categorized as failures because professional help is concentrated in a setting divorced from the site where it should be committed: the real life environment which is the cradle of much of retardation. He would rather see our professionals in that environment and concludes his argument as follows.

> "From Texas to Toronto and indeed throughout the world, reports on mental retardation programs unanimously stress the need to develop community-based services to replace the old institutions. There is even virtual unanimity among the experts about what forms these should take. All these are important: regional planning, improved maternity care, prenatal health counselling, early detection and diagnosis of abnormalities, assessment clinics, family counselling for parents of retarded children, nursery schools, special classes, temporary residential care, guardianship, hostels, workshops, and recreational programs. These services must also be integrated and coordinated with the other health and welfare programs. Thus the needs of the retarded are seen as a part of, not apart from, the rest of the community."[34]

Rehabilitation then would mean not only rehabilitation of a handicapped individual but also rehabilitation of a society.

Qualification standards

Although a retardate may be perfectly capable of performing in a designated labor role, he may be practically prohibited from engaging in that work because of standard testing procedures. It may be required that he obtain a licence or certificate of qualification. Likewise, he may have to satisfy certain requirements in order to be hired by a particular employer.

Commonly, written tests or applications are conditions precedent to qualification or employment. Academic ability and literacy are, however, actually irrelevant to the performance of many jobs: for example, farm hand, messenger boy, and assembly line worker.

This has been recognized by the Government of Canada. It is the normal practice of the Public Service Commission of Canada to require written employment competitions. Section 10 of the *Public Service Employment Act*[35] reads as follows.

> "Appointments to or from within the Public Service shall be based on selection according to merit, as determined by the Commission, and shall be made by the Commission, at the request of the deputy head concerned, by competition or by such other process of personnel selection designed to establish the merit of candidates as the Commission considers is in the best interests of the Public Service."

The damning effect of section 10 to the retarded was lifted by an Order-in-Council,[36] the contents of which read

"AT THE GOVERNMENT HOUSE AT OTTAWA
THURSDAY, the 7th day of DECEMBER, 1967
PRESENT:
HIS EXCELLENCY
THE GOVERNOR GENERAL IN COUNCIL
His Excellency the Governor General in Council, on the recommendation of the Public Service Commission pursuant to section 39 of the Public Service Employment Act, is pleased hereby to approve the exclusion by the Public Service Commission from the provisions of section 10 of the said Act, on initial appointment only, of those persons who because of mental retardation cannot participate in a competitive situation on an equitable basis with persons not so handicapped."

In implementing the spirit of this Order-in-Council, the Public Service Commission has instructed its personnel in relation to the placement and appointment of the mentally retarded.[37]

The staffing officer is expected to identify employment opportunities for the potentially employable mentally retarded person who can perform work in a normal competitive employment climate in situations comparable to his or her own level of achievement; and the less qualified who can perform simple tasks, usually under permanently sheltered (closely supervised, non-competitive) conditions.

Steps to the placement of the mentally retarded are outlined as: identifying jobs which can be filled by such persons; developing suitable methods of selection which permit these individuals to be tried on-the-job; making selections and placements upon the advice of the Department of Manpower and Immigration who will co-ordinate regional and local arrangements to deal with the pertinent associations, provincial or municipal agencies, and educational institutions; and ensuring that the responsible vocational guidance and placement officers advise and assist the Public Service Commission and the departments in the placement and follow-up procedures.

To assist staffing officers, the Commission has identified the following occupations within the Public Service that are now, or can be, performed by mentally retarded persons.

"Building Services – Cleaning and Maintenance
Job: Helper
Duties: Move furniture, boxes; sweep, clean, dust; scrub, mop, wax (machine and hand) floors; wash walls; polish metal work; sort and shelve supplies; mow lawn, trim hedges, shovel snow.

Parks and Grounds Maintenance
Job: Helper
Duties: Paint with brush or spray-gun; pick up trash; sweep walks; clean swimming pool, sprinkle lawns, dig, weed, care for garden and plantings; plant trees, shrubs; roll lawn, track, field, court, operate mowing equipment, assemble or set up outdoor furniture, equipment, supplies.

Clerical Duties in Offices or Libraries
Job: Messenger, clerical or library assistant, helper in mail room, duplicating machine operator
Duties: Messenger service within the organization, or local deliveries on foot or by bus; feed addressograph or postage machine; address envelopes from printed copy; stuff and/or seal envelopes; serialize cards, order by number; file alphabetically; sort, cut, fold, collate, staple punch papers; unpack and/or shelve materials, tie or package for mailing; answer telephone; lay out mail; operate duplicating machine.

Printing Shop Duties
Job: Helper
Duties: Clean rollers or platens, fill machines with ink or fluid, fold, gather, collate paper; stack jogging paper; package or wrap with rope or string; label by stencil; operate wire stitching or stapling machine; move materials.

Building Construction
Job: Helper, unskilled
Duties: Loading, unloading equipment, material, piling or stacking stone, shovelling cement, sand, gravel; picking up scrap lumber, piling, stacking boards; cleaning tools and equipment, greasing and oiling machinery; pushing wheelbarrow; using common hand tools, storing and sorting

tools, sorting brick, painting by hand, raking, stringing wire, shovelling snow, digging with pick and shovel; operating salt or cinder equipment.

Agriculture Work

Job: Farm hand, general: animal, chicken hatchery, grain, greenhouse, fruit farm, dairy

Duties: Loading, unloading, transporting supplies, cleaning barns, buildings, yards, washing miling equipment, miling machines, feeding and watering stock, mowing lawn by hand, using common garden tools, or hand or pump sprayer, picking crops, shovelling snow."[38]

This new program of the Public Service Commission was initially confined geographically to the Ottawa district as a pilot project. In its Annual Report for 1968, the Commission indicated that there would be an extension to the whole of Canada. The Commission reported that those appointed during the pilot project had been most satisfactory in discharging their responsibilities.

We recommend that other governments (provincial and municipal), as well as industry and commerce, follow the exemplary lead taken by the Government of Canada in its policy of hiring on the basis of ability rather than disability.

Occupational licensing and certification bodies, in similar fashion, should also, we recommend, recognize the merit of making their qualification processes more flexible to accommodate the handicapped. Such flexibility is not incompatible with the maintenance of expected performance standards.[39]

Mandatory employment laws

It is almost universally recognized that a handicapped person's development requires his employment and functioning in society in as nearly normal a role as possible. Some countries have gone so far as to make the hiring of handicapped persons compulsory.

The usual scheme of mandatory employment legislation is a requirement that a particular percentage of a company's employees be handicapped persons. Details of this scheme vary from jurisdiction to jurisdiction.

According to a United Kingdom statute,[40] industry and commerce must employ the quota of "handicapped" persons that is fixed by the Ministry of Labour. Information available indicates that this quota is established at 3 per cent. A handicapped person is defined as one deemed registrable by the Ministry as "handicapped but capable of employment". A list of such persons is maintained by the Ministry. Under this legislation, there is no duty on industry to hire any particular individual. The choice is a free one made from the registry. Information received suggests that employers may tend to meet their quota by hiring people with lighter handicaps – such as missing fingers or lameness – rather than those grievously handicapped or mentally retarded.

Other European countries[41] have similar legislation, some with minor differences. West Germany requires all employers to hire a percentage ministerially determined. Luxembourg directs that firms with fifty or more on the payroll employ 2 per cent handicapped. The Netherlands requires the same 2 per cent quota of undertakings with one hundred or more workers.

A Belgian statute[42] requires that industry, commerce, agriculture and public utilities cited by the King and having at least twenty employees, hire a certain number of handicapped persons. The Fonds National discussed earlier under the topic of vocational rehabilitation maintains a registry which takes account of varying degrees of permanent incapacity. The Fonds in liaison with industry sets the quota.

A number of our correspondents have suggested that similar programs would be appropriate in Canada.[43] The potential benefit is clear: employment and training for the handicapped.

There are, however, drawbacks to schemes of mandatory employment.

It is incontrovertible that quotas do result in the placement of large numbers of disabled people. It may well be, however, that forced hiring labels those hired as an inferior group unable to earn their own positions in a market situation. Furthermore, employers may tend to regard their "burdens" as a nuisance, and scarcely more than another form of taxation, to be carried with little incentive to promote the status of the disabled person. Assignment to the lowest grade jobs might be the common result. Fellow workers would, in many cases, resent a handicapped person so hired and reenforce his inferior position when their friendship and encouragement is essential to him.

The most serious criticism of mandatory employment schemes is that they run contrary to the belief that most disabled people have some latent ability that – properly developed – can make the individual productive and self-respecting. Quotas that would brand the disabled as inferior, rejected members of society needing the law to force others to accept them would perhaps have a self-defeating flaw.

The development of vigorous programs of vocational rehabilitation, complemented by adequate provision for securing sheltered and other employment, would be a better solution. We recommend that mandatory employment laws not be adopted in Canada.

Fair employment practices

By virtue of *The Ontario Human Rights Code, 1961-62*,[44] certain discrimination in employment practices is prohibited.[45]

> "No employer or person acting on behalf of an employer shall refuse to employ or to continue to employ any person or discriminate against any person with regard to employment or any term or condition of employment because of his race, creed, colour, nationality, ancestry or place of origin."

An amendment has been suggested which would include in the classes of persons protected those with mental or physical disability. Such a suggestion cannot be supported. Race, creed, color, nationality, ancestry or place of origin are all functionally irrelevant factors to employment performance. Mental or physical ability is very often squarely relevant, and its assessment should be left in the hands of the employer. For one thing, an extension of this nature would negate programs developed by industry for testing aptitude and intelligence, and set progress back many years.

Those who advocate the broadening of human rights laws in this respect claim that there is a need to protect the disabled from social prejudices. These prejudices may, unfortunately, exist. The answer in this case is not, however, government intervention of this nature.[46]

If a retardate secures employment, all laws regulating labor matters apply to him in the same manner as to any other employee. Thus the retardate is protected by Acts governing trades protection, hours of work and vacation with pay, labor relations, rights of labor, and similar legislation however styled from province to province. Since such legislation encompasses no special treatment of retardates, it is not analyzed here.

One topic, however – minimum wage laws – is of particular significance for the retarded. Provisions are found in the statutes and regulations of all provinces and Canada, exempting employers of the retarded from minimum wage laws.

The training, security and growing self-confidence resultant from regular employment among normal workmen cannot be matched elsewhere. It must be recognized, however, that a slower, less efficient or less productive workman is not likely to be the first choice of an employer. Many employers do, nevertheless, evidence a willingness to give the handicapped a needed opportunity.

The principle underlying the enactment of minimum wage laws is clear and sound: the protection of the employee from exploitation. At the same time, it is an imposition on employers requiring them to pay less productive workmen rates equal to those received by competent and efficient staff. Neither employer nor fellow workers would be likely to accept such a situation with grace.

Were minimum wage laws rigid, the result would inevitably be few job and training opportunities for the retarded. The solution is found by way of exemptions – provisions for which exist in all provinces for employers in the case of the handicapped – from minimum wage requirements. These provisions are tabulated in the Canada-wide comparison which follows on pages 66-71.

The governmental departments charged with administering these exemptions proceed with great care. The prime concern is to prevent the exploitation or unfair treatment of any workman. An employer must be issued a permit setting out the name of the employee involved, the hourly wage, the number of hours to be worked and the duration of the permit. Generally, prior to any permit being issued, the case is extensively investigated through examination of medical reports, potential of the employee and nature of the work to be done. Cases are reviewed at regular intervals.

Permits should be applied for, and granted, only in cases where it is established that placement of the handicapped person is not possible at regular pay rates.[47] The minimum wage exemptions should not be allowed to be used as vehicles of exploitation by unscrupulous employers. It is equally important that these exemptions not be the means of the convenient disposition of the handicapped by agencies responsible for job placement.

The appropriate duration of a permit will vary with each case. Some handicapped persons may require only a short period of time to reach a satisfactory level of production. Others may continue to function indefinitely at a level which does not justify minimum wage rates.

Definitions of "handicapped person" embraced by the exemption provisions differ amongst provinces. Alberta, for example, limits the exemption to persons employed by designated or approved rehabilitative organizations. Manitoba requires that it be "fair and reasonable", because of a physical or a mental handicap, for a lower wage to be paid in any venture.

Some of the statutes require that the "employee" be the person who submits a written application for exemption. Should the employer or some counsellor not assist the retardate, how many would be aware of and able to comply with the exemption provisions? Our recommendation here is that it be permissible for anyone to make application for exemption from minimum wage laws on behalf of a mentally handicapped person.

With the accelerated establishment of rehabilitation units in institutions, sheltered workshops and other vocational centers for the handicapped, and their increasing production, there is bound to be an impact on the employment market. Organized labor should, at all times, be sympathetic to the difficulties of the handicapped.

Legislative provisions
dealing with minimum wages

	Statutory Citation	Provision
ALBERTA	*The Alberta Labour Act*, R.S.A. 1970, c. 196, s. 24(10).	"Where an employee is classified by the Board as handicapped the Board upon the written request of such employee (a) may by permit in writing authorize the payment of a wage less than the minim wage fixed under subsection (1), and (b) may limit and define the number of handicapped employees to whom the wag fixed under this subsection may be payable by an employer."
BRITISH COLUMBIA	*Female Minimum Wage Act*, R.S.B.C. 1960, c. 143, s. 6.	"In the case of any employees classified by the Board as handicapped, or as part-ti employees, or as apprentices, the Board may by permit in writing authorize the pay of a wage less than the minimum wage fixed under section 4; and may in any case limit and define the number of handicapped employees, or part-time employees, or apprentices to whom the lesser wage fixed under this section may be payable by an employer."
	Male Minimum Wage Act, R.S.B.C. 1960, c. 230, s. 7.	"In the case of any employees classified by the Board as handicapped, or as part-ti employees, or as apprentices, the Board may by permit in writing authorize the pay of a wage less than the minimum wage fixed under section 5; and may in any case limit and define the number of handicapped employees, or part-time employees, or apprentices to whom the lesser wage fixed under this section may be payable by ar employer.
MANITOBA	*The Employment Standards Act*, R.S.M. 1970, c. E110, s. 13(a).	"The minister may issue a special permit to any employer upon application therefor writing, (a) for the employment of, and fixing a wage or graduated scale of wages to be pai a handicapped employee, and may vary the permit or any provision thereof;"
NEW BRUNSWICK	*Minimum Wage Act*, R.S.N.B. 1952, c. 145, s. 9(2).	"The Board may establish special minimum rates of wages for handicapped and pa time employees, and for apprentices."

Citation of Sample Order or Regulation	Provision	Notes
Regulation 8/69 Order No. 17 (1967) s. 2.	"1. This Order applies to: (a) handicapped persons employed by Edmonton Rehabilitation Society for the Handicapped, Edmonton; Medicine Hat Rehabilitation Society, Medicine Hat; Rehabilitation Society of Calgary for the Handicapped, Calgary; and Rehabilitation Society of Lethbridge for the Handicapped, Lethbridge, who are sheltered workers or who are receiving vocational or educational training; and (b) employees of any other organization which is approved by the Board who are sheltered workers or who are receiving vocational or educational training, and to their employers."	Handicapped person to make written request to Board.
Regulation 21/67	"That for the purpose of the efficient administration of the Male and Female Minimum Wage Acts, the Board, after due inquiry, has exempted from the operation of the said Acts handicapped employees of the Kelowna and District Society for Retarded Children, Kelowna, B.C. Made at Vancouver, B.C., this 21st day of November, 1967."	Handicapped person to make written request to Board.

Regulation 30/60, s. 7.	"(1) Where because of an employee's physical or mental handicap, verified by medical certificate, if the minister so requires, it is fair and reasonable that an employer should employ the employee at an hourly rate less than the minimum hourly rate, the minister may issue a handicapped employee's permit to the employer permitting him to employ the handicapped employee at an hourly wage less than the minimum hourly rate.
	(2) The minister shall set out in the handicapped employee's permit
	  (a) the name and description of the handicapped employee; and
	  (b) the hourly wage that the employer shall pay the handicapped employee.
	(3) The minister may limit the period during which the employer may pay the handicapped employee at an hourly wage less than the minimum hourly rate."
		Employer to make written application to Minister for permit.

Order No. I s. 3(2) & (3) (January, 1968) (Construction, mining and primary transportation industries).	"(2) Subject to subsection (3) the minimum rate of wages which an employer may pay an . . . handicapped person for forty-eight hours of work or less in any one week is 10 cents per hour less than the minimum rate established by subsection (1)." "(3) The minimum rate established by subsection (2) shall not be paid to more than 20% of the total number of employees of an employer in the trade or industry."	The only exemptions from Orders have been where handicapped persons exclusively were employed.

67

	Statutory Citation	Provision
NEWFOUNDLAND	*The Minimum Wage Act*, R.S.N. 1952, c. 260, s. 6(i).	"The board, when it deems it expedient, may and, at the request of the Minister, shall cause an investigation to be made into the terms and conditions of employment of employees in any trade, industry, business, or occupation in any area in Newfoundland and make recommendations to the Lieutenant-Governor in Council which may include (i) special rates of wages for apprentices, inexperienced or handicapped employees"
NOVA SCOTIA	*Minimum Wage Act*, S.N.S. 1964, c. 7, s. 5(2)(g) and s. 5(3).	"(2) Without limiting the generality of subsection (1), the Board may by order, with the approval of the Governor in Council: . . . (g) fix a special rate of wages for apprentices, inexperienced or handicapped employees, and limit the number of such employees to whom the special rate may be payable by any employer;" "(3) The Board, without order, may grant written permission to an employer to pay to any employee who is handicapped a wage fixed by it lower than the minimum wage."
ONTARIO	*The Employment Standards Act*, S.O. 1968, c. 35, s. 17.	"For the purpose of enabling a handicapped person to be gainfully employed, the Director may, upon the application of the handicapped person or his employer and with the consent of the handicapped person, his parent or guardian authorize the employment of such handicapped person at a wage lower than the minimum wage prescribed under a regulation."
	The Industrial Standards Act, R.S.O. 1960, c. 186, s. 7(1)(k).	"The conference may submit to the Minister in writing a schedule of wages and hours and days of labour for the industry affected and the schedule may, . . . (k) authorize the advisory committee to fix a minimum rate of wages lower than the rate fixed by the schedule for any classification of employees or for any individual who performs work included in more than one classification of employees, or whose work is only partly subject of the schedule, or who is handicapped."
PRINCE EDWARD ISLAND	*The Men's Minimum Wage Act*, S.P.E.I. 1960, c. 27, s. 7(h).	"The Board may make orders; . . . (h) Exempting from the operation of this Act or any order made hereunder any group, class or description of employees in any industry, business, trade or occupation."
	The Women's Minimum Wage Act, S.P.E.I. 1959, c. 33, s. 4(2).	"The Board may exempt from the operation of this Act or any order made hereunder any group, class or description of employees or employers in any industry, business, trade or occupation."
QUEBEC	*Minimum Wage Act*, R.S.Q. 1964, c. 144, s. 15.	"The Commission may, by resolution, grant, upon proof deemed sufficient, to any employee of limited physical or mental fitness, a certificate authorizing him to work upon conditions differing from those contemplated in any ordinance applicable."

Citation of Sample Order or Regulation	Provision	Notes
General Order as amended April 1, 1968. s. 14.	"No employer shall pay any wage less than that fixed in this Order, to any handicapped employee unless and until the payment of such wage in each specific case has been approved by the Minimum Wage Board after written application by the employer."	Employer to apply to Board for permit.
		Handicapped person or employer may make application.
O. Reg. 142/69 s. 11.	"The advisory committee is authorized to fix a minimum rate of wages lower than the rate fixed by this schedule for an individual who is handicapped."	Employer to apply to advisory committee and after investigation, if indicated, a permit will issue.
Order of March 1966 as amended March, 1968. s. 6.	"Handicapped Employees: No employer shall pay any wage less then that fixed by this Order to any handicapped employee unless and until the payment of such wages in each specific case has been approved by the Board after written application has been made to it by the employer and a permit setting out such lesser wages has been issued by the Board."	Board for permit. Employer to make written application to
		Reference is to employees of limited physical or mental fitness. Each case is evaluated on its own merits and if deemed warranted, a permit will issue.

	Statutory Citation	Provision
SASKATCHEWAN	*The Minimum Wage Act*, R.S.S. 1965, c. 292, s. 8.	"The minister may, on the recommendation of the chairman of the board, issue to any person who is, in the opinion of the board, a handicapped employee, a learner or an apprentice a special licence authorizing the employment of the licensee under such conditions as may be prescribed in the licence."
CANADA	*Canada Labour (Standards) Code,* S.C. 1964-65, c. 38, s. 13 (1) and (2).	"(1) For the purpose of enabling a person to be gainfully employed who has a disabil that constitutes a handicap in the performance of any work to be done by him for an employer, the Minister may, upon the application of the handicapped person or an employer, authorize the employment of such person at a wage lower than the minimur wage prescribed under section 11 if, having regard to all the circumstances of the case, the Minister is of the opinion that it is in the interests of such person to do so. (2) An applcation made under subsection (1) shall be supported by such evidence disability and handicap as the Minister may require."

itation of Sample order or Regulation	Provision	Notes
		Permits mainly issued to former patients of Provincial Training Schools. Employer and prospective employee make representations to the Department and, after investigation, a permit will issue if deemed warranted.

Workmen's compensation

Workmen's compensation legislation is designed to protect employees from the burden of medical costs and wage losses resulting from injuries incurred on a job. Each province has established a fund from which payments are made to employees whose claims are approved by the Board created to administer the monies.

Such a fund is maintained by premium contributions from industry and other enterprises. There is no absolute premium for all undertakings, but rather a grading and classification system administered by the Board. Employers are classified according to the nature of the enterprise. The premium assessed varies with the severity of accident rates and is calculated as a particular percentage of the payroll.

If an employer falls within the scope of the compensation scheme, he must contribute to it. All employees then have the same status under the plan, whatever their individual circumstances may be. There is no special treatment for the handicapped: their rights are the same as those of any workman. It is, in some jurisdictions, a requirement that employers place handicapped persons in jobs where they are not a danger to themselves or others.[48]

An employer is not exempt from the requirements of contribution by virtue of employing a handicapped person. Some enterprises, such as insurance companies, are exempt ostensibly on the grounds of unlikelihood of accident. However, no dispensation is available to a company merely because a particular employee might be considered a poor risk.

This principle of mandatory coverage is undoubtedly commendable, but it may have the effect of restricting employment opportunities for the handicapped. Whether justified or not, some employers assume the mentally handicapped to be a higher accident risk. Based upon that assumption, the fear of higher premiums (directly or indirectly) is inevitable, because the accident rate will influence the premium level.

In Ontario, an entire class of enterprise is assessed on the basis of an industry-wide average of accident rates.[49] Under such a scheme, even a greater than average number of accidents in a particular company would not impose a significant financial burden on that company.

The fear noted above might be founded upon a false assumption. Some believe that many handicapped persons, aware of their limitations and unsure of themselves, compensate for their disability with greater than usual caution and less inclination to court accident situations in their work. Should such a belief be supportable, the effect may be a lower accident rate for the handicapped.

No attempt is here made to minimize the gravity of the problem of industrial accidents and injuries. If the assumption is made that a retardate faces greater danger than the normal workman, it might follow to consider it common sense and charity to preclude him from that danger. Nevertheless, it is probably true, in most cases, that one cannot predict with certainty the ability of a retardate to avoid injury.

A retardate runs the risk of injury in some employment situations. So, of course, do other persons. The effects of unemployment are as severe for the handicapped as for any other persons desiring work. It is readily conceded that where other workers are exposed to potential injury because of the retardate, his claim to a chance for work and independence is weaker. In the final analysis, all of the various interests involved must be weighed.

For the terms of a workmen's compensation statute to apply to employer or workman, the employment must be considered by the Board to be a true master-servant relationship. The hiring of a worker in a factory to further the trade of the employer in return for a wage is strictly a business arrangement: the purchase of a service. Such an arrangement falls within the scheme of the legislation as a master-servant relationship.

General practice is not to consider the position of persons in training workshops for the retarded as being within the ambit of the statute. The usual arrangement is that only an incentive wage, rather than a salary, is paid to the trainees. Further, the nature of the enterprise is rehabilitative rather than profit-oriented, and the relationship one of teacher-student rather than master-servant.

In the British Columbia scheme, a division of the workshop program into three stages has been made.[50] The first two – evaluation and training with some incentive pay – is considered to be outside the scope of the Act in that Province. The third stage is characterized when a retardate has finished his training, no job can be found for him, and he remains at the workshop receiving a salary relative to his performance. Only the third stage is covered by the Act. It is considered that at this stage the retardate is an employee of the workshop furthering its business interests.

Recognizing that workmen's compensation schemes are a valuable asset to all persons, we recommend that all workmen's compensation boards fairly evaluate programs for the employment of the handicapped and effect coverage of them wherever possible.

Unemployment insurance

Unemployment insurance is a scheme devised to protect the employed, so that if they should at any time be out of work they will not suffer a total loss of income. So long as they meet the requirements which apply to all persons, the mentally handicapped are eligible to seek the benefits of the scheme.

The unemployment insurance plan is administered by the Unemployment Insurance Commission, a federal agency, according to the terms of the *Unemployment Insurance Act*[51] and regulations made thereunder.[52] Under the Act, an employer is required to pay a contribution on behalf of an insurable employee from the wages of the employee, and an equal amount on his own behalf with respect to that employee.[53] Once a designated number of "contribution weeks" have been satisfied within a prescribed period, an employee is considered as having established a "benefit period".[54] Thereupon, should he be unemployed, he is entitled to be paid unemployment insurance benefits.[55]

For periods of employment to be counted in the calculation of contribution weeks, the employment must be of a type deemed "insurable". The Act defines "insurable employment" as "employment that is not included in excepted employment and is . . . employment in Canada, by one or more employers, under any express or implied *contract of service* or apprenticeship, written or oral, whether the earnings of the employed person are received from the employer or some other person and whether the earnings are reckoned by time or by the piece, or partly by time and partly by the piece, or otherwise; . . . ."[56]

To receive benefits, one must claim them from the Commission. The claimant must prove that he has the required number of contribution weeks in insurable employment, and that for each day for which he claims unemployment benefits he was capable of and available for work and unable to obtain it.[57]

If a person is employed within the meaning of the Act, and loses his employment or ceases to work because of illness, he is disqualified from receiving benefit for the duration of the illness.[58] Where, however, the illness arose after he had lost his job for some other reason *and* he had already made a claim, no disqualification applies.[59] This last concession will not in most cases apply to retardation.

Mere institutionalization may deprive one of benefits, even though the individual has the required number of contribution weeks.

> "An insured person is disqualified from receiving benefit while he is an inmate of . . . an institution supported wholly or partly out of public funds. . . ."[60]

An inmate may or may not be capable of work, but in certain circumstances is certainly not available for it as required by the Act. The loss of benefits does not occur upon institutionalization, however, if the institutionalization is a result of an illness that arises after loss of a job and the making of a claim.[61] Presumably, payment of benefits, if suspended, would resume after the individual ceases to be an inmate of the institution. Neither "inmate" nor "institution" are defined in the Act, and it is not clear how far the exclusion for institutionalization will extend into the spectrum of facilities available for the retarded.

When an individual does cease to be an inmate, he may lack the requisite number of contributory weeks because he was institutionalized. The same consideration would apply to the non-institutionalized individual for whom work has for some time been precluded by illness. The Act alleviates the potential hardship accruing from the loss of opportunity to "collect" contributory weeks. After setting out a time limit "period" within which an individual must earn the required number of contributory weeks, the Act provides[62] that if an individual because of illness could not work within any part of the "period", the "period" will be increased by the amount of time lost because of illness.

In the course of habilitating and rehabilitating patients in institutions operating under mental health legislation, they are sometimes placed out to work in the community. Some such placements involve the patient working in the community, but living at the hospital. On other occasions, the patient lives in the community, on probationary status from the hospital. The hope is that ultimately the patient will be able to carry on alone. It might be of significant value for a patient working in the community if he were to participate in the plan of unemployment insurance.

Various considerations are applied to exclude such patients from eligibility for benefits. The employment situation must be one deemed by the Act to be "insurable employment"[63] and that is not included in the definition of excepted employments.[64] Among the list of excepted employments is employment in a non-profit hospital or in a charitable institution.

Even should an employment situation not be one excluded by the Act, coverage for working patients is not available. The Act founds insurable employment upon a "contract of service" which term is not defined. The Commission does not appear to consider that a working patient makes a true contract of service. There seems little ground for the view that an employment contract differs in any essential from other types of contracts. Place of residence should not be a material consideration.

The Commission may be proceeding upon certain assumptions in its interpretation of "contract of service" as applied to patients. Patients of a mental institution are considered to be wards of the institution and as such not free agents working under a contract of service. There is little authority today for such a proposition. The Commission is also unconvincing if it assumes that institutionalization is an indication of a lack of contractual capacity, and that patients are therefore incompetent to make such a contract as the Act requires. Institutionalization does not necessarily indicate incapacity of any specific manner or form. No generalized assumptions are warranted.

The circumstances of each case or group of cases must be considered on the merits, and it is submitted that certain patients of mental institutions do come within the definition of insurability under the statute. Accordingly, we recommend that the Unemployment Insurance Commission reassess the position taken with respect to mental patients with a view to recognizing, where applicable, eligibility for unemployment insurance coverage. Moreover, the Commission might consider it reasonable, even where the employment is not strictly insurable under the defined terms, to take an accommodating view and fashion regulations which would include it under the plan in any event.[65]

A Bill dealing with unemployment insurance has been introduced in the House of Commons.[66] The proposed legislation would generally liberalize the law, although it would not to any considerable extent change the position of the mentally handicapped. Employment in a hospital or charitable institution will no longer be excepted from insurability.[67] Further, a claimant will be considered unemployed and eligible for benefits while he is attending a course of training to which he has been referred by an approved authority.[68] The last provision constitutes a most commendable advance.

References

1 International League of Societies for the Mentally Handicapped, Declaration of general and special rights of the mentally retarded, October 24, 1968, ARTICLE II.
2 *Ibid.*, ARTICLE III.
3 Wolfensberger, *Vocational Preparation and Occupation*, contained in BAUMEISTER (ed.), MENTAL RETARDATION 232 (1967).
4 *Ibid.*, p. 233.
5 COMMISSION ON EMOTIONAL AND LEARNING DISORDERS IN CHILDREN, *one million children* 70-71 (1970).
6 S.C. 1960-61, c. 26.
7 *Ibid.*, s. 3(1).
8 *Ibid.*, s. 2(e).
9 *Ibid.*, s. 2(d).
10 *Ibid.*, s. 3(2).
11 *Ibid.*, s. 3(4).
12 *Ibid.*, s. 5.
13 *Ibid.*, s. 6(1).
14 *Ibid.*, s. 6(2).
15 S.O. 1966, c. 159, as amended by S.O. 1968, c. 141.
16 *Ibid.*, s. 1(b).
17 *Ibid.*, s. 2.
18 *Ibid.*, s. 3.
19 *Ibid.*, s. 4.
20 *Ibid.*, s. 1(f).
21 *Ibid.*, s. 5.
22 *Ibid.*, s. 7(1).
23 *Ibid.*, s. 8.
24 *Ibid.*, s. 9.
25 O. Reg. 64/68, as amended by O. Regs. 122/69 and 356/69.
26 Olshansky, *An Examination of Some Assumptions in the Vocational Rehabilitation of the Mentally Retarded*, 7 MENTAL RETARDATION 51 (Feb. 1969) (U.S.), and Baumeister, *Learning Abilities*, contained in BAUMEISTER (ed.), MENTAL RETARDATION 181 (1967).
27 Baumeister, *ibid.*, at p. 182.
28 Olshansky, *ibid.*, footnote 26, at p. 53.
29 June 5, 1969, during interview by the Project Director with M. A. Maron, Directeur: Fonds National de Reclassement Social des Handicapés, Bruxelles.
30 See COHEN, MANPOWER AND MENTAL RETARDATION: AN EXPLORATION OF THE ISSUES (Proceedings of the Banff International Conference) (1970).
31 Mayo, *Manpower for Mental Retardation, ibid.*, 17, 18.
32 Greenland, *Training Basic and Supportive Personnel: Introductory Statement, ibid.*, 51.

33 Greenland, citing the United States' President's Committee on Mental Retardation as authority, notes that three-quarters of that nation's mentally retarded are to be found in the isolated and impoverished urban and rural slums, and that a child in a low-income rural or urban family is fifteen times more likely to be diagnosed as retarded than is a child from a higher-income family. (See *ibid.*, p. 59.)

34 *Ibid.*, p. 65.

35 S.C. 1966-67, c. 71.

36 P.C. 1967-2283.

37 Public Service of Canada, Staffing Manual, Chapter VI entitled "Disadvantaged Persons".

38 *Ibid.*

39 Matters of professional and occupational licensure are discussed in ALLEN, FERSTER & WEIHOFEN, MENTAL IMPAIRMENT AND LEGAL INCOMPETENCY 354-63 (1968); CHALKE, SWADRON & GRIFFIN, THE LAW AND MENTAL DISORDER (PART TWO: CIVIL RIGHTS AND PRIVILEGES) 64-75 (1967); and LINDMAN & MCINTYRE (eds.), THE MENTALLY DISABLED AND THE LAW 267 (1961).

40 *The Disabled Persons (Employment) Act, 1958*, 6 & 7 Eliz. 2, c. 26.

41 See Report on the International Seminar on Employment of the Disabled, Yugoslavia, May 16-24, 1960.

42 Loi relative à la formation et à la réadaptation professionnelles ainsi qu'au reclassement social des handicapés, 28 avril 1958, art. 4.

43 There is only one instance of the concept of mandatory employment being pursued in Canada. A declaration of the Government of Saskatchewan, reported in the Toronto *Globe & Mail* of March 26, 1970, stated that all contracts between the Province and private firms will contain a clause requiring employment of a percentage of Indian and Métis by the firms. No legislation or regulation is planned, but the effect of the plan is presumably to be achieved through economic pressure.

44 S.O. 1961-62, c. 93.

45 *Ibid.*, s. 4(1). See also subsections (2) and (3) concerning membership in trade unions, and employment applications and advertisements.

46 The statutes relating to more than thirty bodies parallel to the Ontario Human Rights Commission were studied a few years ago and none of them included the mentally and physically disabled for protective purposes.

47 Intradepartmental Information Circular, Ontario Department of Health, September 23, 1969.

48 Letter to the Project Director from the Director of Legal Services, Workmen's Compensation Board of British Columbia, April 23, 1969.

49 *The Workmen's Compensation Act*, R.S.O. 1960, c. 437, ss. 4 and 5.

50 Letters to the Project Director from the Director of Legal Services, Workmen's Compensation Board of British Columbia, May 2, 1969, and June 6, 1969.

51 S.C. 1955, c. 50, as amended.

52 P.C. 1955-1491, as amended.

53 *Supra*, footnote 51, s. 37.

54 *Ibid.*, s. 45. Where contributions were not payable in respect of a person for the reason, *inter alia*, that he was for any time "incapacitated for work by reason of some specific disease or bodily or mental disablement", the period prescribed is increased by such time, up to a specified limit.

55 *Ibid.*, s. 54. An insured person is disqualified from receiving benefit in respect of every day for which he fails to prove that he was capable of and available for work, and unable to obtain suitable employment.

56 *Ibid.*, s. 25(b) (emphasis added).

57 *Ibid.*, s. 54.

58 *Ibid.*, s. 66.

59 *Ibid.*

60 *Ibid.*, s. 64.

61 P.C. 1955-1491, s. 170.

62 S.C. 1955, c. 50, s. 45 (3).

63 *Ibid.*, s. 25.

64 *Ibid.*, s. 27.

65 *Ibid.*, ss. 25(c) and 26(1)(d): with the approval of the Governor in Council, the Commission may make regulations for including in insurable employment "any employment if it appears to the Commission that the nature of work performed by persons employed in that employment is similar to the nature of the work performed by persons employed in insurable employment".

66 Bill C-229, given first reading on March 10, 1971.

67 *Ibid.*, s. 3(2).

68 *Ibid.*, s. 39.

sex
and the
other sex

sex and the other sex

Introduction

This chapter has been the most difficult to write. The topics considered – marriage, being a parent, contraception, sterilization, abortion, annulment, divorce – are each and every one of them contentious. The social values concerning all of them seem constantly to be going through evolution if not revolution. Explosive scientific innovations may cause tremendous changes overnight. The laws governing some of them have, within the past few years, undergone significant modification in Canada and elsewhere. These topics are today subjects of controversial debate, even without regard to the complication presented by handicap.

The subjects considered are interrelated in a complex manner: they are problems of man and woman. We find it meaningless to discuss and analyze any of these subjects without reference to the others because each is interdependent within the whole. For example, it would not be necessary to discuss abortion in the case where an individual has been sterilized: indeed, effective contraceptive methods would preclude a consideration of sterilization. The same that is true in the retrogression is true in the progression.

The sanctity of life and procreation are often considered within a socio-legal framework. Superimposed upon these issues, therefore, are the social institutions of marriage, parenthood and the dissolution of marriage.

Most of the available literature is disappointing. Many of the topics are dealt with in a manner which evades the more difficult issues, to the extent that they cannot withstand logical evaluation. A treatment of one of the topics to the exclusion of others is folly. High-level documents, while unhesitatingly expounding principles of a guiding nature, fail miserably in letting us know how to resolve practical problems which arise on a day-to-day basis.[1]

We have not seen it our place or duty to consider *per se* religious, moral or ideological positions.

Intellectual deficiency does not preclude conjugal and sexual needs and sentiments. The basic right to express them should belong to every human being. "The mentally retarded person has the same basic rights as other citizens of the same country and same age."[2] It follows, therefore, that unless cogent reasons exist, the expression of these rights should be exercisable by all.

An analysis of the pertinent laws in Canada demonstrates that they generally serve a dual purpose. On the one hand, they protect the retarded: all the while, however, these laws restrict them. For example, the law relating to marriage has the effect of shielding some of the retarded from the stresses of marital life. Yet, at the same time, these retardates are unable to reap the benefits of marriage.

An additional illustration is to be found in the terms of the *Criminal Code*,[3] section 140 of which reads as follows.

> "Every male person who, under circumstances that do not amount to rape, has sexual intercourse with a female person
> (*a*) who is not his wife, and
> (*b*) who is and who he knows or has good reason to believe is feeble-minded, insane, or is an idiot or imbecile,
> is guilty of an indictable offence and is liable to imprisonment for five years."

This provision endeavors to prevent the exploitation of retarded girls from those who might take sexual advantage of them. On the other hand, the same provision deprives the "victim" of enjoying intercourse without each time placing her partner in the unenviable position of committing a criminal offence.

References for Sex and the other sex are on pages 97 to 100.

An indication that Parliament is even now mindful of protecting, thereby in a way depriving, mentally handicapped persons is found in a recent amendment to the *Criminal Code*. The offences of buggery, bestiality[4] and gross indecency[5] have been liberalized to exempt from criminal liability any two consenting adults who commit these acts in private. If one of the parties is, and the other party knows or has good reason to believe that he or she is "feeble-minded, insane, or an idiot or imbecile", however, the *Code* deems that no consent can be given.[6] We take no stand, but merely describe the posture of the law.

On the subject of consent, we are confronted with a troublesome matter. In order to be able to give consent in the legal sense, an individual must have knowledge of what is involved and its consequences. A given person may have the capacity to consent for one purpose and not another. Each case must be determined on its merits. The issue is one of fact which, in the final analysis, can be determined only by a court which has knowledge of all material circumstances. The nature and extent of the mental disability of a person is the primary consideration.

To speak of mental retardation and sex is a hollow effort. More definitive guidelines at the practical level must be formulated for discussion. Such guidelines do exist and seem to have been well drawn in Canada in a report submitted to the Association for Retarded Children of British Columbia.[7] The report, dated 1966, prefaces its findings by defining mental retardation as ". . . sub-average general intellectual functioning which originates during the developmental period and is associated with impairment of adaptive behaviour."[8] The report further divides retardates into four classes with a corresponding intelligence quotient level for each:[9]

Borderline	IQ	85-75
Mild	IQ	75-50
Moderate	IQ	50-20
Profound	IQ	20 and below.

The reporting committee notes that "sex drive" is closely linked with other personality and environmental factors and cannot adequately be separated and measured. They note further that little is known how the mentally retarded compare with the "normal" population but add:

> "It is, however, generally agreed that sexual drive is more closely linked with mental age than chronological age. Compared to the normal, therefore, the borderline and mildly retarded will usually exhibit less sexual behaviour and not more as is sometimes believed. The moderately retarded will have markedly less interest and the profoundly retarded virtually none. Fertility patterns follow the same rule."[10]

When discussing the actual sexual behavior of the retarded, the committee writes that profound and lower moderate classes exhibit only simple heterosexual affection, such as holding hands: the higher levels are more interested in and capable of normal heterosexual activity, but probably less so than the general population. Promiscuity is not found greater in the retarded, and in fact illegitimate birth rates are stated to be lower than in the rest of the population. According to them, marriage is more likely, the higher on the IQ scale the retarded person may be. In relation to abnormal behavior, the committee states that homosexuality is probably less common among retardates than it is generally in society. Aggressive behavior, indecent exposure and fetishism are termed rare for a retarded person. Where other-directed sexual interest is lacking, the retardate is said to engage commonly in autoerotic behavior.

One thing is clear. Far more should be known about the matters considered in this chapter. It is recommended that a comprehensive study be undertaken of the domestic and sexual needs of the retarded, determining and weighing all of the interests to be protected. Only then will we be in a position to assess fully the fairness of the laws in this field as they apply to them.

It is noted that the Ontario Association for the Mentally Retarded has recently formed the "Ad-Hoc Committee on Sex, Marriage and Associated Laws". The general purposes of that Committee are

> "to develop a program of education and guidance for parents and the staff who are working in programs and services for the mentally retarded;
> to devise a plan of action to enact whatever legislation is deemed necessary; and
> to develop an effective public education program."

Hopefully, this Committee of the Ontario Association and others like it will serve to further knowledge and public education in these vitally important matters.

Marriage

Whether or not a retarded person should marry depends, of course, upon many factors, and each case should be viewed on its own. The Task Force on Law of the President's Panel on Mental Retardation, USA, emphasizes that marriage should not be categorically denied to all retarded persons.[11]

One assumes that those retardates with respect to whom marriage is considered have similar needs as others for the benefits of marriage. These benefits include companionship, sexual gratification and security of various types. Should these benefits be denied those retardates who wish to marry?

It is sometimes argued that retardates should not marry because of a belief that they may be incapable of undertaking even the basic responsibilities of marriage. Authors have, however, maintained that certain retardates "have the potential to meet the demands of married life and to benefit from this relationship."[12]

The prospects of a successful marriage certainly will depend upon the strength of each party. Those with average or above average ability might compensate for the disability of the other. One man expresses his view in the following way.

> "The problem is with the mildly handicapped.
> a The mildly handicapped man who marries a normal girl (with no psychiatric problem) where the wife looks after the home and the budget may have a successful marriage.
> b The mildly handicapped girl marrying a normal man is not good as the girl cannot look after the home, budget, etc.
> c Two handicapped persons marrying is not recommended."[13]

Some, while recognizing the benefits of marriage for the mentally retarded, recommend that they should have no children.[14] Their concern may stem from fears that the retarded might not be able to cope with the responsibilities of parenthood, the children might suffer from inadequate rearing, and ultimately the public might be burdened with additional charges.

Arguments recommending against marriage because of potential offspring of the union are of doubtful persuasion. The existence of a marriage certificate is not a prerequisite to cohabitation and childbirth. On the other hand, the absence of such a certificate does nothing to minimize the numbers of persons living in "sin" or to enhance the illegitimate birth rates.

According to our Constitution,[15] both Parliament and the Provincial Legislatures have certain jurisdiction in respect of passing laws dealing with marriage.

The solemnization of marriage in a province is a matter about which that province has the power to legislate.[16] Under this power, the provinces regulate such matters as the issuance of licences to marry, the qualifications of persons who may celebrate marriages and, to an extent, the form of the marriage ceremony.

At the same time, Parliament in Ottawa has power to pass laws dealing with marriage. The federal jurisdiction relates to matters of capacity to marry,[17] although Parliament has not seen fit to enact any laws in this respect. The provinces, however, under the guise of regulating the licensing and solemnization of marriage, have enacted legislation which does actually deal with the capacity of a person to marry.

For example, *The Marriage Act*[18] of Ontario prohibits any person from issuing a marriage licence to, or solemnizing the marriage of, any person who is "mentally ill or mentally defective".[19] It is an offence for a licence issuer or person solemnizing a marriage to contravene this provision.[20] Similar provisions exist in some other provinces, as may be seen from the following.

LEGISLATIVE RESTRICTIONS RELATING TO MARRIAGE IN CANADA

Alberta
Marriage Act, R.S.A. 1970, c. 226, s. 27.
A person who . . . issues a licence, or . . . solemnizes a marriage, knowing or having reason to believe that either of the parties to the intended marriage or to the marriage is mentally defective or mentally ill or is under the influence of intoxicating liquor or narcotic drugs, is guilty of an offence. . . .

British Columbia
Marriage Act, R.S.B.C. 1960, c. 232, s. 39.
Every issuer of marriage licences who issues a licence for a marriage, and every minister or clergyman or Marriage Commissioner who solemnizes a marriage, knowing or having reason to believe that either of the parties to the intended marriage or to the marriage is an idiot or is insane or is under the influence of intoxicating liquor, is guilty of an offence. . . .

Manitoba
Marriage Act, R.S.M. 1970, c. M50, s. 22.
Any person who issues a licence, or makes a publication or grants a dispensation, for the marriage of two persons, and any minister, clergyman, or other person, who celebrates the ceremony of marriage between two persons, knowing or believing either of them to be a mentally disordered person within the meaning of the Mental Health Act, is guilty of an offence. . . .

New Brunswick
Marriage Act, R.S.N.B. 1952, c. 139.
No statutory provision relating to this matter.

Newfoundland
Solemnization of Marriages Act, R.S.N. 1952, c. 160.
No statutory provision relating to this matter.

Nova Scotia
Solemnization of Marriage Act, R.S.N.S. 1967, c. 287.
No statutory provision relating to this matter.

Ontario
Marriage Act, R.S.O. 1960, c. 228, s. 48.
Every issuer who issues a licence and every person who solemnizes a marriage, knowing or having reason to believe that either of the parties to the intended marriage or to the marriage is mentally defective or mentally ill or is under the influence of intoxicating liquor or narcotic drugs, is guilty of an offence. . . .

Prince Edward Island
Marriage Act, S.P.E.I. 1969, c. 27, s. 23.
A person who . . . issues a licence, or . . . solemnizes a marriage knowing or having reason to believe that either of the parties to the intended marriage or to the marriage is an idiot or insane, is guilty of an offence. . . .

Quebec
Civil Code, Title V, c. III, article 142.
When the opposition is founded on the insanity of the person about to be married, the opposant is bound to apply for the interdiction and to have it pronounced without delay.

Saskatchewan
Marriage Act, R.S.S. 1965, c. 338, s. 56.
No clergyman or marriage commissioner shall perform a marriage ceremony where to his knowledge either of the parties is a mentally retarded person as defined in *The Mental Health Act,* or is suffering from mental illness as defined in that Act. . . .

A "mentally ill person" and "mentally defective person" are not defined in the Ontario statute, but their meanings are found in *The Interpretation Act*[21] of Ontario. Both of these terms, in definition, provide in part, that the person "requires care, supervision and control for his own protection or welfare or for the protection of others."[22]

The Marriage Act is silent as to the validity of a marriage where one of the parties thereto is mentally ill or mentally defective. Indeed, even if one of the parties comes within the definition and the licence issuer or celebrant is convicted as a result, this does not by itself render the marriage invalid. The validity of a marriage may be determined only by a court applying the law relating to the capacity of a person to marry. There being no legislation on point, reference is made to the common law.

The common law recognizes marriage as a contract and, accordingly, each of the parties must have a certain capacity to enter into such a contract. It is a rule of the common law that a marriage contracted while one of the parties lacks capacity is void from the beginning. Capacity to contract marriage involves the ability to understand the significance and nature of the marriage contract and appreciate the responsibilities normally flowing therefrom.[23]

While some retarded may lack capacity to contract marriage, others may very well be endowed with that capacity. Each case must be determined on its own merits and this is a matter for the court to determine.

Looking at the prohibitions against issuers of licences and celebrants, it is difficult to find any evidence that these officials refuse to issue licences or to celebrate marriages on such grounds. This is scarcely surprising, in view of the fact that issuers and celebrants do not normally spend much time with the persons to be married. Issuers and celebrants, in many instances, lack training and knowledge to make a judgment on this issue. No official guidelines appear to exist for identifying the individuals who come within the proscribed classes. Indeed, there does not seem to be any pressure brought to bear or direction given to these officials to enforce or pay attention to the question of mental capacity. In the final analysis, therefore, there seems to be little, if any, impact resulting from the statutory prohibitions. Consequently, there may be virtually no difference in practice between those provinces having the subject prohibitions and those not having them.

The situation in the United States is similar, where it has been stated that the prohibitory statutes have ". . . thus far . . . invariably proved worthless, chiefly because of the lack of adequate provisions for the identification or diagnosis of the mental status of applicants for marriage licences."[24]

If prohibitive statutory provisions are to be meaningful, there would surely have to be effective ways of identifying persons who lack capacity to marry. The way matters now stand, it may be assumed that those retarded persons who wish to do so are in fact getting married. Such marriages might be prevented if a workable screening process were to be developed, but this would inevitably result in union without the dignity of the marriage label.

Where Provincial Legislatures wish to preserve laws prohibiting the issuance of marriage licences to, and the solemnization of marriages of, the mentally ill and retarded, it is recommended that appropriate criteria be formulated and procedures developed so that the issues may be determined in a sensible manner which seems impossible under much of current legislation.

Being a parent

There is no doubt that some retarded people do have children and do raise them. Probably some of these retarded are inadequate parents. By the same token, there are similar parents who could not be labelled retarded.

Perhaps more so than with any other issue, parental fitness involves a complex weighing of a multiplicity of factors. No general rule can be contrived to decide every case satisfactorily. A balance must be struck weighing all the factors in each individual situation and for each particular family.

Certain universal standards may be formulated by which to judge the quality of parental efforts. Physical cruelty and brutality are clear indices of unfitness. The failure through neglect or inability to provide the necessities of life demonstrates further obvious evidence of incapacity. These negative factors do not constitute a full inventory of points to be considered in determining whether or not a parent is fit.

Also crucial to the role of parent are more intangible matters such as provision of love, affection, emotional stability, guidance and intellectual stimulation. These are factors which cannot be judged by an absolute standard comparable to a requirement that shelter, food, clothing and humane treatment be given to children.

Investigation by social workers and psychiatrists would appear essential to a determination that any child is not receiving the love, moral training and stimulation his healthy development requires. It may well be that the retarded parent is giving the love and emotional security necessary, while at the same time he is inefficient at household management. Such a finding would illustrate the difficulty of this entire question.

The interests of the child are always paramount and no conflict between his best interests and the desires of his parents should be tolerated by anyone. Without questioning this paramount interest, if the welfare of the child is judged by some ideal standard, the parent may suffer by the application of expectations higher than those met by their "normal" counterparts in the community. It is recommended that laws to determine whether an individual is a fit parent should be no more stringently applied to a retarded parent than to others.

All of the provinces have legislation to protect children in untenable family situations. One such piece of legislation, the *Child Welfare Act* of Alberta, enumerates fifteen criteria of "neglect" sufficient to found a decision that the child is in need of protection.[25] A police officer, certain prescribed officials of the Children's Aid Society and other authorities are empowered to enter the home, remove the child to a place of custody and institute a judicial hearing to determine if the child is neglected within the meaning of the Act. If such a finding is made, weighing the various factors discussed above and the provisions of the Act, the child is ordered into permanent custody of the Children's Aid Society for care, protection and possible placement in a foster-home or an institution. Provision is made for the return of the child to the family upon a judicial finding of fitness of the parents and appropriateness of the home situation.

Some guidance of what may be expected of a retarded parent may be found in a judgment of the Supreme Court of Canada in 1950. The Court there considered the fitness of an unwed mother balanced against the opportunities offered by proposed adoptive parents. For the Court, Mr. Justice Cartwright, later Chief Justice of Canada, wrote

> "In the present state of the law as I understand it, giving full effect to the existing legislation, the mother of an illegitimate child, who has not abandoned it, who is of good character and is able and willing to support it in satisfactory surroundings, is not to be deprived of her child merely because on a nice balancing of material and social advantages the Court is of opinion that others, who wish to do so, could provide more advantageously for its upbringing and future. The wishes of the mother must, I think, be given effect unless 'very serious and important' reasons require that, having regard to the child's welfare, they must be disregarded."[26]

Little needs to be said here of the effect of such a dramatic removal upon at least some parents, or the effect on the child of upheaval and dislocation. This measure may be required if the situation has developed to the point that continued residence with the family will have graver consequences for the child.

Remedial social action would logically seem of two types: preventing would-be unfit parents from having children; or assistance to ostensibly unfit parents in rearing their children and, perhaps, at that point, preventing them from having additional children. Sterilization before the couple effect a union would, of course, eliminate the problem of inadequate parenthood. Recommendation of such a step would necessarily involve the decision that the retarded potential parent would be an unfit one. That decision would be to varying degrees based upon speculation, given the characteristics of the individual, scientific understanding of the difficulties of parenthood, and the usual capacity of the retarded to cope with those difficulties. It would appear that scientific opinion has not yet come to a consensus on the last issue.

If sterilization before union is not considered desirable or feasible (given the law relating to sterilization which is analyzed later in this chapter), then social assistance with child rearing would be indicated. Public health nursing and community counselling services are available in many centers. These provide advice and aid in such matters as child care, budgeting, nutrition, discipline and the resolving of emotional crises.

Information about contraception would appear to be an integral part of family management advice, coupled with counselling as to desirability of the practice based on an evaluation of present success of the parents and considered opinion about the effects of further children.

If these supportive services were to be fully utilized by retarded parents, it is not perhaps unrealistic to expect that many such families could be helped through the hardships which make the invocation of the child protection laws essential.

For public services to be of benefit and preclude the necessity of drastic action, the retarded must make use of these services by inviting the assistance or having it offered on public initiative. It may be more practical to have the assistance offered. Experience might suggest that parents with limited intellectual capacity misunderstand the purpose of public intervention even when it is made available only to assist them. Such fear must be overcome if the benefits of counselling are to be realized. Efforts should be made to ensure that legal supervision and social assistance attempts are not seen by the subject family as a threat to be fought or evaded.

Contraception

The prevention of conception may be achieved in various ways, some permanent and others temporary. There seems to be a reluctance on the part of many to condone any measure which is permanent and irreversible, especially if surgery is involved. The same result that would follow from sterilization follows from effective temporary means of birth control.

In the case of mentally handicapped persons, there is a fear – where birth control is indicated – that temporary measures of contraception will fail.

"Contraception is usually found to be unreliable in those of limited ability."[27] Many retarded females no doubt lack an appreciation of the significance of birth control. Where they have some appreciation or accept without question the necessity of practising birth control measures, there may still be problems in following instructions given. They may forget to take their "pill" or lose their sequence. With respect to intra-uterine devices, they may be used only after a pregnancy and the question of consent in inserting them is a difficult question.

The subject of contraceptive methods is something about which one constantly reads of revolutionary scientific developments. There is already a once-a-month injection being used on females in institutions. Moreover, there is talk of the once-a-month pill, an injection lasting three months, the two-year capsule implanted in the womb, and even the lifetime capsule implanted under the skin.

New measures are being projected for males as well, as for example the immunization of the male against his own spermatozoa so that the sperm would no longer be produced.

In order for any measures short of sterilization to accomplish their purpose, those in need of them must be identified and counselled. Until recently, such counselling constituted a crime. By virtue of an amendment to the *Criminal Code*[28] in force August 18, 1969, reference to the words "preventing conception" were dropped. Consequently, the way is open to offering advice and providing means to all persons on this subject, and it is recommended that the fullest use be made of this opportunity in the case of the retarded.

Sterilization

The surgical sterilization procedure in the case of the male is known as the vasectomy, a simple operation which is usually performed in a physician's office. It involves skin incisions in the scrotum and the interruption of each *vas deferens*, the duct leading from the testicle to the ejaculatory duct.

> "It entails, at most, a 20-minute operation under a local anesthetic, one small incision at the front of the scrotum (some doctors favor two), an average fee of $75, a couple of 292s to ease perhaps 24 hours of discomfort, and *voila!* – peace of mind."[29]

Vasectomy is a permanent measure, although it may not be wise to rely fully upon its immediate effectiveness.[30]

Surgical sterilization for the female is, by contrast, more involved than the vasectomy and has to do with the tying or cutting of the Fallopian tubes, down which the egg must travel to the uterus. Various procedures may be adopted. Two of these are known as tubal ligation and salpingectomy. Salpingectomy may be performed abdominally or vaginally. These procedures, all of which require hospitalization on an in-patient basis, are considered permanent.

The permanence of sterilization mentioned relates to its endurance and is not to mean that the resulting conditions are absolutely irreversible. There appears to be a 50-50 chance of reversing a vasectomy[31] and a 15 to 25 per cent rate of success in reversing the sterilized condition caused by tubal ligation.[32] Because the chances of successful reversal are not greater, and perhaps because of legal implications as well, physicians may tend to advise their patients who seek sterilization to do so with an attitude that the procedure will not be capable of reversal.

Neither the male nor the female sterilization measures interfere with the desire for sexual intercourse or with its gratification.[33]

Indications for sterilization in the cases of both sexes are commonly divided into three main categories: eugenic; therapeutic; and contraceptive (sometimes referred to as "sterilization of convenience").

Eugenic

The essence of eugenics is the concept of improving the racial strain through the prevention of transmission of defective genes. It seems to be the thinking of some that this improvement would be accomplished by sterilizing all who presently "carry" genetic defects which are said to be harmful and burdensome to society.

Eugenic sterilization has been and is still recognized by statutes of a number of jurisdictions as an appropriate measure to be employed in defined circumstances.

A man described as a pioneer American gynecologist wrote:

> "I am, indeed, not sure that in the progressive future it will not be deemed a measure of sound policy and of commendable statesmanship to stamp out insanity, by castrating all the insane men and spaying all the insane women."[34]

In the United States, the greatest impetus for eugenic sterilization statutes was present during the early years of this century. The State of Indiana was the first to pass such a law, but this and other Acts enacted prior to 1925 eventually were declared unconstitutional. The Virginia law was argued before the United States Supreme Court in 1927 in the celebrated case of *Buck v. Bell.*[35] Justice Oliver Wendell Holmes, in upholding the Virginia law, made a comparison to the sacrifice required of soldiers during war. "The Holmes decision was based on the assumption that the defects were hereditary in the absence of any scientific evidence challenging this theory, and on the precedent of the Massachusetts compulsory vaccination law which, however, provided that those who 'should deem it important that vaccination should not be performed' had merely to pay a fine of five dollars to escape the procedure."[36]

> "The principle that sustains compulsory vaccination is broad enough to cover cutting the Fallopian tubes. . . . Three generations of imbeciles are enough."[37]

It is reported that there are currently twenty-six states of the United States with eugenic sterilization laws, twenty-three of which are compulsory.[38]

Only two Canadian provinces – Alberta and British Columbia – carry sexual sterilization laws on their statute books. The Alberta law[39] was first enacted in 1928, receiving its Royal Assent on March 21 of that year. In original form, the Act made reference to "the danger of procreation with its attendant risk of multiplication of the evil by transmission of the disability to progeny."[40] A sexual sterilization law was passed some five years later in British Columbia[41] and came into operation on July 1, 1933.

The Sexual Sterilization Act in Alberta applies to patients proposed for discharge from a mental hospital and mentally defective persons who have been under treatment or observation at a mental hygiene clinic. The medical super-intendent of the hospital or physician in charge of the clinic "may cause" the individual to be examined by, or in the presence of, the Eugenics Board. The Board is a four-member body appointed by Cabinet, two and only two of whom must be physicians.

In all cases the Board may act only on the basis of unanimous opinion. The machinery of the statute deals with various diagnostic categories in different ways, the main difference in procedure relating to the giving of consent.

"Mentally defective person" is defined as "a person in whom there is a condition of arrested or incomplete development of mind existing before the age of eighteen years, whether arising from inherent causes or induced by disease or injury." If upon the examination of a mentally defective person the Board is unanimously of the opinion that the exercise of the power of procreation by that person "would result in the transmission of any mental disability or deficiency to his progeny" or "involves the risk of mental injury either to such person or his progeny", the Board may in writing direct such surgical operation for surgical sterilization as may be specified and appoint a surgeon to perform the operation. The statute is silent on the matter of consent in the case of sterilization of a mentally defective person. As a matter of interpretation, consent would not appear to be a condition precedent.

Also contained in the Act are similar measures for persons suffering from a psychosis; neurosyphilis with deterioration not amounting to psychosis but not responsive to treatment; epilepsy with psychosis or mental deterioration; and Huntington's Chorea. In these instances, consent of the individual involved is required. However, with respect to a psychotic person who in the opinion of the Board is not capable of giving a valid consent, the consent may be given by his or her spouse, or if unmarried by a parent or guardian who is resident in Alberta.

Protection by way of exemption from civil liability for anything done in good faith in purported pursuance of the Act is given to a number of persons, including the medical superintendent who initiates the examination, Board members, anyone giving consent to the operation, and the surgeon and persons assisting or working with him in the performance of the operation.

The Eugenics Board of Alberta meets on an average of five times a year at various provincial facilities. Approximately 25 cases may be evaluated in a two-day session of the Board.[42]

Once cases are presented to the Eugenics Board, it seems fairly certain that they will be passed for surgery. In 1967, the Board considered a total of 89 cases, 82 of which were passed for surgery. Four cases were "deferred" because they did not fall within the scope of the Act and three cases were "represented". Of the 82 passed (27 male and 55 female) 19 were passed subject to their consent. Sixty of the 82 had first been examined at an Alberta Guidance Clinic, although some of these had been institutionalized prior to presentation.

During 1967, 97 operations were performed: 34 on males and 63 on females. All of these operations were done at the Alberta Hospitals at Edmonton and Ponoka and the Alberta School Hospital at Red Deer. Two surgeons of the Board performed all of the operations.

Statistical data over the years show that between 1929 and 1967, there were a total of 4,430 cases (2,064 male, 2,366 female) presented to and passed by the Board. Of these, there were 2,572 operations (1,082 male and 1,490 female) actually performed during that period. No significant trends appear as may be seen from the figures.[43]

CASES PRESENTED AND PASSED
To December 31, 1967

Years	YEARLY TOTALS			CUMULATIVE TOTALS		
	Male	Female	Totals	Male	Female	Totals
1929-1933	87	201	288	87	201	288
1934-1938	557	438	995	644	639	1283
1939-1943	339	299	638	983	938	1921
1944-1948	237	311	548	1220	1249	2469
1949-1953	187	239	426	1407	1488	2895
1954-1958	302	275	577	1709	1763	3472
1959	32	62	94	1741	1825	3566
1960	37	65	102	1778	1890	3668
1961	44	75	119	1822	1965	3787
1962	48	71	119	1870	2036	3906
1963	45	80	125	1915	2116	4031
1964	43	63	106	1958	2179	4137
1965	28	53	81	1986	2232	4218
1966	51	79	130	2037	2311	4348
1967	27	55	82	2064	2366	4430

OPERATIONS ONLY
To December 31, 1967

Years	YEARLY TOTALS			CUMULATIVE TOTALS		
	Male	Female	Totals	Male	Female	Totals
1929-1933	48	158	206	48	158	206
1934-1938	198	240	438	246	398	644
1939-1943	122	151	273	368	549	917
1944-1948	87	124	211	455	673	1128
1949-1953	84	162	246	539	835	1374
1954-1958	207	160	367	746	995	1741
1959	40	50	90	786	1045	1831
1960	21	48	69	807	1093	1900
1961	53	52	105	860	1145	2005
1962	33	65	98	893	1210	2103
1963	31	61	92	924	1271	2195
1964	37	44	81	961	1315	2276
1965	45	47	92	1006	1362	2368
1966	42	65	107	1048	1427	2475
1967	34	63	97	1082	1490	2572

The British Columbia *Sexual Sterilization Act* differs in a number of respects from the Alberta law. It applies to inmates of "institutions": "institution" meaning any provincial mental health facility as defined in the *Mental Health Act, 1964* or a training-school as defined in the *Training-schools Act*.

Where it appears to the Superintendent of an institution that any inmate "if discharged therefrom without being subjected to an operation for sexual sterilization, would be likely to beget or bear children who by reason of inheritance would have a tendency to serious mental disease or mental deficiency," he may submit a recommendation to the Board of Eugenics that a surgical operation for sexual sterilization be performed.

The Board is composed of three persons appointed by Cabinet: one being a judge; another a psychiatrist; and the third, a person experienced in social-welfare work.

The recommendation by the Superintendent must be written and accompanied by a statement reciting the inmate's relevant history as shown in the institutional records and the reasons why sexual sterilization is recommended. The Superintendent "may cause" the inmate to be examined by or in the presence of the Board of Eugenics. If upon such examination the Board is unanimously of the opinion that the criteria are satisfied, it may by a written order direct "such surgical operation for sexual sterilization of the inmate as is set out in the order," and may appoint a physician to perform the operation. It is, by law, open to the inmate or person acting on his or her behalf to select and employ, at the inmate's expense, a physician to attend in consultation at or to perform the operation directed by the Board's order.

Written consent to the operation is in all cases an absolute requirement. If, in the opinion of the Board, the inmate is capable of giving consent, he or she must be the one to give it. Where, in the Board's opinion the inmate lacks capacity to give consent, it is the husband or wife of the inmate, or the parent or guardian of the unmarried inmate, whose consent is required. In case an inmate without capacity to consent has no spouse, or parent or guardian resident in British Columbia, the Provincial Secretary is empowered to give the consent.

The Act protects the physician appointed by the Board to perform the operation, he not being liable to any civil action by reason of the performance of the operation, except in the case of negligence in performing it.

Information received from British Columbia[44] in mid-1969 disclosed that the Board of Eugenics "dealt with a number of matters over the last few years and operations have followed from consultation, the figures being as follows:

1966 – five cases (no breakdown as to male and female)
1967 – one female
1968 – one female
1969 to date – one female."

An examination of scientific literature relating to genetics casts serious doubt on the strength of the foundations upon which these statutes are erected.

"When considered in the light of recent scientific thinking the validity of sterilization for eugenic purposes is certainly open to serious questioning. In evaluating the advisability of compulsory sterilization it is important to keep in mind that mental illness and epilepsy have shown an increased response to medical treatment. It is also important to remember that though there is some relationship between heredity and mental deficiency, it has been estimated that about 89 per cent of inheritable mental deficiency is passed on by individuals not themselves deficient. At the present time there is no way of ascertaining who these normal carriers are. Thus, if it were possible to sterilize collectively all the feeble-minded, their number in the following generation would be cut down only about 11 per cent. It has been asserted that at present there is no scientific basis for any plan to eliminate completely the problem of mental deficiency."[45]

The preliminary report of the Mental Incompetency Study in the United States noted that the Task Force on Law of the President's Panel on Mental Retardation and several state mental retardation planning committees have equivocated on the matter of involuntary sterilization, and added that: "We have been unable to find persuasive scientific proof . . . of the inheritability of the defects for which sterilization is now being imposed. . . ."[46]

Likewise in Canada, questions have been raised about the propriety of the sexual sterilization laws here. It has been suggested as a reasonable query "if any of the individuals who have been sterilized under [the British Columbia] Act to date would have been if a geneticist had been involved in the decision?"[47]

A recent critique[48] of the Alberta *Sexual Sterilization Act* describes it as "reminiscent of the sterilization laws of National Socialist Germany"[49] and states that the statute is antiquated from a genetic point of view "because it singles out in a rather incoherent way partly genetically induced and partly environmentally induced syndromes, which, in the opinion of the modern geneticist constitute only minor contributions to the genetic burden of the population."[50] The same critique dismisses the Act as "scientifically illiterate" and "a disgrace to the whole of Canada."[51]

Therapeutic

Therapeutic sterilization is a measure designed to preserve the life or health of a female who should not medically undergo childbirth, either again or at all. The procedure is sometimes performed as a separate operation, or could be done in conjunction with a therapeutic abortion. "There is a growing tendency on both sides of the Atlantic for surgeons to combine sterilization with therapeutic abortion in suitable cases, because the same condition that indicates the abortion may indicate that the woman should not become pregnant again."[52]

Indications for therapeutic sterilization certainly include a number of medical conditions such as malignant tumors, severe heart or kidney diseases, recurrent toxaemia of pregnancy and repeated Caesarian section.[53] Therapeutic sterilization may also be indicated on psychiatric grounds relating to emotional stresses of parenthood.

Contraceptive

As indicated by its name, contraceptive sterilization is performed on an individual who wishes a failsafe method of birth control. Social and economic factors often play a part in the reaching of a decision that sterilization is desired. Medical, including psychiatric reasons, are not here present.

Outside the two statutes dealing with eugenic sterilization, there would appear to be no law in Canada dealing with the subject of sterilization: no law prohibiting it and no law sanctioning it. Reviewing the probable legal situation with respect to therapeutic and contraceptive sterilization, there seems to be little difference between the two.

Sterilization involves the use of "force" upon an individual. The *Criminal Code* sees the intentional application of force, directly or indirectly, as an "assault" unless consent is first obtained.[54] Presumably, therefore, a surgeon who sterilizes a person is protected from criminal liability where he performs the operation under the authority of the consent of the patient. Indeed, the surgeon should not fear criminal charges arising out of the operation, even where no consent is obtained, providing certain circumstances prevail.

> "Every one is protected from criminal responsibility for performing a surgical operation upon any person for the benefit of that person if
> (*a*) the operation is performed with reasonable care and skill, and

(*b*) it is reasonable to perform the operation, having regard to the state of health of the person at the time the operation is performed and to all the circumstances of the case."[55]

This protection afforded by the *Code* relates only to immunity from criminal responsibility, and is probably restricted to cases where consent is not obtained to sterilization procedures of a therapeutic character. It seems doubtful from the wording of this section that it would protect a surgeon sterilizing a person without consent for contraceptive reasons.

On the civil side, the need for consent arises as a more significant issue. Proper consent is a prerequisite to sterilization unless the circumstances are such that medical necessity dictates immediate action in the absence of such consent.

"In MURRAY *v.* McMURCHY, [1949] 2 D.L.R. 442; 1 W.W.R. 989 (B.C. Sup. Ct.), in the course of a Caesarian operation the surgeon discovered a number of fibroid tumors in the uterus wall. After consultation with another surgeon he tied off the Fallopian tubes to prevent the hazards of a second pregnancy. The plaintiff sued the surgeon and recovered $3,000 damages. MACFARLANE, J., distinguished the case where an operation was 'necessary' as involving 'urgency' and 'immediate decision'. In the present case the possibility of future hazard did not absolve the surgeon from obtaining consent no matter how 'convenient or desirable' in order to prevent danger in a later contingency. That risk must be left to the decision of the plaintiff."[56]

There seems to have been in Canada a reluctance by physicians to perform sterilization operations generally. Exceptions are reported, but these relate only to consenting adult males. The combination of prevailing legal uncertainties and problems of consent in the case of the retarded has, so far as we can determine, militated against sterilization of the retarded. Because of this, perhaps, another measure – equally effective – seems to have developed. This measure is commonly referred to as "institutional sterilization".

Institutional sterilization is the detention of persons in mental institutions to prevent them from producing children. Although no statistical data are available, there are unquestionably a significant number of retardates currently institutionalized mainly – if not entirely – for this purpose. Whether the use of institutional sterilization is a fair, or even proper, approach is currently the subject of heated debate.[57] Considering the logic of the concept, it is difficult, indeed impossible, to support it. Bearing in mind that surgical and institutional sterilization accomplish the same end, how can compulsory institutionalization be justified when freedom is at the same time available? Surely any retarded person would prefer sterilization and freedom to sterilization and incarceration?

There are indications of a new trend in Canada on the subject of sterilization. The Canadian Medical Association passed a resolution in 1970 accepting as policy "any procedure for the purpose of producing sterilization of either male or female" under certain conditions: it must be performed by a qualified physician in adequate facilities and be based upon written permission of the patient stating that he understands the likelihood of permanency.[58] The Association, at the same time, dropped any reference to sterilization from its Code of Ethics.[59] The physician is now, to all intents and purposes, on his own to decide the question. This recent professional liberalization may well be reflected in the practice of sterilizing retardates and special guidelines developed in that regard.

Still, the issue of consent looms large, and sterilization may be indicated where the person has not the capacity to give that consent. Nothing short of legislation can overcome this problem. It is recommended that laws be enacted by the Legislatures encompassing appropriate procedures for sexual sterilization where the individual lacks capacity to consent. Any new laws in this regard should, of course, be based upon sound scientific principles, and guarantee individual rights in every way possible.

Abortion

According to the *Criminal Code* which, of course, applies across Canada, a person who "with intent to procure the miscarriage of a female . . . uses any means for the purpose of carrying out his intention" is guilty of an offence.[60] Likewise, a pregnant female who "with intent to procure her own miscarriage, uses any means or permits any means to be used for the purpose of carrying out her intention" is guilty of an offence.[61] However, recent amendments[62] to the criminal law, proclaimed in force on August 26, 1969, exempt physicians and pregnant females from criminal liability in respect of abortions performed under prescribed circumstances.

Performance of the abortion will not attract such liability to these persons where it is done by the physician in good faith in an accredited or approved hospital and he is in possession of a certificate from the therapeutic abortion committee of the hospital. The new law contemplates that the board of a hospital will appoint such a committee which must have at least three members each of whom is a physician. A therapeutic abortion committee may act on a majority decision. The physician who performs the operation must not be a member of the committee.

In order for an abortion to be considered legal under the new legislation, the committee must be of the opinion that "the continuation of the pregnancy . . . would or would be likely to endanger her life or health".

There has, as yet, been no Canadian court decision which would shed light on what constitutes a danger to life or health. As medical science advances, there is a decreasing number of conditions of a physical nature which can be considered a risk to life or health of a pregnant woman.[63] Consequently, more and more pressures seem to be exerted on those seeking abortions to achieve their purposes on psychiatric grounds. Indications are that therapeutic abortions are now most often performed on the basis of threat to the mother's mental health.[64] The practice is not without contention: "A Canadian woman's chances of getting a legal abortion depend mainly on whether she can find a 'dishonest' psychiatrist. Women must hope to find psychiatrists who will strain for a diagnosis that would permit the operation. . . . Those who gain hospital committee permission for an abortion are often as healthy as those who are rejected."[65]

While the *Criminal Code* refers to the "life or health" of the expectant mother, there is no mention whatsoever of the expected child. A therapeutic abortion in this country is not legally available on the ground that the child may be born with a physical or mental disability. This is so even though the risk of a serious disability in the child is 100 per cent. The probability – or even the certainty – of a disability in the child may, however, be seen by the psychiatrist as ultimately endangering the mental stability of the mother, thus enabling him to find a danger to her "life or health".

Other jurisdictions have seen fit to include within their therapeutic abortion laws specific grounds relating to the potential birth of an abnormal child.

Since 1956, Denmark's *Pregnancy Act* has provided for abortions, amongst other reasons, where the child is likely to be born with any serious form of mental illness or deficiency or serious physical abnormality.[66]

The *Abortion Act*, passed in 1967 in the United Kingdom,[67] recognizes as lawful an abortion performed on the ground of the genuine belief of two physicians that the fetus would be born with a physical or mental deformity.[68]

In the State of Colorado, a therapeutic abortion may be legally obtained on the ground that the pregnancy would result in the birth of a child with grave physical deformities or mental retardation.[69]

Widening our abortion laws to include consideration of the interests of the expected child was advocated by Canadian lawyers even before our recent abortion laws were passed. In 1966, the Canadian Bar Association resolved (on a vote of 153 to 94) that abortions be lawful if "there is a substantial risk that the child may be born with a grave mental or physical disability."[70]

"There are, to-day, modern medical techniques for predicting in some instances, on a statistical basis, when a defective child can be anticipated. The potential for mongolism and various types of severe, hereditary, mental, and physical defects can be uncovered by genetic typing, ..."[71] For example, a testing of the amniotic fluid of a pregnant woman during the first three months of gestation may support a prediction of the birth of a mongoloid.[72] Many would argue in favor of abortion under such circumstances. Indications are that there may be a greater frequency of abortion coming on the basis of potential abnormality.

> "Therapeutic abortion on genetic grounds is, at the present time, rarely done. As more is learned about inherited diseases, however, there is likely to be an increasing demand from both the physician and the patient for interruption of pregnancy when there is a substantial risk of congenital malformation as a result of a likely combination of parental genes."[73]

Certain countries, in formulating the grounds for legal abortion, have gone further than simply looking directly at the mother or the child.

In Denmark, for example, permission for a legal abortion is granted where the woman is deemed unfit to take proper care of her child because of serious physical or psychic defects or other medical reasons.

> "This provision, which was introduced in 1956, has special reference to conditions where, by reason of any severe mental or physical defect (mental deficiency, severe defects of character, severe physical disability), the woman is not able to care for her child, and where termination of the pregnancy is not indicated for health or hereditary reasons. In principle, it is a social indication, it being the interests of the child, not of the woman herself, that are safeguarded. In accordance with its terms, the provision has been applied in only a few cases. The current debate about extending the range of indications has touched upon the possibility of applying a broader construction to this provision so as to include, for instance, a larger number of mentally retarded persons."[74]

The law in the United Kingdom goes further. The so-called "social clause" of *The Abortion Act* authorizes an abortion where the physical or mental health of existing children in the family would be injured.[75]

In the State of New York, the law has recently been liberalized to the extent that abortion is now basically a matter to be determined between a woman and her physician.[76] A similar posture has been recommended by the American Medical Association[77] and, as well, by the Canadian Psychiatric Association.[78]

Whatever the law relating to abortion, consent of the woman to be aborted is considered a condition precedent. There should be an appropriate and expedient procedure to allow abortion where otherwise indicated and the individual lacks capacity to consent. Since legislation would be required to accomplish this purpose, and in Canada this is a matter of criminal law, it is recommended that the

Criminal Code be amended accordingly. Needless to say, such an amendment should fully secure individual rights.

Annulment

Capacity to marry was earlier defined as ability to understand the significance and nature of the marriage contract and appreciate the responsibilities normally flowing therefrom. If that capacity is lacking, the marriage is invalid. The same effect follows from an incapacity in law to give a good consent. Where a person has not legal capacity to marry, the proper legal method of dissolution is annulment.

Defective marriages fall into two classes: void *ab initio* (from the beginning) and voidable. The distinction has clearly been described as follows.

> ". . . a void marriage is one that will be regarded by every court in any case in which the existence of the marriage is in issue as never having taken place and can be so treated by both parties to it without the necessity of any decree annulling it; a voidable marriage is one that will be regarded as a valid subsisting marriage until a decree annulling it has been pronounced by a court of competent jurisdiction."[79]

The grounds for finding a marriage voidable and declaring it a nullity, such as impotence or consanguinity, raise no special issues for retarded persons.

Grounds for holding a marriage void *ab initio* include legal incapacity to marry because of mental incompetence or because there was no real consent to the marriage.[80] These grounds are crucial to this study.

Whether a marriage is void from the beginning or is rendered void at a later time is a most important consideration where there are children of the union. The legitimacy of children of a marriage that is annulled may be protected by provincial statutes dealing with legitimacy. Some of these statutes provide that the children of a voidable marriage shall remain legitimate provided that they would have been legitimate if the marriage had been dissolved by divorce rather than annulled. These statutes also confer legitimacy on children of a void marriage if the marriage substantially complied with local laws regulating form and if either of the parties reasonably believed the marriage to be valid.[81]

A petition for annulment where the marriage is void may be initiated by any person as well as a party to the "marriage",[82] and even after the death of either partner. The power of a third party to intervene makes sense, for example, where the annulment is sought on the ground of mental deficiency: action by such an individual is essential to protect a defective party to the "marriage". By contrast, where the marriage is merely voidable, only a party to the marriage may seek an annulment.[83]

Whoever petitions for the decree of annulment must bear a heavy onus of proof. The validity of a marriage is a presumption of law, and if the petitioner cannot rebut the presumption, the marriage persists whatever the extent of the respondent's reply to the petition. The proof required to rebut the presumption is not that of a criminal trial – beyond any reasonable doubt. The burden of proof is, however, greater than the mere balance of probabilities required in a civil action.[84] The court will have to be convinced that one of the parties to the marriage was so defective mentally as not to have comprehended the nature of his undertaking.

Divorce

Mental retardation is not a ground for divorce in Canada. The *Divorce Act*[85] allows for dissolution of a marriage if a marital offence is committed[86] or if there has been a permanent marriage breakdown under named circumstances.[87]

There is no legislative provision treating retardates as a special class for this purpose, and where a divorce is desired by or from a retarded person, the action must proceed in the normal fashion by establishing one of the grounds in the Act.

Assume that a petitioner alleges commission of a marital offence by a retarded spouse. The issue arises whether the retarded respondent may plead lack of capacity to form the intent to commit that offence, and inability to appreciate the consequences of his act. The courts have considered the matter where the offence alleged was cruelty and the mental condition pleaded in defence was insanity. In *Novak v. Novak*[88] it was held that the insanity of the husband did not disentitle the petitioning wife to a divorce decree on the ground of cruelty. The Supreme Court of Nova Scotia in *Herman v. Herman*[89] adopted the words of the House of Lords in the English case of *Williams v. Williams*[90] as follows.

> ". . . Where, however, the conduct would be held to be cruelty regardless of motive or intention to be cruel, insanity would not bar relief."

It may be generally assumed that a divorce petition indicates that one of the parties no longer wishes marriage and cohabitation. Whether the respondent is deserving of blame or not, continued union is intolerable for the petitioner. The matter is not yet clarified, but it may be that the courts will give no more effect to a defence of retardation than they appear to give to insanity.

Some extremely tricky issues could conceivably be raised where a retarded petitioner seeks divorce on a marital offence ground, and a "normal" partner tries to defeat the petition by arguing that the petitioner lacked mental capacity to appreciate the nature of the offence done to him.[91]

For a marriage breakdown to be established, it must be shown that the parties are living "separate and apart" in circumstances expressed in the *Divorce Act*. The meaning of "separate and apart" is discussed in *Rushton v. Rushton*[92] by Mr. Justice McIntyre.

> "The words 'separate and apart' are disjunctive. They mean, in my view, that there must be a withdrawal from the matrimonial obligation with the intent of destroying the matrimonial *consortium*, as well as physical separation. The two conditions must be met."

In that case, living "separate and apart" was found although the parties were living in the same apartment. They were withdrawn from one another with the intent of considering marital union totally ended. Physical proximity is not a guideline. Conversely, parties are not living "separate and apart" merely because of geographical distance: ". . . as long as the spouses treat the parting or absence, be it long or short, as *temporary* and *not permanent*, the couple is not living separately even though physically it is living apart."[93]

While this legal concept is of general application, it may have particular relevance where a retarded spouse must be placed in a special residential setting. The couple then are physically separated. In the British Columbia case of *Kennedy v. Kennedy*[94] a wife was hospitalized as a schizophrenic and after some years the husband determined never to see her again and not to contribute to her maintenance. It was the finding of the court that from that point the parties were "separate and apart". A similar decision was reached in Ontario where the required status was not found to have existed until the wife ceased to visit her hospitalized husband.[95]

In addition to four listed circumstances which evidence permanent marriage breakdown (imprisonment, addiction, disappearance and non-consummation), the statute provides a catch-all remedy. To come within the catch-all framework, the parties must meet intent and time requirements. *Animus* or intent is here an essential element of being separate.[96] This intention may be mutual, leading to a consensual separation, or unilateral (desertion).

The requisite time period for so living as proof of marriage breakdown varies depending whether the intention is mutual. If both spouses agree to be apart and intend to end their marriage, the waiting period before petitioning for divorce is three years. If only one spouse desires to end the marriage, and deserts the other, the waiting period before applying would be three years for the deserted partner and five years for the one deserting. Consequently, desertion and a five-year waiting period may be the only recourse for an aggrieved spouse.

A mental disability may preclude capacity to form the intent to live "separate and apart". But such incapacity does not make it impossible for the other party to desert. It is not necessary that the deserted spouse know or be capable of knowing of the desertion.[97]

References

1 See, for examples, INTERNATIONAL LEAGUE OF SOCIETIES FOR THE MENTALLY HANDICAPPED, CONCLUSIONS: SYMPOSIUM ON GUARDIANSHIP OF THE MENTALLY RETARDED (1969) (hereinafter cited as SYMPOSIUM) and THE PRESIDENT'S PANEL ON MENTAL RETARDATION, REPORT OF THE TASK FORCE ON LAW (1963) U.S.A. (hereinafter cited as TASK FORCE).
2 International League of Societies for the Mentally Handicapped, Declaration of general and special rights of the mentally retarded, October 24, 1968, Article I. The entire declaration is reprinted as Appendix A.
3 S.C. 1953-54, c. 51.
4 *Ibid.*, s. 147.
5 *Ibid.*, s. 149.
6 *Criminal Law Amendment Act, 1968-69*, S.C. 1968-69, c. 38, s. 7, adding s. 149A.
7 Bradley, Kendall and Bland, How May the Mentally Retarded Be Trained So That Their Sexual Behaviour Will Be Generally Acceptable, February 14, 1966.
8 *Ibid.*, p. 1.
9 *Ibid.*
10 *Ibid.*, p. 2.
11 TASK FORCE 22.
12 Abbott and Ladd, . . . *any reason why this mentally retarded couple should not be joined together . . .*, 2:8 MENTAL RETARDATION (U.S.) 45, 45 (April, 1970).
13 Dr. N. Speijer, quoted in 19:3 MENTAL RETARDATION (Can.) 19 (July, 1969).
14 See authorities cited in Bass, *Marriage for the Mentally Deficient*, 2 MENTAL RETARDATION (U.S.) 198, 199-200 (August, 1964). See, also, SYMPOSIUM 15, wherein it is stated as follows: In so far as marriage is considered inseparable from the raising of children, the rights of the children to proper care and nurture must be considered in the light of the capability of the retarded parent to give proper care.
15 *British North America Act* (1867), 30 & 31 Vict., c. 3 (U.K.).
16 *Ibid.*, s. 92, head 12.
17 *Ibid.*, s. 91, head 26. Saskatchewan has gone further in its *Marriage Act*, R.S.S. 1965, c. 338, than constitutional law would seem to permit. See s. 55 which reads as follows: "No person who is a mentally retarded person as defined in *The Mental Health Act*, or is suffering from mental illness as defined in that Act, . . . shall marry within the province."
18 R.S.O. 1960, c. 228.
19 *Ibid.*, s. 6. See discussion of this section in ONTARIO LAW REFORM COMMISSION, REPORT ON FAMILY LAW (Part II: MARRIAGE) 59 (1970).
20 *Ibid.*, s. 48.
21 R.S.O. 1960, c. 191.
22 *Ibid.*, s. 30, clauses 17 and 19 respectively.
23 For a discussion of this rule, see *Re Capon, Capon and O'Brien v. McLay* (1965), 49 D.L.R. (2d) 675, at pp. 680-83 (Ont.).
24 DEUTSCH, THE MENTALLY ILL IN AMERICA 377 (2d ed., 1949).
25 S.A. 1966, c. 13, s. 14.
26 *Martin et al v. Duffel*, [1950] 4 D.L.R. 1, 9.
27 Bradley, Kendall and Bland, How May the Mentally Retarded Be Trained So That Their Sexual Behaviour Will Be Generally Acceptable, February 14, 1966, p. 10.
28 S.C. 1968-69, c. 41, s. 13, re-enacting s. 150(2)(*c*).

29 Cobb, *The Operation – Then No More Children*, THE CANADIAN MAGAZINE (September 20, 1969).

30 *Ibid*. The author cites the recommendation that contraceptives should still be used for up to one year.

31 *Ibid*.

32 Dr. Lindsay Curtis writing in *Toronto Daily Star*, May 20, 1970, p. 31.

33 DEUTSCH, THE MENTALLY ILL IN AMERICA 371 (2d ed., 1949).

34 Goodell, *Clinical notes on the extirpation of the ovaries for insanity*, 38 AMERICAN JOURNAL OF INSANITY 249, 295 (1882). Dr. Goodell's statement is reprinted in Paul, *The Psychiatrist As Public Administrator. Case in Point: State Sterilization Laws*, 38 AMERICAN JOURNAL OF ORTHOPSYCHIATRY 76 (1968), wherein a comprehensive history and analysis (1890-1968) of sterilization in the United States is to be found.

35 274 U.S. 200, 1927.

36 ROBITSCHER, PURSUIT OF AGREEMENT: PSYCHIATRY & THE LAW 81 (1966).

37 *Ibid*., footnote 35 at p. 207.

38 Allen, *Legal Norms and Practices Affecting The Mentally Deficient*, 38 AMERICAN JOURNAL OF ORTHOPSYCHIATRY 635, 638 (1968).

39 *The Sexual Sterilization Act*, S.A. 1928, c. 37.

40 *Ibid*., s. 5.

41 *Sexual Sterilization Act*, S.B.C. 1933, c. 59.

42 Blair, *Mental Health in Alberta* (A Report on the Alberta Mental Health Study, 1968) 267 (1969).

43 Province of Alberta, Department of Health, Annual Report, 1967.

44 British Columbia Department of Attorney General, August 1, 1969.

45 DEUTSCH, THE MENTALLY ILL IN AMERICA 373-74 (2d ed., 1949).

46 Allen, *Legal Norms and Practices Affecting The Mentally Deficient*, 38 AMERICAN JOURNAL OF ORTHOPSYCHIATRY 635, 638 (1968).

47 Subcommittee to the Professional Advisory Committee of the Association for Retarded Children of British Columbia, reported in 14:3 MENTAL RETARDATION 25 (September, 1964).

48 McWhirter and Weijer, *The Alberta Sterilization Act: A Genetic Critique*, 19 UNIVERSITY OF TORONTO LAW JOURNAL 424 (1969).

49 *Ibid*., p. 425.

50 *Ibid*., p. 431.

51 *Ibid*., p. 430.

52 WILLIAMS, THE SANCTITY OF LIFE AND THE CRIMINAL LAW 76 (1957).

53 *Ibid*., pp. 76-77.

54 S.C. 1954-54, c. 51, s. 230.

55 *Ibid*., s. 45. For a restrictive interpretation of the protection conferred by this section, see Fisher, *Legal Implications of Sterilization*, 91 CANADIAN MEDICAL ASSOCIATION JOURNAL 1363 (1964).

56 WRIGHT, CASES ON THE LAW OF TORTS 81 (2d ed., 1958).

57 See, in the Uinted States, Birnbaum, *Eugenic Sterilization* 175 JOURNAL OF THE AMERICAN MEDICAL ASSOCIATION 951 (1961)) and Bass, *Marriage, Parenthood, and Prevention of Pregnancy*, 68 AMERICAN JOURNAL OF MENTAL DEFICIENCY 318 (1963). In Canada, see Hunsberger, *The Adult Female Retardate as an Unwed Parent*, 11:8 JOURNAL OF THE ONTARIO ASSOCIATION OF CHILDREN'S AID SOCIETIES 4 (October, 1968) and Bell, *Segregation of the Retarded*, 12:4 JOURNAL OF THE ONTARIO ASSOCIATION OF CHILDREN'S AID SOCIETIES 7 (April, 1969).

58 *Toronto Globe and Mail*, June 16, 1970, p. 1.

59 *Toronto Daily Star*, June 18, 1970.

60 S.C. 1953-54, c. 51, s. 237(1).

61 *Ibid*., s. 237(2). For a discussion of the state of the law in Canada prior to 1969, reference should be made to GRAY, LAW AND THE PRACTICE OF MEDICINE 37 *et seq*. (rev'd. 1955).

62 S.C. 1968-69, c. 38, s. 18, adding subss. (4) and (5) to s. 237.

63 ROBITSCHER, PURSUIT OF AGREEMENT: PSYCHIATRY & THE LAW 85 (1966). Also, see comments of A. A. Sarchuk, Esq., reported in 49 PROCEEDINGS OF THE CANADIAN BAR ASSOCIATION 83 (1966).

64 ". . . , [many hospitals and doctors] require that one of the examining doctors be a psychiatrist and the onus of the decision thus falls on him.": Gillian Robertson in *Toronto Telegram*, July 10, 1970.

65 Statement by Dr. Stanley Greben, President of the Ontario Psychiatric Association to Canadian Psychiatric Association Annual Conference in Winnipeg, as reported in *Toronto Daily Star*, June 22, 1970.

66 Skalts and Norgaard, *Abortion Legislation in Denmark*, contained in SMITH (ed.), ABORTION AND THE LAW 144, 156 (1967).

67 *The Abortion Act*, Elizabeth II 1967 Chapter 87.

68 See Gunn, *The Legal Termination of Pregnancy*, 65 NURSING TIMES 1130 (1969).

69 See a description of the initial practice of the Colorado law in *The First Year of the "Modernized" Colorado Abortion Law*, 33 BRIEFS: FOOTNOTES ON MATERNITY CARE 67 (1969).

70 49 PROCEEDINGS OF THE CANADIAN BAR ASSOCIATION 74 (1966).

71 Ryan, *Humane Abortion Laws and the Health Needs of Society*, contained in SMITH (ed.), ABORTION AND THE LAW 60, 64 (1967).

72 Interview with Dr. Donald E. Zarfas, Director, Mental Retardation Branch, Mental Health Division, Ontario Department of Health, July 23, 1969. Indeed, amniocentesis can predict a great number of conditions: see Zarfas, *The mentally retarded and the physician*, 102 CANADIAN MEDICAL ASSOCIATION JOURNAL 733, 733 (1970).

73 Niswander, *Medical Abortion Practices in the United States*, contained in SMITH (ed.), ABORTION AND THE LAW 37, 48 (1967).

74 Skalts and Norgaard, *Abortion Legislation in Denmark*, contained in SMITH (ed.), ABORTION AND THE LAW 144, 156 (1967).

75 *Ibid.*, footnote 67, s. 1(1)(a).

76 Laws of New York, Chapter 127, 1970 Regular Session, s. 1, amending subdivision three of s. 125.05 of the penal law to read, in part, as follows: "An abortional act is justifiable when committed upon a female with her consent by a duly licensed physician acting (a) under a reasonable belief that such is necessary to preserve her life or, (b) within twenty-four weeks from the commencement of her pregnancy". This amendment was placed in effect on July 1, 1970.

77 *Toronto Daily Star*, June 22, 1970.

78 *Toronto Telegram*, July 10, 1970.

79 *De Reneville (otherwise Sheridan) v. De Reneville*, [1948] p. 100, 110.

80 POWER, THE LAW & PRACTICE RELATING TO DIVORCE (2d ed., 1964 by PAYNE) 194.

81 For examples, see in Saskatchewan, *The Legitimacy Act*, R.S.S. 1965, c. 343, ss. 3 and 5 respectively; in Manitoba, *The Legitimacy Act*, S.M. 1962, c. 38, ss. 3 and 5 respectively.

82 *Ibid.*, footnote 80, at p. 188.

83 *Fleming v. Fleming*, [1934] 4 D.L.R. 90 Ont.

84 *Smith v. Smith*, [1952] 2 S.C.R. 312; *Forster v. Forster*, [1955] 4 D.L.R. 2d 710.

85 S.C. 1967-68, c. 24.

86 *Ibid.*, s. 3, the text of which reads as follows: ". . . a petition for divorce may be presented to a court by a husband or wife, on the ground that the respondent, since the celebration of the marriage,

(*a*) has committed adultery;

(*b*) has been guilty of sodomy, bestiality or rape, or has engaged in a homosexual act;

(*c*) has gone through a form of marriage with another person; or

(*d*) has treated the petitioner with physical or mental cruelty of such a kind as to render intolerable the continued cohabitation of the spouses."

87 *Ibid.*, s. 4, the text of which reads as follows: "(1) In addition to the grounds specified in section 3, . . . , a petition for divorce may be presented to a court by a husband or wife where the husband and wife are living separate and apart, on the ground that there has been a permanent breakdown of their marriage by reason of one or more of the following circumstances as specified in the petition, namely:

(*a*) the respondent

(i) has been imprisoned, pursuant to his conviction for one or more offences, for a period or an aggregate period of not less than three years during the five year period immediately preceding the presentation of the petition, or

(ii) has been imprisoned for a period of not less than two years immediately preceding the presentation of the petition pursuant to his conviction for an offence for which he was sentenced to death or to imprisonment for a term of ten years or more, against which conviction or sentence all rights of the respondent to appeal to a court having jurisdiction to hear such an appeal have been exhausted;

(*b*) the respondent has, for a period of not less than three years immediately preceding the presentation of the petition, been grossly addicted to alcohol, or a narcotic as defined in the *Narcotic Control Act*, and there is no reasonable expectation of the respondent's rehabilitation within a reasonably foreseeable period;

(*c*) the petitioner, for a period of not less than three years immediately preceding the presentation of the petition, has had no knowledge of or information as to the whereabouts of the respondent and, throughout that period, has been unable to locate the respondent;

(*d*) the marriage has not been consummated and the respondent, for a period of not less than one year, has been unable by reason of illness or disability to consummate the marriage, or has refused to consummate it; or

(*e*) the spouses have been living separate and apart

(i) for any reason other than that described in subparagraph (ii), for a period of not less than three years, or

(ii) by reason of the petitioner's desertion of the respondent, for a period of not less than five years,

immediately preceding the presentation of the petition.

(2) On any petition presented under this section, where the existence of any of the circumstances described in subsection (1) has been established, a permanent breakdown of the marriage by reason of those circumstances shall be deemed to have been established."

88 (1969), 68 W.W.R. 524 (B.C.).
89 (1969), 3 D.L.R. (3d) 551 (N.S.) at 559.
90 [1964] A.C. 698.
91 In *Boswell v. Boswell*, [1951] 2 D.L.R. 847, it was held that the mental condition of the petitioner was not a bar to a divorce founded in adultery.
92 (1968), 2 D.L.R. (3d) 25 (B.C.), at 27.
93 *Herman v. Herman, ibid.* footnote 89, at 555.
94 (1968), 2 D.L.R. (3d) 405.
95 *Rowland v. Rowland* (1969), 6 D.L.R. (3d) 292.
96 *Ibid.*, at 295.
97 *Kennedy v. Kennedy, ibid.* footnote 94, at 408.

property
and
property
management

property and property management

Introduction

This chapter deals with money and other property: not only that which the retarded person owns, but also that which he is entitled to and that which may otherwise come his way.

It has been noted earlier that ARTICLE III of the Declaration of general and special rights of the mentally retarded recognizes their right to economic security and to a decent standard of living.[1]

Some have suggested that the question of protecting the assets of a retardate is in most instances academic since the retarded generally are without property. While this suggestion may have had some substance at one time, the picture is rapidly changing. Contemporary rehabilitative schemes, particularly in the field of labor, now see a significant segment of the handicapped earning a living once unknown to them. Governments are becoming increasingly sophisticated in making available to the disabled various forms of monetary benefits. Indeed, there is a school of thought which recognizes eligibility for benefits of this nature as being itself property. Estates in expectancy as, for example, through gifts or inheritances, have always been a possibility. This once possibility seems often to be emerging now as a probability. Partly this is so through the enactment of such legislation as that embracing dependants' relief. As well, it stems from the accelerating social competence of those classed as retarded. It stands to reason that parents and other relatives are more apt to make direct provision to the retarded in circumstances where they are confident that the fund will be secure from undue influence and dissipation. The days of the indigent citizen are dwindling.

From the viewpoint of those who may wish to provide for a retarded person and others in their family, factors of efficiency and economy must receive primary attention. It makes good sense to put one's money to the best use possible by maximizing its positive effects in delivering it to those whom he wishes to look after.

Property management by the statutory committee has to do mainly with the conservation of assets of those who are institutionalized and need such conservation. Mental incompetency proceedings are available essentially to achieve protection and management of property of individuals who require it without reference to institutionalization. Various social benefits are available to handicapped persons. Their nature and delivery are crucial. Other matters considered in this chapter include insurance on the life of the retardate, legislative schemes of dependants' relief, and implications of income and estate taxation.

In this chapter, as in certain of the others, it is extremely difficult to offer detailed advice. Matters of estate planning are peculiar to the individual estate and to the jurisdiction of domicile. What is a sound device for one might be totally inappropriate for another. There are numerous variables of a highly complex and technical nature involved. Each situation can be properly assessed only on its own merits with competent professional guidance and advice.

Property management by statutory committee

An individual who is admitted to a mental hospital or mental hospital school may or may not be competent to manage his financial affairs. Chances are that there is in such facilities a concentration of persons who are incompetent in this respect. Most jurisdictions have seen fit to appoint an official, generically known as a

References for Property and property management are on pages 126 to 129.

statutory committee, to serve as a trustee in conserving and protecting a person's assets while he is in the facility, and sometimes beyond that period. This type of protection is, as will be shown, an essential part of the mental health program of a province. Procedurally, it makes available estate protection on a relatively simple basis compared with cumbersome, costly and time-consuming mental incompetency proceedings described in the following section of this chapter which are generally the appropriate proceedings in the case of those who are not identified with an institution.

As in the case of mental hospitalization itself, this is a matter of provincial legislative authority. Surprisingly, not all provinces provide a statutory committee. The need for such an official operating within an appropriate legislative framework is clear and we strongly recommend that those provinces not having one take the necessary steps in that direction.

Most provinces have an official who serves as statutory committee. He is known by different titles in various jurisdictions. In Alberta,[2] British Columbia,[3] and Ontario,[4] he is designated the Public Trustee. Both New Brunswick[5] and Saskatchewan[6] call him the Administrator of Estates. Quebec's[7] official is called the Public Curator. The Official Trustee is the counterpart in Prince Edward Island.[8] In Manitoba,[9] the Administrator of Estates of Mentally Disordered Persons serves in that capacity. Newfoundland[10] and Nova Scotia[11] do not maintain offices of the statutory committee.

The last few years have seen a significant change in the manner in which the services of the statutory committee are engaged.[12] Typically, this official would or would not become committee of the estate of a patient depending upon the mode of his admission to the institution: it was automatic.[13]

The trend has been to allow for an individual determination in each case: a procedure which makes far greater sense. Whether, for example, an individual is admitted to an institution on an involuntary basis or otherwise, is often a poor, if at all a proper criterion of one's competence to manage his assets. While a system of individual determination and decision in each instance makes more work and creates some problems for those who must make the decision, it is an eminently more sound and satisfactory system than one which involves automatic deeming of incompetency.

It is not uncommon for institutional authorities to question the need for invoking a statutory committeeship, particularly where the patient is a minor or is indigent. These authorities are overlooking a number of tasks which such an official may perform which are not dependent upon the individual having any assets. Examples are found in the application for and collection of various disability allowances or other social benefits for which the patient may be eligible, and the representation of the patient with respect to an interest he may have in the estate of a deceased person.

For the information of the reader, the scheme of statutory committeeship in one province has been selected for description: that in New Brunswick. Since the laws vary from province to province, an accurate picture in the other provinces may be had only by reference to the statutes themselves.

The administration of estates of patients in psychiatric facilities in the Province of New Brunswick is dealt with under the *Mental Health Act*,[14] new in 1969.

Where a patient is admitted to a psychiatric facility, he must be examined "forthwith" by a physician to determine whether he is competent to manage his estate.[15] The attending physician may perform such an examination at any time during the period of institutionalization.[16]

Criteria for determination are not expressed in the statute, but factors which should be considered include: (a) the degree of retardation; (b) the nature and size of the retardate's assets; (c) the effect of the retardation on the management of his assets; (d) any added difficulty in managing his assets while in the institution.[17]

In the event that the examining physician is of the opinion that the patient is not competent to manage his estate, he is required to issue a certificate of incompetence and the officer-in-charge of the psychiatric facility is, in turn, to forward the certificate to the Administrator of Estates,[18] a public official appointed by the Provincial Cabinet.[19] Upon receipt of a certificate of incompetence, the Administrator of Estates becomes committee of the estate of the patient and is bound to assume its management.[20] Where it appears that the patient's estate should have the benefit of immediate protection and a certificate of incompetence has been issued, the officer-in-charge must notify the Administrator in the fastest manner possible that the certificate has been issued. The Administrator becomes committee upon receipt of such notice.[21]

It may be that, under the circumstances, the examining physician is of the opinion that a certificate of incompetence should not be issued. In such case, the patient may, at any time, in writing appoint the Administrator of Estates as committee of his estate while he is a patient in the psychiatric facility,[22] and upon receipt of this written appointment the Administrator will assume management of the estate.[23]

Sometimes it occurs that arrangements will have been made for the protection of the estate of a retardate prior to his admission to an institution. These arrangements, in the form of mental incompetency proceedings, are discussed in the next chapter: a private committee of the estate will have been appointed. Such a private committeeship is left undisturbed by admission to a psychiatric facility.[24] There is still provision, however, for the Administrator of Estates to apply to court to have himself appointed as committee in the stead of the private committee where he believes the same to be indicated.[25] Likewise, under mental incompetency procedures, an application may be made to have a private committee appointed to displace the Administrator of Estates.[26]

As statutory committee, the Administrator of Estates "has and may exercise all the rights and powers with respect to the estate of the patient that the patient would have if of full age and of sound and disposing mind."[27]

A number of provisions in the Act enable the Administrator of Estates better to perform his function of conserving the estate of the retardate. These include those dealing variously with lawsuits brought on behalf of the retardate,[28] against him,[29] and the avoidance of any earlier power of attorney.[30] Another example is to be found in the following section.

> "Every gift, grant, alienation, conveyance or transfer of property made by a person who is or becomes a patient shall be deemed to be fraudulent and void as against the Administrator of Estates if the same was not made for full and valuable consideration actually paid or sufficiently secured to such a person or if the purchaser or transferee has notice of his mental condition."[31]

The provision recited above recognizes that the mentally retarded or those in similar categories may have been victimized and gives power to the Administrator of Estates to rectify the situation.

A section in the Act which provides that "[n]othing in this Act makes it the duty of the Administrator of Estates to institute proceedings on behalf of a patient or to intervene in respect of his estate or any part thereof or to take charge of any of his property,"[32] deserves special mention here. This section could be the subject of criticism insofar as it might be construed to mean that the Administrator of Estates could, in an arbitrary manner, fail to take any measures to administer an estate. On the contrary, the content of this provision has merit.

It is conceivable that the Administrator of Estates may not be aware, even after taking reasonable steps to determine the entire inventory of an estate, of the existence of certain assets. The Administrator should not be responsible for the protection of assets of which he has no knowledge. The section has clear advantages. Under certain circumstances, part or all of the patient's assets may already be looked after in an appropriate and secure way, as for example by a relative. If such is so, the Administrator may recognize that he could, with safety, leave a satisfactory situation undisturbed. Without this statutory flexibility, the Administrator would be bound to administer and keep under his absolute and direct control every penny of the assets. Indeed, the provision permits a patient himself to manage a portion of his estate. In Ontario, for example, the Public Trustee – the counterpart of the Administrator of Estates – has agreed to permit patients to retain up to a maximum of $100.00 for "pin money" account purposes. Such schemes are invaluable in the habilitation and rehabilitation of patients. As an illustration, a retarded person could be taught how to handle his money by opening up a bank account in his own name, in the initial stages with small amounts of funds. The flexibility could see each case tailored to suit the needs of the individual retardates. An "all or nothing at all" policy is certainly not indicated.

Out of the funds being administered by the Administrator of Estates for a patient, he is authorized to pay charges for the maintenance of the patient in the psychiatric facility, and he may also pay such sums as he deems advisable to the patient's family or other persons dependent upon him. The payments to the family and dependants may be made despite the fact that they may preclude the payment of maintenance charges.[33]

The statutory committeeship may be terminated while the patient is still in the psychiatric facility. The attending physician may, after examining the patient for that purpose, cancel the patient's certificate of incompetence, and the officer-in-charge is then required to forward a notice of cancellation to the Administrator of Estates.[20] Upon receipt of that notice, the Administrator of Estates ceases to be the committee of the estate of the patient and is required to relinquish management thereof to the patient.[35]

Where a patient whose estate is being managed by the Administrator of Estates is about to be discharged from a psychiatric facility, the attending physician is required to examine him to determine whether he will be competent to manage his estate upon discharge.[36] In the event that the attending physician feels that the patient will not be incompetent in this regard, he takes no action, and upon receipt of the notice of discharge, the Administrator of Estates automatically ceases to be committee of the estate.[37] Should, however, the attending physician be of the opinion that the patient will not, upon discharge, be competent to manage his estate, he must issue a document known as the notice of continuance, which document is to be forwarded to the Administrator of Estates by the officer-in-charge of the psychiatric facility.[38] Under these circumstances, the statutory committeeship will endure for a period of three months after the discharge of the patient.[39] This post-discharge period, often a vital one of adjustment in the community, may in some instances be a sufficient length of time after which the individual could himself assume management of his own estate. If it appears, on the other hand, that he will continue beyond the three-month period to be incompetent to manage his estate, more permanent arrangements may be made under mental incompetency procedures upon private application.[40] Based on a report of the attending physician or evidence available to the Administrator of Estates that a person will not be competent to manage his estate beyond the three-month period, there is special provision in the *Mental Health Act* itself for the Administrator to apply to continue the statutory committeeship for an indeterminate length of time.[41] The committeeship so extended may, upon application to the court, be terminated.[42]

A patient, not found to be incompetent to manage his estate, but who in writing appoints the Administrator of Estates to be committee of the estate,[43] may in similar fashion revoke that appointment at any time.[44] Upon receipt of the written revocation, the Administrator of Estates ceases to be committee of the estate of such a patient.[45] Such a committeeship may not, in any event, endure later than the patient's discharge from the facility.

The Administrator of Estates is liable to account for the manner in which he has managed property in the same way and subject to the same responsibilities as any trustee duly appointed for a similar purpose may be called upon to account, but he is liable only for wilful misconduct.[46]

There is a statutory right of independent review available to a patient or an ex-patient who feels he should not have been made the subject of an estate committeeship in the first instance or on a continuing basis. Where a certificate of incompetence or a notice of continuance has been issued, the patient or discharged patient may apply to a review board to inquire into whether he is competent to manage his estate.[47] The review board consists of a county court judge who is chairman, a psychiatrist and a third person.[48] Applications for such reviews are restricted in frequency to once in any twelve-month period.[49]

To a lay person, much of the above may seem complex. Patients and family members alike are sometimes at a loss to know how the office of the statutory committee operates.[50] Certain provinces have issued descriptive and informative pamphlets to explain the services of these offices. In Ontario, the Public Trustee makes available a brochure entitled "Management of Patients' Assets by the Public Trustee" which is reprinted as Appendix E to this Report. Appendix F is a document outlining the services of "La Curatelle Publique", the Public Curator in the Province of Quebec.

As already noted, the laws dealing with the statutory committee differ from province to province. A knowledge of the precise law in any jurisdiction may be had only by direct reference to the applicable statute or statutes.

The statutory committee has a hard job to perform. Many of the criticisms levelled at this office are unjustified. In many instances, they come from persons who may be antagonistic from the outset: persons who, perhaps because of their mental disorder, resent what they feel is interference with their property, but which is actually intended for their protection.

Looking at the practical side, there would appear to be a number of modifications which could be implemented to improve the image of the office of statutory committee. It is difficult to discuss these matters at the general level, since the size, nature and operations of the statutory committee's office also vary from one jurisdiction to another. Some of the discussion which follows will not, consequently, apply universally.

A common complaint is that the office of statutory committee is understaffed and overworked. The protection of the estates of incompetent persons is a task which the state has properly undertaken with respect to mental hospital patients. Every measure should be taken to ensure that this important program works well. It should not suffer because of inadequate numbers of staff. We recommend that every statutory committee's office be assessed with this in mind and, where understaffing exists, appropriate steps be taken to remedy the situation.

In most provinces, the statutory committee is committee of the estate of the patient only and not of the person of the patient. While his is true, it would be wrong to think that the personal welfare of a patient is unaffected by the management of his assets. Major decisions concerning the handling of property cannot help but affect the well-being of the individual concerned. For this reason, we recommend that the staff of the statutory committee receive special training as to the problems facing institutional professional staff and learn how they, even though their transactions are limited to property, can assist in the habilitation and rehabilitation of the patient. In turn, we recommend that institutional professional staff generally, and social service staff particularly, receive special instruction involving the functions of the statutory committee to learn in what ways they can facilitate his work.

Being more specific, there is some suggestion that institutional staff have had difficulty from time to time in obtaining information from the office of the statutory committee concerning the financial status of a patient. Knowing a patient's means is a vital ingredient in planning for his future. It should be made abundantly clear, and we so recommend, that the members of the professional staff of the institution in which the individual is a patient be permitted direct and swift access to information in the hands of the statutory committee.

Needless to say, the statutory committee and his staff should rely heavily upon institutional staff as to the diagnosis and prognosis of the patient whose estate he is administering. Without a good knowledge of the expected course of a patient's institutionalization and future needs, it is questionable whether solid decisions can be made as to the management of an estate. For example, it might be poor management to retain highly depreciable assets where the patient is expected to be institutionalized on a long-term basis. Likewise, it might be unfortunate to liquidate assets which would have to be replaced at a much higher cost in the near future. Accordingly, there should be frequent consultation of institutional authorities by the staff of the statutory committee. There seems to be a tendency to reduce this type of consultation to a routinized form which impairs and even negates its worth. To ask simply what are the diagnosis and prognosis and neglect to set forth the context within which the question is posed is to thwart the opportunities for a reply that has meaning and value. The chances of a helpful response would be increased inmeasurably where the particular purpose or purposes of the query are set forth. Using this approach, the professional staff of the institution could direct their special attention to the matters requiring resolution. By way of illustration, the focus of the reply could vary greatly if the question were posed with a view to claiming unemployment insurance benefits on the one hand; or endeavoring to vary the terms of the will under dependant's relief legislation on the other. We recommend, therefore, that the statutory committee consult frequently with professional staff of the facility, outlining the particular circumstances under which the consultation is made. It follows as a recommendation that those who are consulted should be as helpful as possible in assisting the personnel of the statutory committee in the performance of his duties by supplying information relevant and suitable to the character of the inquiry. In short, the personnel of both the institution and the statutory committee should complement each other with a view to the total well-being of the patient.

The fact that the person has been found incompetent to manage his affairs does not mean that he should be considered out of the picture. Indeed, while incompetent to deal with his affairs, he may well have certain desires as to the handling of his financial matters which often can be respected in manner consistent with estate protection. The best and sure way to ascertain a person's feeling is, of course, by personal interview. Depending upon the degree of the retardation or other mental disorder, consultation with the individual himself may or may not accomplish a useful purpose. Nevertheless, it would certainly restrict the scope of an all-too-common complaint that the operations of the statutory committee are deficient in the personal and human elements. With this in mind, it is our recommendation that the statutory committee be encouraged, subject to the advice of the professional staff of the institution in each case, to consult the wishes of the patient through personal interview.

There may be merit in the complaint – a frequently and relatively consistent one – that a statutory committeeship suffers because it lacks the personal touch. This may, in part at least, be due to its very structure which is highly centralized. One can sometimes readily sympathize with the dissatisfaction emanating from the situation which sees a decision affecting the property of a private individual being made several hundred miles away in some office building in the provincial capital. For obvious reasons, a certain amount of centralization is necessary and desirable. Yet, the blow could be somewhat softened if employees or official agents of the office of statutory committee were strategically deployed in various centres throughout a province. The existence of a network of such employees or agents – clothed with a certain amount of authority – would certainly strengthen the accessibility factor, fortification of which is unquestionably indicated. In this light, the recommendation is put forward that the office of statutory committee be decentralized as and where required through the establishment of regional or local offices with a view to providing a greater measure of accessibility to affected citizens. This approach would undoubtedly enhance the chances of the statutory committee offering estate protection on a much needed more personal level.

Reference has already been made to the desirability in given instances, of allowing an individual to manage part of his estate. Through proper training, many retardates can pass from what the law considers incompetence to what it recognizes as competence. All the while acknowledging the need to protect an estate, it would seem possible to facilitate the gradual strengthening of a person's competency to manage his affairs through a sensible program geared to the individual case. It is our recommendation that the statutory committee be permitted, by legislative clarification if necessary, to allow a degree of flexibility, consistent with the potential of the particular patient and in keeping with protection of his estate, to enable him to manage a portion of his financial affairs. This recommendation re-emphasizes the need for a close liaison between the institutional authorities and the statutory committee.

Essentially, estate administration by the statutory committee arises only upon institutionalization. The word "institutionalization" has, in the discussion of this topic, been used loosely until this point. Not too many years ago, the institutional placement of the retarded meant admission to the typically large installation commonly termed a mental hospital school or training school for mental defectives. These facilities do, of course, still exist, but many other facilities have been established in which the retarded are placed initially or subsequent to placement in the large institutions mentioned. As, from the residential point of view, patterns of programming change, the classes of facilities with respect to which the system of statutory committeeship applies should be reassessed. Doubtless, there will, in the foreseeable future at least, be a need for laws permitting private arrangements for estate committeeship. However, where there is a concentration of persons who may be incompetent to manage their affairs as, for example, the mentally retarded, in a particular class of facility, serious consideration should be given to the extension of the system of statutory committeeship to that class of facility. The procedural simplicity involved in a determination of incompetency, one of the positive factors of contemporary laws governing statutory committeeship, may represent a logical solution. Consequently, we are prepared to and do recommend that there be an on-going assessment of classes of facilities with respect to which patients or residents thereof may fall within the estate administration jurisdiction of the statutory committee.

More is said about the statutory committee in "mental incompetency proceedings" which follows.

Mental incompetency proceedings

As stated in the introduction to this chapter, mental incompetency proceedings are available essentially to achieve protection and management of property of individuals who require it without reference to institutionalization.

All provinces have legislation dealing with mental incompetency proceedings. Oddly enough, each of the pertinent statutes go under different titles.[51] The provisions of each of these statutes vary from province to province and reference should be had to the laws of a particular province to see what is the situation there.[52] For in-depth description, the relevant statute of Saskatchewan has been selected.

The statute in Saskatchewan which embraces mental incompetency proceedings is *The Lunacy Act*.[53] The Supreme Court of that Province may, upon application supported by evidence, by order declare a person a "lunatic" if satisfied that the evidence establishes "beyond reasonable doubt" that he is a lunatic.[54] A "lunatic" is defined to include "an idiot and a person of unsound mind".[55] The application may be brought by the Attorney General, by any one or more of the next of kin of the alleged lunatic, by the spouse, by a creditor or by any other person.[56] The alleged lunatic and any other person aggrieved or affected by the order has the right to appeal from it.[57]

Where, in the opinion of the court, the evidence does not establish the alleged lunacy beyond a reasonable doubt, or where for any other reason the court deems it expedient to do so, the court may – instead of making an order declaring the person a lunatic – direct an issue to try the alleged lunacy.[58] The issue may be tried with or without a jury.[59] An alleged lunatic is entitled to demand a jury trial and, unless he withdraws the demand before trial, or the court is satisfied by personal examination that he is not mentally competent to form and express a wish for a trial by jury and so declares by order, the issue must be tried by a jury.[60] For the purpose of the personal examination referred to, or where it is deemed proper for any other purpose, the court may require the alleged lunatic to attend at such convenient time and place as the court may appoint.[61] Also, the court may by order require him to attend and submit to examination by one or more medical practitioners at such time and place as the order directs.[62]

On the trial of the issue the alleged lunatic, if he is within the jurisdiction of the court, must be produced, and is to be examined at such time and in such manner, either in open court or privately, and where it is a jury trial before the jury retire to consider their verdict, as the presiding judge directs, unless the court (by the order directing the issue) or the judge (presiding at the trial) dispenses with the production of the alleged lunatic or with his examination.[63]

The inquiry on the trial of the issue is restricted to the question "whether or not the person who is the subject of the inquiry is at the time of the inquiry of unsound mind and incapable of managing himself or his affairs".[64]

There is provision for allowing the alleged lunatic and any person aggrieved or affected to move against a verdict or to appeal from an order made upon or after the trial.[65]

The court is empowered, subject to *The Administration of Estates of Mentally Disordered Persons Act*,[66] to make orders for "committing the custody of lunatics and the management of their estates."[67]

Where a committee of the estate of a lunatic has been appointed

"(*a*) the committee shall, within six months after being appointed, file in the office of such officer as may be appointed for that purpose, a true inventory of the whole real and personal estate of the lunatic, stating the income and profits thereof, and setting forth the debts, credits, and effects of the lunatic, so far as the same have come to the knowledge of the committee;

(*b*) if any proprty belonging to the estate is discovered after the filing of an inventory, the committee shall file a true account of the same as it is discovered;

(*c*) every inventory and account shall be verified by the oath of the committee;

(*d*) the committee shall give security with two or more sureties in double the amount of the personal estate and of the annual rents and profits of the real estate, or in such less amount as the court may direct, for duly accounting for the same once in every year, or oftener if required by the court, for filing the inventory and for the payment into court of the balances in his hands forthwith after the same have been ascertained or otherwise as the court directs; and

(*e*) the security shall be taken by bond in the name of the local registrar of the Court of Queen's Bench and his successors in office or legal assigns, and shall be filed in his office."[68]

The powers conferred by the statute relating to the management and administration of a lunatic's estate are exerciseable in the discretion of the court for the maintenance or benefit of the lunatic or of his family, or, where it appears to be expedient, in the due course of management of the property of the lunatic.[69] Nothing in the Act subjects a lunatic's property to claims of his creditors further than it would otherwise be subject according to law.[70]

By order, the court may authorize the committee of the estate of a lunatic to do any of a number of specified acts, which include:

"(*a*) to sell any property belonging to the lunatic;

(*b*) make exchange or partition of any property belonging to the lunatic, or in which he is interested, and give or receive any money for equality of exchange or partition;

(*c*) carry on any trade or business of the lunatic;

(*d*) grant leases of any property of the lunatic for building, agricultural or other purposes;

(*e*) grant leases of minerals forming part of the lunatic's property, whether the minerals have been already worked or not, and either with or without the surface or other land;

(*f*) surrender any lease and accept a new lease;

(*g*) accept a surrender of any lease and grant a new lease;

(*h*) execute any power of leasing vested in the lunatic where he has a limited estate only in the property over which the power extends;

(*i*) perform any contract relating to the property of the lunatic entered into by him before his lunacy;

(*j*) surrender, assign or otherwise dispose of with or without consideration any onerous property belonging to the lunatic;

(*k*) exercise any power or give any consent required for the exercise of any power where the power is vested in the lunatic for his own benefit or the power of consent is in the nature of a beneficial interest in the lunatic;

(*l*) exercise a right or obligation to elect belonging to or imposed upon the lunatic;

(*m*) give consent to the transfer or assignment of a lease where the consent of the lunatic to the transfer or assignment thereof is requisite."[71]

The enactment also makes provision for "temporary unsoundness of mind". Where it appears to the court that there is reason to believe that the unsoundness of mind of a lunatic so found is in its nature temporary, and will probably be soon removed, and that it is expedient that temporary provision should be made for the maintenance of the lunatic, or of the lunatic and the members of his immediate family who are dependent upon him for maintenance, and that any sum of money arising from or being in the nature of income or of ready money belonging to the lunatic, and standing to his account with a banker or agent, or being in the hands of any person for his use, is readily available, and may be safely and properly applied in that behalf, the court has the power to proceed in a special way. Under these circumstances, the court may allow such amount as may be proper for the temporary maintenance referred to and instead of ordering a grant of the custody of the estate, order the payment of such sum of money, or part of it, to such person as under the circumstances it is thought proper to entrust with its application and direct that it be applied by that person towards the temporary maintenance.[72] The person so receiving the money is required to pass an account when and as the court directs.[73]

There is provision for applying the terms of the Act relating to management and administration to certain persons who are not declared to be "lunatics". Such a person is one with respect to whom it is proved "to the satisfaction of the court" that he is "through mental infirmity, arising from disease, age or other cause, or by reason of habitual drunkenness or the use of drugs, incapable of managing his affairs."[74] In such case, the powers conferred by the Act that would normally be exercisable by a committee of the estate are to be exercised by such person as the court directs, and the court may confer upon that person authority to do any specified act or exercise any specified power, or may confer a general authority.[75] Every person so appointed is subject to the jurisdiction and authority of the court as if he were the committee of the estate of a lunatic so declared.[76] The person in respect of whom the order is made and any person aggrieved or affected by an order made in proceedings of this nature has a right of appeal.[77]

A declaration of lunacy may be superseded. Upon application at any time after the expiration of one year from the date of the order by which a person has been declared a lunatic, or sooner (but only by leave of the court), the court may make an order declaring that the person has become of "sound mind and capable of managing his own affairs" if it is satisfied that the same is so.[78] Any such order is subject to appeal.[79] Instead of making a superseding order, the court may direct an issue to try the question of "restoration to sanity".[80] As with the initial proceedings leading to the declaration of lunacy, there is provision for a jury trial and appeal.[81] The statute makes the effect of the superseding order clear. It supersedes, vacates and sets aside the order declaring the lunacy of that person for all purposes except as to acts or things done in respect of the person or the estate of the lunatic while the order was in force.[82]

The Administrator of Estates is kept fully informed of orders made under this statute: the local registrar of the court is required to transmit to him a certified copy of an order declaring a person a lunatic, appointing a committee of the estate, finding a person incapable of managing his affairs (short of lunacy), and of superseding orders.[83]

Mental incompetency proceedings, and this is generally true in all provinces, are complicated, cumbersome, slow and expensive. This is unfortunate because a great measure of protection flows from them. The involvement of a lawyer is almost essential. Relatively small estates might not be able to withstand the costs of the proceedings. There may sometimes be no apparently suitable person to take the initiative: family members may be reluctant. It might be difficult to find committees of the estate unless there are sizeable assets to be administered.

We believe that the adoption of certain recommendations would have a positive effect on making the protection afforded by mental incompetency proceedings more accessible.

Such proceedings are usually within the jurisdiction of the Supreme Court of a province. Ontario, in 1964,[84] divested most of the jurisdiction in these proceedings from the Supreme Court to a lower court (County or District Court). In the event that the transfer of jurisdiction in mental incompetency proceedings to a lower court would be otherwise appropriate and increase their availability (by reducing costs, increasing speed, etc.), we recommend that this be done.

We further recommend that provision be made in any legal aid plan so that it embraces mental incompetency proceedings in a manner which would involve an assessment of the means of the person alleged to be mentally incompetent and, where the value of the estate is relatively a small one, the court should not order costs of the proceedings to be taken out of the estate.

Where there is any doubt that a statutory committee has the power to initiate mental incompetency proceedings, we recommend that he be given express statutory authority to do so in instances where there is no other suitable person who is willing or able to initiate them.

To ensure that there is always a committee available, even for small estates, we recommend that the statutory committee (where it is not clear that he has authority for the purpose) be clothed with legislative authority to become committee of the estate of a person who is declared mentally incompetent under mental incompetency proceedings.

It should be noted at this point that mental incompetency proceedings, by statute, purport to deal not only with protecting the estate of a person, but also with protecting the person. They refer not only to the appointment of a committee of the estate of a person, but as well to the appointment of a committee of the person. Such proceedings are, however, very rarely used to obtain the appointment of a committee of the person. The basic tenor of the relevant statutes is such that it relates essentially, if not entirely, to the protection of assets as opposed to the welfare of the individual. This is a matter which is considered in expanded detail in the following chapter in dealing with amplification of mental incompetency proceedings.

Social benefits

Some retardates are able to care for themselves, manage their affairs with some degree of confidence and function reasonably in the community. Others are so deficient in necessary skills that they must be institutionalized. The great majority fall between these poles, unable to support themselves adequately by working, but not so retarded as to be accepted by an institution. For these, financial assistance is essential to survival in the community.

Governments have moved to provide this assistance from public funds. Disability pensions and welfare payments are of significant help to the retarded and their families upon whom may fall the onerous burden of support. As with most such assistance plans, the amounts received by the beneficiary may be inadequate for proper care, but are the difference between survival and disaster.

The benefit programs are complex and to some extent diversified. Many persons with a mental disability will have no notion of the assistance and services available to them. In addition, a certain amount of competence, energy, perseverance and confidence in one's rights is necessary to secure the benefits that are available. The retarded should not be presumed to know the law, nor how to use it. Imagine, for example, a retardate endeavoring to complete an "Application for an Allowance" – even if he knows of his entitlement – prescribed by the Government of Ontario.[85] In many instances, the families attempting to maintain retardates are equally adrift.

Social assistance programs are provided by each of the three – federal, provincial, and municipal – levels of government.

The Government of Canada disburses each month under the *Family Allowances Plan*[86] sums of money designed to supplement family income for the benefit of children. The current monthly rate is $6 for each child under ten years of age, $8 for each child between the ages of ten and sixteen, and $10 for each child aged sixteen or seventeen who is either a full-time student or incapable of attending school because of physical or mental impairment.

Income supplement for the elderly is provided under the *Old Age Security Act*.[87] At present the monthly sum paid is $80.00 to all persons who meet the eligibility requirements. These requirements relate to residence – a minimum of 10 years in Canada – and age – a minimum of sixty-five years. If these standards are met the payments are made regardless of any other income received by the beneficiary. If other income is very low or nil, a "Guaranteed Income Supplement" may be added to the Old Age Security Benefit.[88] These benefits to the elderly must be applied for and cannot be granted until an application is approved. If a person is late in applying, the application may be approved as of the earlier date of attainment of the age of sixty-five years, with the stipulation however that the retroactive payment may not be for a period exceeding one year.[89]

The primary assistance scheme at the federal level is the *Canada Pension Plan*.[90] The benefits under that Plan, termed "pensions", are of seven types:

1 a monthly retirement pension;
2 a monthly disability pension if one is disabled and cannot work at a substantially gainful level;
3 a monthly pension for children of a disabled person;
4 a lump-sum payment to one's estate upon death;
5 a monthly widow's pension;
6 a monthly pension to dependent children upon one's death; and

7 a monthly pension to a disabled widower who was dependent financially upon his deceased wife.

The *Canada Pension Plan* is based upon compulsory contributions deducted from an individual's wages and matched by his employer in accordance with a rate schedule. Self-employed persons must make their own contributions. Contributions may be made only on income from employment, and may not be made on any other type of income such as income from investments, an annuity or any pension plan.

It has been noted that there is a rate schedule for contributions to the Canada Pension Plan. Briefly described, that rate is 1.8% of employment income up to a maximum called the "Year's Maximum Pensionable Earnings", which for 1970 was $5,300. If one earns more than that amount the same contributions are made as if the total income was $5,300. As well, the first $600 of one's annual income is deducted from consideration. Therefore in 1970 no one could contribute more than $84.60.

There is no means of enrolment in the Plan and establishment of eligibility for pensions other than by contributions from earned income. A person who is not employed and in receipt of more than $600 per year is in a very unfortunate position.

Of the seven types of pensions available under the Plan, only disability pensions, pensions for dependent children of the disabled, widow's pensions, and dependent widower's pensions will be here analyzed as of special relevance to the retarded.

Disability pensions are available only to an applicant who has been a contributor for five whole or part years and who has a physical or mental disability both severe and prolonged. "Severe" means incapacity to regularly pursue any substantially gainful occupation, and "prolonged" means that the disability is likely to be long continued and of indefinite duration or likely to result in death. Medical evidence is required, usually in the form of a report to a disability determination board. Rehabilitation measures at the expense of the Plan may be required. Employability is an important factor in the assessment.

If a disability pension is approved, payments begin four months after the month in which the disability started, provided, however, that a contributor cannot under the Act be determined to have been disabled more than 12 months before his application. The amount of the disability pension payable in 1970 was a flat-rate component of $26.53 a month plus 75 per cent of the current value of his monthly retirement pension (25% of average of annual earnings up to $5,300 per year from January 1, 1966, or age 18 if later, to the month before age 65). The formula is complicated, and the amounts vary with age and employment record, but it is fair to say that the resulting pension is not a particularly significant amount of money.

However significant the amount of a disability pension, many retardates will not meet the eligibility requirement of five prior years of employment and contributions. This is always, of course, assuming that the retardate was able to apply and secure the appropriate medical reports.

As of 1970, each child of a disabled "contributor" receives $26.53 per month. It is a condition, of course, that the parent be approved as a disabled person.

A widow receives $26.53 per month plus 37½ per cent of the current value of her deceased's husband's monthly retirement pension. A woman who marries a man receiving a disability pension does not qualify for a widow's pension unless he had ceased to be disabled and resumed contributions to the Plan. She would, however, receive the lump-sum death benefit pension which is six times the deceased person's monthly retirement pension.

A widower who was and remains disabled within the meaning of the Act, and was wholly dependent upon hisw ife for support, may receive $26.53 per month plus 37½ per cent of the value of his wife's retirement pension at her death.

With the exception of the *Old Age Security Act,* the federal schemes do not apply in the Province of Quebec. There provincial plans have been established to almost exactly the same effect as those enacted by the Government of Canada.

If a retarded individual does not qualify for a pension under the Canada Pension Plan, as many will not, or if further assistance is needed, an application may be made to provincially-administered programs.

Provincial schemes are based upon a "means" or "needs" test for eligibility. There is no emphasis upon employment as a condition for support. Assets of an applicant are calculated, his needs assessed, and if indicated a monthly payment authorized. An example of such a plan is that established by *The Family Benefits Act, 1966,* in Ontario.[91] Similar schemes administered by municipal administrations and termed "welfare", "relief" or "the dole" are designed to meet short-term, crisis situations.[92] Long-term needs are referred to the provincial plans, which offer more security, more money, and less social stigma.

Under the provincial programs, benefits will most often be directed to those suffering under a disability. In the Ontario plan, a disabled person is defined to mean

> "a person who has a major physical or mental impairment that is likely to continue for a prolonged period of time and who, as a result thereof, is severely limited in activities pertaining to normal living, as verified by objective medical findings accepted by the medical advisory board."[93]

It will be noted that no direct mention of employment is contained in the above definition. Of some 25,000 persons currently receiving Ontario disability pensions, some 15.4 per cent are mentally deficient and a further 11 per cent described as mentally ill.[94] There are no set benefit rates, since payments are based solely upon need in each case.

The most successful programs are probably those providing hospitalization and medical care insurance. Again, however, application is a prerequisite to coverage, and difficulties are compounded for the retarded by the necessity of renewal and the consequent correspondence. Sometimes partial or even full premium assistance is available but still only upon application.

We have canvassed the possibility of parental prepayment of premiums in programs such as that of hospital insurance with the view to achieving a perpetual benefit period for a retardate. In this way, a parent during his or her lifetime, could rest assured that the son or daughter would be entitled at least to that particular essential service for life without the necessity of any further positive step. It would seem feasible to determine what should be the present cost of the lifetime coverage. No doubt many parents of the retarded would want to take advantage of any such scheme offered to them. There are, however, certain difficulties which would have to be resolved. Governments might not see fit to commit themselves to current premium rates nor to project what these rates would be in the future. In the event that partial or full premium assistance is now provided for, an individual may qualify for such assistance during one period and not another. Moreover, such assistance may be introduced, varied or withdrawn in future years. Another consideration may relate to the determination of longevity so that lifetime prepayment will be actuarially ascertainable. This could create administrative difficulties in the event that it were decided to establish numerous classes with different life expectancies. Despite these problems, we recommend that serious consideration be given to making provision for prepayment on a lifetime or long-term basis as part of social benefit programs which require periodic premium payments.

If a retardate is on the lists for payment of support money, he will often need assistance in the proper management of the funds. The practicalities of the situation would appear to require that, in most cases, a third person be the one who receives the cheques. Money would be disbursed by him to the retardate as necessary. Such a system does operate in many areas, but the indications are that dissatisfaction is prevalent and well-founded.

The use of a third-party trustee to receive and disburse benefit payments does not appear to be formalized to any reasonable degree. In some areas, voluntary organizations – such as the Salvation Army – receive welfare cheques on behalf of beneficiaries, pay their rent and provide them with portions of the balance of the proceeds. The Salvation Army is able to give supportive counselling because of the opportunity available to see the beneficiaries regularly.

In other cases, an unsuitable person may be receiving the cheques. If a retardate does not have any immediate family, the agency providing the benefits often chooses some person who knows the recipient to administer the cheques. The choice is not always well made. In some instances, a local grocer or other storekeeper handles the money. It happens that some of the storekeepers give credit in their own stores in return for the cheques, a system which could harbour abuse. Other abuses may occur where the person administering the money spends it with little regard for the retarded beneficiary.

Whatever approach is taken, we recommend that the legislation authorizing payment over of these funds to a third person to administer for the benefit of the retardate be such as to foster and ensure that sound selections are made.

The incidence of abuse may not stem from an unwillingness of the authorities to find more suitable persons to administer the funds. Many people are unwilling to take on this job. Usually a considerable amount of work is involved, with no remuneration. Alternatives are to provide remuneration to private persons or to have public employees appointed trustees.

A complaint that is vigorously made about all governmental support to the needy applies to the retardate. Benefits are reduced or cut off if the recipient acquires any other source of income. It is no longer open to question that a job and involvement in the community are essential to a retardate. In no other manner can he develop the self-confidence and social skills which are necessary in his rehabilitative process.

Immediate loss of benefit may inevitably have the effect of preventing or militating against efforts by the retardate to undergo training and begin working Reports are not rare of families keeping retardates in the home because of the desire to continue receiving benefit cheques. Some of these situations are immeasurably tragic. Little can be imagined that is more prejudicial to the retardate. Essential to his self-advancement is a period of time in which to accumulate a financial base to support independence.

It is our recommendation that all programs which provide benefits that diminish or disappear as other income is received be reassessed to determine whether the diminution is such as to negate or destroy altogether any incentive. In the event that it does, it is our further recommendation that consideration be given to the establishment of formulae which, under given circumstances, will ease the lessening of benefits to a degree which is consistent with the preservation of the incentive feature.

When social benefit programs are seen in perspective, it would appear that the medium for financial assistance is established in the provincial assistance plans. It would be desirable, of course, if benefit payments were higher. Crucial, however, is the necessity to ensure that all persons eligible actually apply, and that benefits, once paid, are managed in a manner provident of the welfare of the retardate. The need for an instrument of such personal guidance and assistance to the retarded is clear.

Insurance on the retardate

The type of insurance referred to here is life insurance, a protective device which has been suggested as appropriate for the retarded.

The matter was discussed in a memorandum to State Presidents and State Executive Directors of the Member Associations of the National Association for Retarded Children in the United States. In that memorandum, the Chairman of the Insurance Committee of the National Association wrote as follows.

> "It is my opinion that insurance on the lives of retarded persons of lower grade is not an economic necessity and that the family's insurance dollars can be better spent for the purchase of additional insurance on the life of the person who provides the financial support of the retarded person. The death of the retarded person may cause a temporary financial hardship. The death of a breadwinner who does not have adequate life insurance will cause a financial hardship which will continue for years into the future."[95]

He had been discussing a program of life insurance on retarded persons issued by a certain company which would have granted policies to each person without any evidence of insurability provided a minimum number of persons participated in the plan. The Chairman continued by noting that retarded persons of higher grade who are capable of self-support may need life insurance, adding that those who do can usually obtain insurance at more favorable rates than the particular plan then under consideration. He indicated a justification for these higher rates inasmuch as the company could fairly assume that the mortality rates would be high as the plan was offered to all classes of retarded without requiring evidence of insurability.

In the absence of exceptional circumstances, we fail to see any special need for or particular advantage to the purchase of insurance on the life of a person simply because he is retarded. The factors which would normally be considered in determining a matter such as this should apply. One of these factors might be the planning for final expenses but, again, this is not unique to the retarded.

Dependant's relief legislation

A will is a private and individual document, arranging the disposition of property and assets in whatever way the testator desires. The law does not restrict a testator's complete freedom. It may, however, intervene after his death to disrupt his scheme of distribution if dependant's relief standards are not met. Where a testator, deliberately or otherwise, cuts a dependant off from a share in his estate, that dependant may apply to vary the terms of the will.

Relevant legislation in various provinces is basically similar.[96] The *Family Relief Act*[97] of Alberta provides as follows.

"Where a person . . . dies testate without making in his will adequate provision for the proper maintenance and support of his dependants or any of them, . . . a judge, on application by or on behalf of the dependants or any of them, may in his discretion, notwithstanding the provisions of the will . . . order that such provision as he deems adequate be made out of the estate of the deceased for the proper maintenance and support of the dependants or any of them."[98]

The right to make the application for a part of, or an increase in one's share of, an estate is limited to the dependants of the deceased. The definition of dependant is a narrow one restricted to immediate family members, specifically.

" (i) the spouse of the deceased,
 (ii) a child of the deceased who is under the age of 21 at the time of the deceased's death, and
 (iii) a child of the deceased who is 21 years of age or over at the time of the deceased's death and unable by reason of mental or physical disability to earn a livelihood."[99]

The last clause of the definition can be interpreted to mean that, however old he may be, a retarded person has a claim against the estate of either of his parents, if he is unable to earn a livelihood. A very serious question is raised for those mentally handicapped who are able to earn a livelihood but have been "forgotten" by a parent. The statute contemplates that such problems will be resolved by the court in its assessment of what would constitute "adequate provision" for "proper" maintenance and support.

When an application is made by a dependant alleging that adequate provision was not made for him, the judge to decide the question

"(a) may inquire into and consider all matters that he deems should be fairly taken into account in deciding upon the application,
 (b) may in addition to the evidence adduced by the parties appearing direct such other evidence to be given as he deems necessary or proper, and
 (c) may accept such evidence as he deems proper of the deceased's reasons, so far as ascertainable,
   (i) for making the dispositions made by his will, or
   (ii) for not making adequate provision for a dependant,
  including any statement in writing signed by the deceased."[100]

There is no absolute duty on a testator to leave part of his estate to any dependant. The dependant may have been adequately provided for by the testator during his lifetime through gifts or other financial benefits. The dependant may be financially successful on his own and not need any of his parents' money, however much he may desire it or feel that he should have it. Family circumstances may be such that other members need all the money for adequate provision so that the applicant would have no claim if he could provide well for himself.

"What constitutes 'proper maintenance and support' is a question to be determined with reference to a variety of circumstances. It cannot be limited to the bare necessities of existence. For the purpose of arriving at a conclusion, the court on whom devolves the responsibility of giving effect to the statute, would naturally proceed from the point of view of the judicious father of a family seeking to discharge both his marital and his parental duty; and would of course (looking at the matter from that point of view), consider the situation of a child, wife or husband, and the standard of living to which, having regard to this and the other circumstances, reference ought to be had. If the court comes to the decision that adequate provision has not been made, then the court must consider what provision would be not only adequate, but just and equitable also; and in exercising its judgment upon this, the pecuniary magnitude of the estate, and the situation of others having claims upon the testator, must be taken into account."[101]

Although the court may inquire into all circumstances, it would be well for a testator who leaves no bequest to a particular dependant to leave a written statement of reasons for his action.

Some persons may conceive the law to be such that no bequest need be left to any dependant whom the state will support, such as an institutionalized or pensioned retardate. The view would be that the retardate is adequately provided for in those circumstances: "why should I make provision when the state will provide?" The cases are not clear on whether such a stratagem is acceptable.

In *Zajac v. Zwarycz*,[102] a decision of the High Court of Justice for Ontario, the applicant was the widow of the testator. The widow lived in Russia on a state-owned collective farm. Believing that any money left her would not be received by his wife, the testator made no provision for her in his will. On the application, defence evidence showed that Soviet regulations did not allow citizens to receive legacies from abroad and that the Soviet Government retained all such monies. Evidence also showed that the applicant would be able to live on the collective farm all her life and would receive a pension from the farm.

The Court dismissed the application.

> "An order can be made under the Act only after it has been made to appear to the Judge that the testator has so disposed of his property that adequate provision has not been made for the future maintenance of the dependant applying, and then the relief to be granted is limited to *such* maintenance. In other words, the scope and purpose of the Act is only to provide adequately for the future maintenance of dependants who are entitled to relief. Any order made should be limited to this purpose and be effective therefor. In this case it is not established that any order which might be made would provide maintenance for the widow; on the other hand it would appear from the testimony which is not disputed that the only effect of such an order would be to add to the treasury of the government in whose jurisdiction she now resides. The statute must be literally followed and its provisions strictly observed. In view of the special circumstances of the present case it would defeat the purposes of the Act to make an order."[103]

The circumstances of this case, with the special foreign element, do not, in our view, render it an authoritative legal proposition that the courts recognize state support as being adequate provision, although they do fortify that argument. On the other hand, since everyone is eligible for state support through social welfare programs, every testator could rely on this fact in an attempt to justify an omission of a dependant from testamentary provision, thereby rendering the legislation meaningless.

In *Re Beyor Estate*,[104] the testator left most of his estate to his executors, directing them to maintain and support his wife who was then in a mental hospital. Upon her release, the widow applied for an order varying the will to make adequate provision for her. The Chief Justice of Ontario accepted[105] the assumption that the testator provided as he did in the belief that his wife would spend the rest of her life in the hospital and that he could do no more for her. The court held that the meager amount provided for support was not adequate to a person living in the community. The question is whether the adequacy of the provision must be assessed at the time of the making of the will – when it was adequate because of the hospitalization; at the testator's death – when the provision was still adequate; or at the time of the application – when the provision once adequate had become inadequate. In this case the court found the crucial time to be that of the making of the application.[106] Although he provided adequately given the circumstances at his death, the testator did not consider changes in those circumstances.

> "I think that because the testator, by the terms of his will, created a situation which was likely to bring about the existing state of affairs, it cannot be said, having regard to all the existing facts and circumstances, that he has made adequate provision for the future maintenance of his widow."[107]

It may be, then, that a testator cannot conclude that institutionalization or pension support constitutes adequate provision, since circumstances may and do change.

An application may be brought on behalf of the dependant

> "(a) by the committee of the estate of a dependant, on behalf of the dependant, where the dependant is one for whose estate a committee has been appointed by the court or designated by statute, and
>
> (b) by a parent or by a guardian appointed by the court or by the Public Trustee, on behalf of an infant dependant."[108]

If a new division of an estate is ordered so that benefits do go to an institutionalized or pensioned retardate, these benefits may find their way to the institutional coffers as maintenance charges, or serve to reduce a pension.

Where a retardate provided for by the state could become independent with the portion of the estate claimed, then it stands to reason that he should reap the benefit.

Should relief be barred by fact of state support, then the right to the relief would presumably crystallize upon the ending of that support, such as by discharge from an institution. At that point, the time limit for applying to vary the will would be crucial. The statutes impose a limitation period upon applications (in Alberta, six months from granting of probate of the will), but allow judicial discretion.

> "A judge may, if he deems it just, allow an application to be made at any time as to any portion of the estate remaining undistributed at the date of the application."[109]

The right to apply when circumstances change may often be hollow in practice, since the applicant if outside the prescribed limitation period, would have access only to any of the estate undistributed.

In the event that an application is made some considerable time after probate of the will, it may be a case in which a change of circumstances is relied upon to show inadequate provision. A change in circumstances is not a conclusive fact, however, but merely evidence tending to show inadequate provision. Even if a dependant were destitute at the time of making an application, adequate provision may have been made by the testator. In *Re Hull Estate*,[110] an application was dismissed against an impoverished widow who, during the eight years following her husband's death, had dissipated a bequest which was by any consideration adequate provision.

Where a court finds that an applicant has proven that adequate provision was not made for him, the judge will then order that

> ". . . provision for maintenance and support be made out of and charged against the whole or any portion of the estate in such proportion and in such manner as to him seems proper. . . . Such provision may be made out of income or corpus

DEPENDANT'S RELIEF LEGISLATION

or both and may be made in one or more of the following ways, as the judge deems fit:

(*a*) an amount payable annually or otherwise;

(*b*) a lump sum to be paid or held in trust;

(*c*) any specified property to be transferred or assigned absolutely or in trust or for life, or for a term of years to or for the benefit of the dependant."[111]

The successful applicant may receive his share of the estate in various forms. If he does not wish to transfer a lump sum, the judge may order periodic payments. Periodic payments may be computed by granting for each year a portion of the lump sum which would otherwise be ordered. Alternatively, the amount of the periodic payments could be computed as the amount necessary for support each year spread over life. In either alternative, the life expectancy of the retardate is relevant since there may be an upper limit[112] beyond which the portion of the estate received by the retardate could not extend.

The trend in the courts is now to grant periodic payments rather than lump sum payments. The calculation of that proportion of the capital of the estate to be set aside to yield these payments will depend upon a prediction about the likely length of the life of the retarded dependant. Retardates tend to have shorter lives than others, particularly where concomitant disabilities exist. Each case must be determined on its own merits based upon medical judgment.

Should a judge grant relief to an applicant, he may order that monies be paid to some other person or agency for administration in the best interests of the dependant.

"The judge in any order making provision for maintenance and support of a dependant may impose such conditions and restrictions as he deems fit."[113]

This last provision is of obvious utility in the case of some retarded persons, to prevent dissipation of legacies.

The effect of the statutes is then that it may be difficult to omit benefit in a will for a retarded dependant. The effect of dependant's relief legislation could, of course, be avoided, by disposing of one's assets before death.

It may be possible even to vary the effect of the laws governing devolution of estates in an intestacy. *The Family Relief Act* in Alberta covers this very situation. All of the provisions of that Act discussed here apply when a person

"dies intestate and the share under *The Intestate Succession Act* of the intestate's dependants or of any of them in the estate is inadequate for their proper maintenance and support, ..."[114]

Income tax implications

The structure of income taxation in Canada is contained in the *Income Tax Act*,[115] a federal statute. Under this enactment, schedules of taxation rates are established at various levels of income. The percentage rates are progressive as income increases.

The Act allows a taxpayer certain personal exemptions and permits him to deduct designated expenses from his income to arrive at the taxable figure upon which tax is calculated. Income tax is relevant to retardation for two groups: the retarded themselves; and parents or others who support them.

A retarded person is treated no differently under the *Income Tax Act* than any other taxpayer. He must pay taxes on any income he receives and is allowed the same deductions to which he would be entitled were he not retarded. The financial circumstances of retardates vary, but few would seem to receive large incomes. Like other low-income persons, most retardates probably pay little or no income tax. The implications of the Act, consequently, are probably not of great significance for most retardates personally.

Needless to say, however, an individual retardate would probably have a great deal of difficulty in knowing how to complete an income tax return properly. Those who require assistance in this regard are not, of course, limited to the retarded. Many retardates would not know that income tax returns must be completed. This is an area in which the retarded certainly require assistance.

The matter of income tax may be significant for parents and others supporting the retarded. One of the rationales underlying deductions for tax purposes is that the taxpayer has had to spend the money thought to be deducted for a socially useful purpose. Whatever the desirability of necessity of the expenditure, the money is lost to him and he has less money than other persons who do not have such expenses. The right to deduct those expenses for tax purposes is an indirect measure of compensation.

What, then, is the position of a person responsible for a retardate and who expends extra money in his care? It is certainly socially desirable that a retardate receive satisfactory care and training, and someone, or society itself, must ensure that he does. It is a very important question whether parents of retardates are actually put to greater expense than other parents. Little satisfactory information is available.

One study[116] estimated that in Alberta the educational costs for mentally retarded children is three to four times that for normal children. Special schools, equipment and teachers are often required. Medical expenses are in many cases higher for the retarded, involving heavy expenditures to maintain and advance psychological as well as physical health. Often, a family maintaining a retardate in the home must employ personnel to care for and watch over him, particularly when the parents are out of the home. It should be noted that all of these expenses are of a long-term nature, often required during the whole of the parental lifetimes.

While the retarded may require special programs, the extent to which parents bear the costs of these is not known. School systems, workshops, and medical and hospital insurance schemes are progressively extending their coevrage. Certainly some of the extra expense engendered by retardation is, in this manner, absorbed by society.

There is a pressing need for extensive study to provide a clear indication of who is paying what. If it is the fact that parents of retardates are being subjected to greater expenses than other parents, then it is most desirable that they should be able, for tax purposes, to deduct from their income those expenditures that are in excess of a statistical social norm.

The *Income Tax Act* allows all parents to make deductions for their children. All parents may deduct $550. for each dependent child who is over sixteen years but not yet twenty-one years of age, and $300. for each such child under sixteen.[117] A taxpayer may claim a $2,000. deduction if he supported his spouse, or alternatively not claim for his spouse and apply the $2,000. deduction to a child.[118] This would be practicable where there is no spouse or where the spouse is working and not eligible as a dependant for income tax purposes. The same arrangement may be utilized where the child is over twenty-one years of age and "dependent by reason of mental or physical infirmity." We interpret mental retardation to be included within the term "mental infirmity". The taxpayer who is most burdened would be the one supporting both a spouse and a retarded child needing costly training and care.

These deduction provisions may afford adequate tax relief for parents with no financial problems who are maintaining a retardate whose needs do not exceed $2,000. in a year. For many other families, the relief will not be adequate. If, for instance, special education outside the public system is needed, the tuition and boarding costs for that program alone could well exceed $2,000.

The Act does allow a deduction of medical expenses that are in excess of 3% of the taxpayer's taxable income.[119] These expenses must be to secure actual medical or hospital care, full-time nursing home fees, medications, or similar care. As noted above, more and more of such expenses are being met by social welfare schemes. It would appear that the main areas of concern are the costs of special education and home attendants, both of which are not deductible.[120]

The foregoing analysis relates to the taxation of income by the Federal Government. Each of the provinces has enacted parallel statutes taxing income for their own purposes. In all provinces, with the exception of Quebec, provincial income tax payable is assessed as a percentage of tax payable under the federal statute.[121] No specific deductions are provided by the provincial legislation: the provincial tax is merely an additional surcharge levied as a percentage of the tax payable atfer deductions in the federal sphere.

Percentage of the federal tax which is payable to the provinces varies among provinces and from year to year.[122] By virtue of collection agreements, the Federal Government collects provincial income tax as agent for these provinces. It follows naturally that these provinces take account of the special problems of the handicapped to the same extent precisely as does the Federal Government.

The Province of Quebec has established its own criteria for income taxation rather than adopt federal criteria by reference.[123] The Quebec provisions are, however, very similar to those of the federal statute in respect of deductions.[124] Quebec collects its own income tax levies.

The law in the United States provides an interesting comparison. Taxpayers there may deduct fees paid to private educational institutions for the retarded[125] and transportation costs to and from such schools.[126] They may also deduct $600. per year for salaries paid to attendants in the home while the taxpayer and his spouse are working or incapacitated.[127]

It is recommended that extensive studies be conducted to determine whether parents of the retarded and the handicapped generally are put to actual greater cost for that reason. In the event that they are, we recommend that this be recognized and reflected by amendment to the *Income Tax Act* (Canada) to allow special and appropriate deductions. Should the Federal Government fail to give recognition and relief in this way, we recommend that the Provincial Legislatures be urged to do so through the vehicle of their income tax statutes.

If tax relief is granted along these lines, the effect may be to hinder efforts directed at persuading governments to extend their social welfare schemes to embrace these special needs of the retarded. In the overall picture, therefore, these problems are compound and the proper direction in which to move is not at all so simple to resolve.

Estate tax implications

Both the federal and provincial levels of government are constitutionally authorized to tax property upon the death of its owner. Only the Federal Government and the Provinces of British Columbia, Ontario and Quebec do in fact impose such taxes at the present time. The other provinces receive compensatory payments from the Federal Government.

The federal tax on the one hand and the provincial taxes on the other, are imposed from different directions. The *Estate Tax Act*[128] (Canada) levies taxation upon the estate of a deceased person in proportion to its value. The three taxing provinces tax, not the estate, but on the value of the inheritance of each of the heirs.[129] Each of the other provinces receives from Canada 75 per cent of the estate taxes collected in that province in return for not exacting succession duties.[130]

The same rate of Federal estate taxation applies, of course, in all parts of Canada. Succession duty rates vary among the provinces which exact them. For various reasons, the provinces of Alberta and Saskatchewan, which have no succession duties, also return to the estate of persons dying domiciled there the whole of the estate tax rebate recovered from the Government of Canada under the scheme noted above.[131]

Estate taxes and succession duties are matters of considerable complexity. This is further complicated by the significant disparity in taxes payable dependent upon the province of domicile. As a crucial element in estate planning, these taxes and the provisions surrounding them must in every case be the responsibility of an expert able to tailor-make an estate plan appropriate to the facts before him. The analysis here must be restricted to those principles and provisions of general relevance to the disabled. It should be noted that the whole field of income and estate taxation is currently undergoing searching study and debate. Massive changes may result in the near future.

Estate taxes are levied upon the value of an estate. Like income tax, however, certain exemptions are allowed from the total value of an estate before taxable value is calculated.[132] Thus, property left outright by a husband or wife to a spouse is totally exempt. Property left in trust for a spouse where the benefitting spouse alone is indefeasibly entitled to the income, and in whose favor alone capital can be expended during survivorship, is also exempt.

A child of the deceased is allowed a deduction of $10,000 from the value of property inherited by him, provided that he acquires complete title to the property by age 40. That deduction is increased for a "healthy" child by $1,000 for each year the child is under 26 years of age at the testator's death.

For a child of the deceased who was by reason of infirmity wholly dependent upon the deceased or his spouse, a significantly greater exemption is allowed. Such a child is entitled to an estate tax exemption of $10,000 plus

> "an amount equal to the product obtained when $1,000 is multiplied by the number of full years in the period commencing on the day of the death of the deceased, and ending on the day on which the child will, if ever, become 71 years of age . . .".[133]

As will be seen, the maximum exemption possible for an infirm dependent child would be $80,000. Such an exemption should be quite sufficient for almost all cases. From the point of view of a few infirm children heir to great wealth, it would perhaps be preferable to allow them the complete exemption accorded to spouses. There does not, however, seem to be any pressing problem in this regard or much merit in advocating such a change.

Estate taxes cannot be avoided by giving one's property away before death. All gifts made within three years of the death of the testator are "brought back" into the estate for tax purposes. The taxes cannot even be defeated by giving one's property away three years before death, should such a feat of scheduling be arranged. The Federal Government imposes a tax upon such past gifts, using a complex formula, as part of the *Income Tax Act*.[134] In each year, all gifts made by an individual taxpayer are considered in the aggregate. From that aggregate will be subtracted certain exempt gifts, and deductions allowed in respect of certain other gifts, to arrive at an "aggregate taxable value". On that latter figure the tax is computed at graduated rates of from 12 to 75 per cent.

Gifts exempted from taxation are, basically, those of a value less than $2,000; gifts between husbands and wives; a trust created for a spouse; and gifts to registered charities.

Deductions of $2,000 from the value of any gift, and $10,000 from the value of farm land given to a child, are authorized by the Act.

The three provincial succession duty statutes essentially differ from the federal scheme only in taxing property as it is received by each heir, rather than the whole estate upon the deceased person's death. Again, the formulae used in computing taxable values are very complex, and the schemes of allowable deductions convoluted. It will suffice to note that inheritances by immediate family members receive significant exemptions from succession duties and that no problem appears in that regard. The provincial enactments also impose gift taxes upon most classes of gifts made by the deceased, within five years of his death in Ontario and Quebec, and three years of his death in British Columbia. The Province of Ontario has clearly indicated its intention to repeal its succession duties and instead receive federal compensatory payments.[135]

References

1 International League of Societies for the Mentally Handicapped, October 24, 1968.

2 See *The Public Trustee Act*, R.S.A. 1970, c. 301.

3 See the *Patients' Estates Act*, S.B.C. 1962, c. 44.

4 See *The Mental Health Act, 1967*, S.O. 1967, c. 51.

5 See the *Mental Health Act*, S.N.B. 1969, c. 13.

6 See *The Administrator of Estates of Mentally Disordered Persons Act*, R.S.S. 1965, c. 347.

7 See the *Public Curatorship Act*, R.S.Q. 1964, c. 314.

8 See *The Mental Health Act*, S.P.E.I. 1968, c. 37.

9 See *The Mental Health Act*, R.S.M. 1970, c. M110.

10 Although the *Public Trustee Act*, S.N. 1962, c. 77 deals with such an office, the statute has not been proclaimed in force.

11 By virtue of s. 33(1) of the *Nova Scotia Hospital Act*, R.S.N.S. 1967, c. 210, where, in the case of a mentally disordered patient confined in the Hospital, "no guardian of the person and estate of such patient has been appointed under provisions of the Incompetent Persons Act [R.S.N.S. 1967, c. 135] or otherwise, the Minister [of Public Health] shall have a right to appoint a person as guardian of the person and estate of such patient and the person so appointed shall have all the powers of a guardian appointed under the Incompetent Persons Act."

12 The situation with respect to when the statutory committee would assume management of an estate under the legislation of the various provinces as it prevailed in 1967 is contained in CHALKE, SWADRON & GRIFFIN, THE LAW AND MENTAL DISORDER (PART TWO: CIVIL RIGHTS AND PRIVILEGES) (1967): see Chapter Three entitled "Administration of Estates", pp. 19-42.

13 For example, see in Ontario, *The Mental Hospitals Act*, R.S.O. 1960, c. 236, ss. 80 and 83. The Public Trustee would automatically become committee of every patient admitted to an institution unless he were a voluntary patient, a patient remanded by a judge or magistrate in accordance with the Act and regulations, or an habitué patient during the period he was admitted temporarily.

14 S.N.B. 1969, c. 13.

15 *Ibid.*, c. 36(1).

16 *Ibid.*, s. 36(2).

17 See CHALKE, SWADRON & GRIFFIN, THE LAW AND MENTAL DISORDER (PART TWO: CIVIL RIGHTS AND PRIVILEGES) 39-40 (1967).
18 *Ibid.*, footnote 14, s. 36(3).
19 *Ibid.*, s. 35(1).
20 *Ibid.*, s. 38(a).
21 *Ibid.*, s. 38(b).
22 *Ibid.*, s. 36(5).
23 *Ibid.*, s. 38(c).
24 *Ibid.*, s. 36(6). A private committeeeship is created under the terms of the *Infirm Persons Act*, R.S.N.B. 1952, c. 144 (new title by S.N.B. 1961-62, c. 61).
25 *Ibid.*, s. 37(1).
26 *Ibid.*, s. 37(2). See also, s. 37(3) which prohibits the making of an order under the *Infirm Persons Act, supra*, footnote 10, for the appointment of a committee without the consent of the Administrator of Estates unless seven days notice of the petition has been given to him; and s. 37(4), which ensures that acts of the Administrator while estate committee are not rendered invalid by the making of an order appointing another committee.
27 *Ibid.*, s. 35(2).
28 *Ibid.*, s. 43.
29 *Ibid.*, s. 44.
30 *Ibid.*, s. 46.
31 *Ibid.*, s. 50.
32 *Ibid.*, s. 56.
33 *Ibid.*, s. 54.
34 *Ibid.*, s. 39.
35 *Ibid.*, s. 41(a).
36 *Ibid.*, s. 40(1).
37 *Ibid.*, s. 41(c).
38 *Ibid.*, s. 40(2).
39 *Ibid.*, s. 41(d).
40 In this regard, see the *Infirm Persons Act*, footnote 24 *supra*.
41 *Mental Health Act*, S.N.B. 1969, c. 13, s. 53(1).
42 *Ibid.*, s. 53(2).
43 *Ibid.*, s. 36(5). See footnote 22 *supra*.
44 *Ibid.*
45 *Ibid.*, s. 41(b).
46 *Ibid.*, s. 52.
47 *Ibid.*, s. 42(1).
48 *Ibid.*, s. 30(2).
49 *Ibid.*, s. 42(2).
50 For a descriptive view of the internal operation of the office of statutory committee in one jurisdiction (Ontario), see Thompson, *The Public Trustee (Official Administration of Mental Incompetents' Estates)*, SPECIAL LECTURES OF THE LAW SOCIETY OF UPPER CANADA 35 (1963).
51 In Alberta – *The Mentally Incapacitated Persons Act*, R.S.A. 1970, c. 232; in British Columbia – *Patients' Estates Act*, S.B.C. 1962, c. 44; in Manitoba – *The Mental Health Act*, R.S.M. 1970, c. M110; in New Brunswick – *Infirm Persons Act*, S.N.B. 1961-62, c. 61, giving only a new title to *Mental Incompetency Act*, R.S.N.B. 1952, c. 144; in Newfoundland – *Mentally Incompetent Persons' Estates Act*, S.N. 1968, c. 3; in Nova Scotia – *Incompetent Persons Act*, R.S.N.S. 1967, c. 135; in Ontario – *The Mental Incompetency Act*, R.S.O. 1960, c. 237; in Prince Edward Island – *The Chancery Act*, R.S.P.E.I. 1951, c. 21; in Quebec – *Civil Code*; and in Saskatchewan – *The Lunacy Act*, R.S.S. 1965, c. 346.
52 A concise tabulation of the procedural ingredients in the statutes of the provinces is contained in CHALKE, SWADRON & GRIFFIN, THE LAW AND MENTAL DISORDER (PART TWO: CIVIL RIGHTS AND PRIVILEGES) 36 and 37 (1967).
53 R.S.S. 1965, c. 346.
54 *Ibid.*, s. 5(1).
55 *Ibid.*, s. 2(e).
56 *Ibid.*, s. 5(2).
57 *Ibid.*, s. 5(3).
58 *Ibid.*, s. 6(1).
59 *Ibid.*, s. 6(2).
60 *Ibid.*, s. 7.
61 *Ibid.*, s. 8(1).
62 *Ibid.*, s. 8(2).
63 *Ibid.*, s. 6(4).
64 *Ibid.*, s. 6(5).

65 *Ibid.*, s. 6(7).

66 R.S.S. 1965, c. 347.

67 R.S.S. 1965, c. 346, s. 3.

68 *Ibid.*, s. 11(1). The court may reduce or increase the amount of security to be given by the committee: *ibid.*, s. 11(2).

69 *Ibid.*, s. 14.

70 *Ibid.*, s. 15.

71 *Ibid.*, s. 18.

72 *Ibid.*, s. 25(1).

73 *Ibid.*, s. 25(3).

74 *Ibid.*, s. 42(1).

75 *Ibid.*, s. 42(3).

76 *Ibid.*, s. 42(4).

77 *Ibid.*, s. 42(5).

78 *Ibid.*, s. 9(1).

79 *Ibid.*, s. 9(2).

80 *Ibid.*, s. 9(3).

81 *Ibid.*, s. 9(4).

82 *Ibid.*, s. 9(5).

83 *Ibid.*, s. 10.

84 See S.O. 1964, c. 60, amending *The Mental Incompetency Act*, R.S.O. 1960, c. 237.

85 See Form 1 prescribed under *The Family Benefits Act, 1966*, S.O. 1966, c. 54, by O. Reg. 102/67, s. 13, which form is reprinted as Appendix G to this Report.

86 R.S.C. 1952, c. 109.

87 R.S.C. 1952, c. 200.

88 *Ibid.*, s. 7, amended by S.C. 1970, c. 9, s. 4(1) and (2) (in force January 1, 1971).

89 *Ibid.*, s. 4(1)(*a*), added by S.C. 1964, c. 51, s. 121.

90 S.C. 1964, c. 51 (in force May 5, 1965).

91 S.O. 1966, c. 54.

92 See, for example, *The General Welfare Assistance Act*, R.S.O. 1960, c. 164.

93 O. Reg. 102/67, s. 1(4)(*b*), made under *The Family Benefits Act, 1966*, S.O. 1966, c. 54.

94 ONTARIO DEPARTMENT OF SOCIAL AND FAMILY SERVICES, REPORT 105 (1969-70).

95 Dr. Franklin C. Smith, May 17, 1968.

96 See, for example, *The Testators Family Maintenance Act*, R.S.M. 1970, c. T50; *The Dependants' Relief Act*, R.S.O. 1960, c. 104.

97 R.S.A. 1970, c. 134.

98 *Ibid.*, s. 4(1)(*a*).

99 *Ibid.*, s. 2(*d*).

100 *Ibid.*, s. 4(2).

101 The Supreme Court of Canada in *Walker v. McDermott*, [1931] S.C.R. 94, 96; followed by that Court in *In Re Jones, McCarvill v. Jones et al.*, [1962] S.C.R. 273.

102 [1963] 39 D.L.R. (2d) 6.

103 *Ibid.*, at p. 10 (per Grant, J.).

104 [1949] O.W.N. 289.

105 *Ibid.*, at p. 290.

106 *Ibid.*, at p. 293.

107 *Ibid.* (per Hogg, J.).

108 *Ibid.*, footnote 97, s. 14(2).

109 *Ibid.*, s. 16(2).

110 [1943] O.W.N. 685.

111 *Ibid.*, footnote 97, s. 6(2) and (3).

112 Indeed, legislation may impose a specific limit. See, for instance, *The Dependants' Relief Act* (Ontario), R.S.O. 1960, c. 104, s. 10 which restricts an applicant to receiving no more under that Act than he would have received on an intestacy.

113 *Ibid.*, footnote 97, s. 6(1).

114 *Ibid.*, s. 4(1)(*b*).

115 R.S.C. 1952, c. 148.

116 Letter written by Executive Director of the Alberta Association for Retarded Children, June 23, 1969.

117 R.S.C. 1952, c. 148, s. 26(1)(*c*).

118 *Ibid.*, s. 26(1)(*a*).

119 *Ibid.*, s. 27(1)(*c*).

120 *Ida Tate v. Minister of National Revenue*, 69 D.T.C. 777. See, also, *Cohen v. Minister of National Revenue* (1959), 23 Tax Appeal Board Cases 82.

121 *The Alberta Income Tax*, R.S.A. 1970, c. 182; *Income Tax Act, 1962*, S.B.C. 1962, c. 27 (British Columbia); *The Income Tax Act (Manitoba)*, R.S.M. 1970, c. I 10; *Income Tax Act*, S.N.B. 1961-62, c. 2 (New Brunswick); *The Income Tax Act*, S.N. 1961, c. 1

(Newfoundland); *Income Tax Act*, R.S.N.S. 1967, c. 134 (Nova Scotia); *Income Tax Act, 1961-62*, S.O. 1961-62, c. 60 (Ontario); *The Income Tax Act, 1961*, S.P.E.I. 1961 (2d Sess.), c. 1 (Prince Edward Island); and *The Income Tax Act*, R.S.S. 1965, c. 62 (Saskatchewan).

122 The current surcharges in these provinces are the following percentages of federal income tax payable: Alberta: 33% – R.S.A. 1970, c. 182, s. 4(3); British Columbia: 28% – S.B.C. 1967, c. 1, s. 3; Manitoba: 39% – R.S.M. 1970, C. I 10, s. 4(3)(*f*); New Brunswick: 38% – S.N.B. 1969, c. 42, s. 1(*c*); Nova Scotia: 28% – R.S.N.S. 1967, c. 134, s. 2(3); Newfoundland: 33% – S.N. 1969, c. 74, s. 2; Ontario: 28% – S.O. 1970, c. 111, s. 1; Prince Edward Island: 28% – S.P.E.I. 1966, c. 2, s. 2; and Saskatchewan: 34% – S.S. 1970, c. 31, s. 2.
123 *Provincial Income Tax Act*, R.S.Q. 1964, c. 69.
124 *Ibid.*, s. 13.
125 Revenue Ruling 64 – 221, CB 1964-1, 46.
126 Rev. Proc. 64 – 15, I.R.B. 1964-9-34.
127 See *Action Together*, issue AT-73, February 1, 1970 (published by the National Association for Retarded Children).
128 S.C. 1958, c. 29, as amended by S.C. 1968-69, c. 33.
129 *Succession Duty Act*, R.S.B.C. 1960, c. 372.
   The Succession Duty Act, R.S.O. 1960, c. 386.
   Succession Duties Act, R.S.Q. 1964, c. 70.
130 *Federal-Provincial Fiscal Arrangements Act, 1967*, S.C. 1966-67, c. 87.
131 *The Estate Tax Rebate Act*, R.S.A. 1970, c. 126 and *The Estate Tax Rebate Act, 1969*, S.S. 1969, c. 17.
132 *Estate Tax Act*, footnote 1, *ibid.*; see, generally, s. 7, amended by S.C. 1968-69, c. 33, s. 3(1).
133 *Ibid.*
134 R.S.C. 1952, c. 148, Part IV, as substituted by 1968-69, c. 33, s. 1.
135 See discussion in NEIL, ESTATE AND GIFT TAX HANDBOOK, 1969, 83.

laws
and
flaws

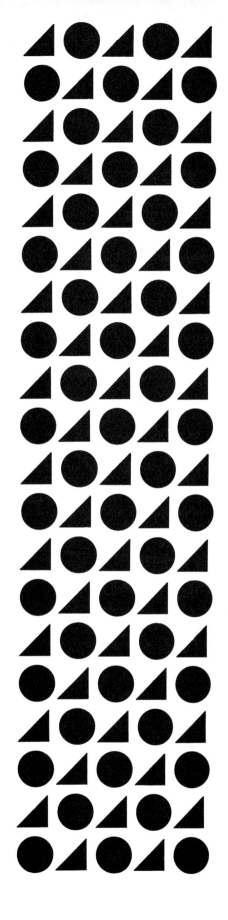

laws and flaws

Introduction

Statutory committee as guardian

Amplification of mental incompetency proceedings

Legislation concerning infants

Testamentary guardian

Child protection laws
Grounds for a separation
Procedure for the separation
Seizure · Interim custody · The hearing
Nature of the remedy
Return to parents · Adjournment · Temporary commitment ·
Permanent commitment · Commitment to a training school

State guardianship by court order · *Minnesota*

State guardianship by contract · *California*

Local authority guardianship · *England*

Supervisory guardianship · *Israel*

Special trust arrangements · *Maryland* · *Massachusetts* ·
British Columbia · *Ontario*

Citizen advocacy

Legal Aid

Ombudsman

References

Introduction

In this chapter, we describe and assess certain legislative frameworks which embrace some aspects of guardianship. We devote considerable attention to various integrated schemes of actual guardianship that have been established in other countries. An analysis is presented of certain programs that would appear to have developed because of the absence of a functional guardianship mechanism. Finally, recognition is given to the potential of general protective devices of an essentially legal nature.

The role of the statutory committee, and the intricacies of mental incompetency proceedings, were dealt with earlier. It has been a common suggestion that within one or both of these frameworks a full guardianship plan should be implemented. Precedents for such developments exist, and we describe and evaluate an example of each.

Some of the provinces have legislation designed to regularize the rights of parents to the custody of, and access to, their children. Parental guardianship and its ramifications is the prime focus of our assessment of legislation concerning infants.

In certain of the provinces, provision is made in legislation for the devolution of guardianship responsibility through testamentary instrument. The utility of that procedure is evaluated.

Every province has legislation detailing minimum standards for the care of children, and providing for public intervention when those standards are not met. The remedy of the commitment of children in need of protection to responsible authorities is made available. Because of the importance of the child welfare statutes, and because many people see them as models for the protection of persons of all ages, we examine them in detail, comparing their provisions and considering the lessons to be learned from experience with them.

Full-fledged guardianship schemes all have in common the assignment of a certain legal status and general core of responsibilities. Many differences exist among the schemes with respect to criteria for eligibility, identity of the guardian, and appointment procedures. We describe and assess systems based upon state guardianship by court order, state guardianship by contract, local authority guardianship and guardianship under court supervision. There are others.

Because the needs of the retardate for support and protection are great, they often develop various attempts to fill the void in services resulting from an absence of guardianship plans. Special trust arrangements and citizen advocacy programs are considered as illustrations of remedial attempts.

Finally, social developments which ensue from a recognition of the needs of the general population often hold out hope for better service to the retarded as well, when they can benefit from the new services. The legal aid and ombudsman concepts are treated in that light in this chapter.

Statutory committee as guardian

The functions and practices of the statutory committee have already been described. It was noted that this official – whether known as the Public Trustee, Public Curator, Administrator of Estates, or Official Trustee – serves essentially as trustee of the property of mental hospital patients deemed incompetent to manage their affairs.

References for Laws and flaws are on pages 168 to 171.

Considerable interest has been shown in the possibility of the statutory committee assuming the role of committee of the person, as well as the estate. Such a scheme exists in Manitoba.

The *Mental Health Act*[1] of Manitoba provides that the Administrator of Estates of Mentally Disordered Persons shall be the committee of both the estate and the person of every individual who has no committee and is:

1 declared to be incapable of managing his affairs;[2] or
2 mentally disordered and detained as a patient at a hospital or institution; or
3 mentally disordered and on probation or leave from a hospital or institution; or
4 is placed under supervision[3] or custody.

Indications are that the assumption of such personal committeeship on a supervision order is to a large extent used for older people.

Although the Administrator is not appointed by a court, he has all the powers of a court-appointed committee. The Act makes express reference, however, only to estate matters: making binding contracts for the patient, conveying title to land, and administering his estate after death. The Administrator is also liable to render an account of his stewardship in the same manner as a court-appointed committee.

There would seem little question that the Manitoba provision for committeeship of the person as an added duty of the Administrator is a step in the right direction: it fills a vacuum.

As a matter of interest, it has been suggested to us that statutory committees in other jurisdictions have recoiled violently from accepting such an additional responsibility. This is understandable. The operation of a statutory committee is similar to that of a trust company in the private sector. Simply, he and his staff are neither trained nor equipped to handle matters of a purely personal nature. A statutory committee charged with personal committeeship would probably be able to do no more than rely upon the services of other individuals or agencies. Such seems to be the experience in Manitoba. Moreover, most of the experience statutory committees have had in respect of the mentally handicapped has related to those confined to institutions. It is questionable that this experience is an adequate foundation upon which readily to build services geared to an integral community program.

Amplification of mental incompetency proceedings

Earlier in this work, a full and comprehensive discussion has been afforded the topic of mental incompetency proceedings. It has been noted that while mental incompetency proceedings in Canadian jurisdictions embrace the matters of protection of the person as well as the estate, the emphasis appears to have been placed upon the property aspect.

With very little alteration in legislation, the Province of Prince Edward Island has endeavoured to utilize existing mental incompetency laws to afford a system of personal guardianship. The statute in Pirnce Edward Island embracing mental incompetency proceedings is *The Chancery Act*.[4]

Under *The Chancery Act*, a "mentally incompetent person" is defined as a person "(i) in whom there is such a condition of arrested or incomplete development of mind, whether arising from inherent causes or induced by disease or injury, or (ii) who is suffering from such a disorder of the mind, that he requires care, supervision and control for his protection and the protection of his property.[5]

At the same time as the Province of Prince Edward Island was reviewing its mental health legislation with a view to comprehensive amendment, regard was given to the question of guardianship. In the end result, the vehicle of *The Mental Act*[6] was employed to incorporate guardianship provisions. In essence, the new mental health legislation lends "teeth" to the use of Part VI of *The Chancery Act*, which Part deals with "Mentally Incompetent Persons".

By virtue of *The Mental Health Act*, which was placed into force on May 8, 1968, a "person in need of guardianship" is defined as a mentally incompetent person as that term is defined in *The Chancery Act*.[7] In other words, the concept of a "mentally incompetent person" as contained in *The Chancery Act* is undisturbed.

Part IV[8] of *The Mental Health Act* is entitled "Guardianship". That Part contemplates the services of a government official known as the Official Trustee. The Official Trustee is a new officer created, *inter alia*, to be statutory committee for the Province. Until the recent mental health legislative package was passed, the Province did not make provision for a statutory committee *per se*.

There is a duty placed upon the Official Trustee to bring the appropriate petition under *The Chancery Act* under prescribed circumstances. Where the Official Trustee has reason to believe that a person "in the community or in an institution" may be in need of guardianship and require a committee for that reason, he is required to bring a petition under the relevant section of *The Chancery Act*. Where such a petition is brought the Official Trustee must, at the direction of the court, furnish such information as is deemed necessary to assist the court to determine whether the person is in need of guardianship.

Once the court is satisfied that a person who is the subject of the petition is in need of guardianship, the Official Trustee is required to bring to the attention of the court what are the appropriate and available resources in the community to assist the court to determine into whose custody the person or his estate, or both, should be committed. The statute expressly mentions that the appropriate and available resources in the community for the purposes of guardianship include relatives, friends, private social agencies, the Office of the Official Trustee, and welfare and health agencies of government.

The statute makes it clear that the Official Trustee is required to serve as a residual resource in respect of guardianship. Where it appears to the court that there is no other fit and proper person or body to act as committee, the court must appoint the Official Trustee to act in that capacity in making an order under the pertinent provision of *The Chancery Act*.

For the services rendered by the Official Trustee concerning a person in need of guardianship, he may be allowed compensation not exceeding the amount that a Trustee would be allowed for like services, but in cases or poverty or hardship, the Official Trustee has the power to forego any claim for compensation.

The Lieutenant-Governor-in-Council is authorized to make regulations respecting the guardianship of persons and patients.[9]

Prince Edward Island deserves a great deal of credit for having embarked on such a legislative scheme. It does pinpoint responsibility where none has existed before. A number of exemplary ingredients are incorporated in these few provisions. It may be that for a relatively small jurisdiction such as Prince Edward Island, its current legislation embraces a workable system of guardianship. It is questionable, however, whether a larger province could get along without a more complex statutory plan.

Legislation concerning infants

Every child at birth has two guardians. Basically both parents have equal powers, rights and duties in respect of their children. When marital discord such as to divide the parents occurs, the courts are authorized to determine the issues of custody, access and maintenance that are involved. When custody is given to either parent, that parent becomes the sole guardian of the child or children of the marriage. If the court approves, a separation agreement between marriage partners may accomplish the same devolution of sole guardianship authority.

Guardianship may, in some provinces, be transferred from a parent without marital disharmony being involved. All provinces have legislation directed to the welfare and protection of children providing that where a child is in any degree of danger, public authorities may seize him and entrust his custody and care to a public agency.[10] The purview of the following discussion is limited to those four provinces which provide, in legislation concerning infants, for the appointment of guardians as a means of avoiding problems.[11]

The relevant statutes of Alberta,[12] Ontario,[13] and Saskatchewan[14] provide that if an infant has any real estate, stocks, leases or similar property, the court may order their sale, letting or other distribution under the control of an appointed custodian, if such action will benefit the infant. An infant is in any province anyone under the age of majority declared by that province.

In Ontario, the Surrogate Court may with the consent of the father and mother of an infant, or the survivor of them, appoint the father, mother, or some other suitable person or persons to a formal guardianship.[15] If the infant is 14 years of age, he too must consent to the guardianship appointment. If the father and mother are both dead and no guardian has been appointed, or if the infant is 14 and refuses his consent, then upon application of a friend of the infant and 20 days notice in a newspaper, the court may appoint a suitable person or persons.[16] The court may remove a guardian for improper conduct. In Saskatchewan, very much the same provisions exist for judicial appointment and removal of guardians.[17]

Both Ontario[18] and Saskatchewan[19] delineate the authority of a guardian. Unless that authority is limited, a guardian is to act for and on behalf of the infant, and to have charge and management of his estate, real and personal, and the custody of his person and care of his education.

The above-noted guardianship appointments must be made by a court upon application. British Columbia depends upon much less formal procedures.[20] Either parent may by will appoint a person to act in his or her place as guardian upon the parents' death if the child is then still an infant.[21] In the absence of the appointment of such a testamentary guardian, a surviving parent becomes sole guardian. However, if a testamentary guardian has been named, his powers, rights and duties are equal to those of the surviving natural parent.[22] Saskatchewan has the same provision for appointing a guardian in one's will.[23] It should also be noted that British Columbia has authorized a surviving parent or a guardian at any time before a female child is 12 years old (14 if male) to transfer guardianship to some "respectable trustworthy person."[24]

Indications are that the provisions for appointment of guardians of infants are only rarely utilized. The reasons for such scant use of this opportunity are readily apparent.

Firstly, even if such a guardian is appointed, his mandate ends with the infancy of his ward, now usually 18 and at most 21 years. Secondly, most infants have parents during the greater part of their minority and most parents do not transfer their duties to someone else. Thirdly, those parents who would be prepared to have their responsibility transferred will often, by the nature of their parenthood, see the initiative to displace them coming from authorities intervening to protect a child. Finally, in the complete absence of parents, children's aid agencies, Public Trustees, Official Guardians and similar institutions take up the slack in child protection.

In essence, only a very few families would ever find themselves in a position susceptible to assistance by the guardianship provisions of these statutes. Other legislation has superseded the infants Acts, which, so far as guardianship is concerned, are now directed at the one time of life – childhood – when a new guardianship scheme is not urgently needed.

Testamentary guardian

A parent is the legal guardian of his infant children. That guardianship continues until such time as a child attains his majority, the parent dies, the courts sever the parental relationship, or (where permitted in law) the parent transfers his authority to another.

While alive, most parents retain the care and custody of their children, and have no desire whatsoever to surrender their parental duties to anyone else. Such being the case, however, the death of both parents could be seen as leaving a child to survive by his own initiative. Historically, parents have sought to prevent that eventuality by the naming in a will of a person to succeed in the care and custody of the child.

There is no longer any need for such a process. Legislation in all jurisdictions in Canada seeks to provide care for any children left to fend for themselves. Indeed, since a testamentary guardian is not only unnecessary but could in fact be an obstacle to proper social assistance, some jurisdictions have specifically abolished the parental right to make such an appointment. As well, when it is unnecessary, there is something unpleasant about the concept of a parent leaving to an heir some money, property and children.

The modern trust fund and trust company are the closest practical parallel to the old testamentary guardian, although the powers of the company are strictly limited to the financial management of a sum of money left in the name of the child. If parents wish a more personal element – usually desirable – they may create a trust fund with relatives or trusted friends as trustees.

Two at least of the provinces of Canada have seen fit to retain the procedure of appointing a testamentary guardian in the statute books.[25] One cannot imagine that the retention serves any useful purpose. Even where it is available, a court will not be bound by the testamentary appointment of a guardian and, at any rate, its effect will not endure beyond the age of majority which seems to be moving in the direction of 18 years.

Child protection laws

The most significant system of guardianship presently operating in Canada is that established by child welfare legislation.

Each province has a statute[26] directed to discovering and caring for children who may be "neglected" or "in need of protection." Children found to be in that state are removed into the custody of a public agency to receive such guidance, assistance or treatment as may be necessary.

It has long been the basic premise of judicial supervision of the family that a child should be reared in the love and security of his natural parents.[27] Legislation imposes itself unto that premise by providing for interference with the liberty of parents to do with their children as they see fit. The immediate effect of child welfare legislation would seem rather negative: public intervention into and disruption of a family unit. There is a much more elevated view.

> "The view of the child's welfare conceives it to be, first, within the warmth and security of the home provided by his parents; when through a failure, with or without parental fault, to furnish that protection, that welfare is threatened, the community, presented by the Sovereign, is, on the broadest social and national grounds, justified in displacing the parents and assuming their duties."[28]

The statutes here under discussion authorize the seizure of children from their parents, and a temporary or permanent separation. These statutes will be analyzed under the following heads:

A   grounds for a separation;
B   procedure for the separation;
C   nature of the remedy.

A   *Grounds for a separation*

Each of the provincial statutes provides that if a child may be "neglected" or "in need of protection" certain persons may seize him wherever he may be. Seizure institutes a judicial process which, finding neglect or need of protection, will sever the parent-child relationship. The crucial issue is what constitutes "neglect" or "need of protection."

The statutes define one or the other of these grounds by listing a great many situations and behaviors which, if proven, evidence the necessity of separation and retroactively justify the public intervention. These great lists purporting to be definitions, contain much in the way of imprecision and vagueness, not to say exotica. Many of the "definitions" could themselves stand definition, which would perhaps be a horrendous task.

A point of significance is that the provinces differ in the extent to which they specify conditions of neglect. Ontario prefers general standards: "unfitness" of a home, or association with "improper" persons. Quebec is the most generalized of all, relying almost solely upon a requirement that a child be "unmanageable", or exposed to "moral or physical danger." Other provinces, to varying degrees, have provided specific lists of behaviors, character types and conditions which should inspire official action.

Whether particularity of definition is to be preferred to generality is a difficult question. For most statutes authorizing interference with the citizen, the civil libertarian would probably prefer that grounds be very specific and that as little discretion as possible be left to officials. General provisions may shelter abuses and arbitrariness.

Generality however may have desirable aspects. Official hands are not bound, and implementation of the purpose of the legislation is thereby made much easier. Unease about wide bureaucratic discretion may be tempered where the discretion is given to permit rapid action in aid of children in serious trouble.

Where legislative draftsmen have chosen particularity in defining grounds for public intervention, many difficulties appear. The specific activities disapproved of are not uniform across the country, varying, one assumes, with local conditions. A reasonable parent would not approve or accept his child being involved in any of the situations enumerated in the statutes. Many of those situations are tragic and pathetic.

Some of the definitions are intriguing for other reasons. Manitoba and Saskatchewan term a child to be in need of protection if he is associating with a vicious, dissolute or disreputable person, unless that person is his parent. British Columbia holds a child to need protection – seizure – if he is associating with a person "reputed criminal, immoral or disorderly." Reputed by whom, and for what? One also wonders at the meaning of "habitually", "immorally" and "guilty" when applied to the conduct of children.

When it is noted that these definitions apply to all persons until age sixteen (and in two provinces age eighteen) faith must be placed in the common sense of public authorities. At the age of fifteen many minors do use "obscene" language, "frequent" poolrooms, and associate with "disreputable" people. It is most unlikely in practice that child welfare legislation would be utilized at this level. The criminal law process would probably, in most provinces, be relied upon.

Considerable publicity has followed seizure of children meeting one of the definitions because of religious principles of the parents, rather than mere neglect. The school truancy aspect of neglect authorizes public intervention to remove a child from his home when he is kept out of the public system. Parental consent to a truancy is no justification for it.

In an even more controversial matter Saskatchewan and British Columbia are the only provinces which do not define the failure or refusal to obtain medical care for a child to be evidence of neglect.[29] Bitter disputes have arisen when this provision is used to ensure blood transfusions to children of Jehovah's Witnesses.

Of particularly direct interest is the action of British Columbia and Newfoundland which authorize seizure of any child subject to such feeble-mindedness as is likely to make him a charge on the public. Also provided for is seizure of a child suffering from such a lack of medical or surgical care as is likely to interfere with his normal development.

If any of the definitions of neglect or need for protection appears to be satisfied by a situation, forcible intervention into a family will probably occur. Because of the tender age of the children involved, someone with their care and control is usually behaving improperly. If the system covered persons who are, by age at least, adults, the "negative" quasi-criminal orientation would not have to follow into the extension of coverage.

B   *Procedure for the separation*

All of the statutes contain lengthy provisions regulating seizure, custody, hearing and appeals.[30] In search of clarity the analysis will concentrate on each stage of the process individually.

i   Seizure

The grounds previously discussed provide the rationalization for a seizure. The question of the persons authorized to act in the belief that one of the grounds exists is of utmost importance.

In all provinces except Quebec, any police officer may remove a child. The Director or Superintendent of Welfare or his officers may intervene in all provinces but Quebec. In addition to these public officials, in British Columbia, Manitoba, Nova Scotia, Ontario, Quebec and Saskatchewan, officers of independent children's aid societies are vested with the power of seizure. Probation officers are so authorized in British Columbia and truancy officers in Manitoba.

Quebec merely grants seizure power to "any person in authority." That phrase is elsewhere defined to mean a father, mother, teacher, priest (curé), school commissioner, and officer of any social organization for child welfare approved by the Minister. The Minister himself may intervene if no "person in authority" does so.

The authority of all these persons is particularly interesting when it is noted that no warrant is required before entry of a home and removal of a child. One wonders whether such an untrammelled discretion need be held by so many groups and persons. The system would perhaps not suffer if one agency was empowered to intervene in a situation and all other groups restricted their activities to reporting instances of need for protection.

In no province is seizure without warrant the only recourse available to the authorities.

In Alberta, British Columbia, Manitoba, Prince Edward Island and Quebec, any person authorized to seize a child may instead swear an information before a judge. The judge may issue a warrant for seizure on reasonable and probable grounds that a neglect situation exists. Such warrants allow entry by force, but do not require that the child to be seized be named in the information or warrant.

Ontario has the warrant provision, but limits it to cases where a sworn information alleges that a child has been taken from a children's aid society or is being unlawfully concealed. The warrant allows a general search not limited to any particular premises.

Most interesting of all is a procedure available in New Brunswick, Newfoundland, Nova Scotia, Quebec and Saskatchewan. On the swearing of an information before him, a judge may issue a summons to parents to bring a child before him for a hearing on a specified date. Failure to appear then results in the issuing of a warrant for the seizure of the child.

ii Interim custody

After a child is removed from a situation, he must be held in a shelter until his case is disposed of. Several provinces expressly provide that the child is not to be held in a jail or mixed with adult prisoners during his detention.

In some provinces, the Director of Welfare or a children's aid society are to be notified of all seizures.

Interesting problems of discretion must arise in Alberta and British Columbia, where the seizing officer is empowered to leave a child in his home/life-style until the judicial process is complete. In Newfoundland, that discretion is vested only in the Director of Welfare.

During custody, the care of the child is the responsibility of the authority in whose charge he is. Any measure required, including medical treatment may be ordered by that authority without parental consent. The effect is that even during the period preceding a judicial determination of the case, the custodian assumes the role and functions of a guardian.

iii The hearing

Every child removed into custody must be taken before a judge for a hearing of all allegations of neglect or need of protection. In all but three provinces,[31] a time limit for convening a hearing is specified, varying from seven to twenty-one days.

Only New Brunswick does not require that parents receive notice of the hearing into the disposition of their child. The other provinces provide that notice must be given a certain period of time in advance of the hearing, varying from five to fourteen days to "reasonable time". In Nova Scotia, notice must also be given of the grounds to be relied upon to prove neglect.

Counsel for parents at the hearing is generally expressly authorized. The Director of Welfare in Saskatchewan may provide counsel for the parents, and in Ontario the Official Guardian will act as guardian *ad litem* if the parent is not twenty-one. Counsel for the child involved may be appointed by the Director in Alberta.

The nature of the hearing to be held is not expressly set out, but general principles concerning natural justice are not excluded. Since various rights may be affected, the hearings must be, and are, in judicial form. Standard courtroom procedure is followed, and the judge has all the usual powers of compelling the attendances of witnesses and production of documents. Evidence is on oath and recorded. In most provinces, decisions and orders must be in writing and contain reasons for judgment.

The task of the judge at the hearing is to determine whether the child is "neglected" or "in need of protection" as defined in the appropriate statute. The quantum of neglect necessary has been considered by the Manitoba Court of Appeal in *Dauphin v. Director of Public Welfare*.[32] It was there that in determining whether the definition of neglect is met, the court should not put the various acts, conduct or situations alleged in separate compartments and say that since none of them by itself fully satisfied the definition, the totality cannot. This decision is consistent with the priority of the interests of the child in these cases. The implication is also clear that the onus may not be heavy on the "prosecuting" authority. The courts will not take chances with a life and leave a child in a home on any principle of benefit of the doubt to him or his parents.

C   Nature of the remedy

If the judge at a hearing finds that a child is not "neglected" or "in need of protection", then the child is returned whence he came and the case dismissed.

If the definition is met, the judge may, depending upon the province, have as many as five options.

i   Return to parents

If he considers the interests of the child and society best served thereby, the judge, in six provinces,[33] may return the child to the place from which he was taken. The return is made subject to inspection and supervision of the home by the Director of Welfare or a children's aid society.

ii   Adjournment

Only Newfoundland does not provide for an adjournment of the hearing without the making of an order after the definition is found satisfied. In three provinces,[34] this adjournment cannot extend beyond twelve months, although the others provide for adjournment *sine die*. The detention of the child may continue for this period or he could be released to function as before. Only Saskatchewan provides for supervision of a family during the time the decision as to final disposition is postponed.

iii   Temporary commitment

Most provinces permit the commitment of a child, as ward, to either the Director of Welfare or an agency for a temporary period. The variations are allowing commitment only to the Director[35] or only to a society as wards of the society.[36]

Consideration of the facilities and abilities of the children's aid societies would be very material to this work. In nearly all jurisdictions, these societies play a crucial and often dominant role in the administration of child welfare. Particularly is this the case when they accept and assume very great guardianship powers over children committed to them.

Unfortunately, an analysis of the societies is completely beyond the scope of this book. It must suffice here to note that there are many societies in each province, and that these must inevitably vary in resources, policies and staff quality. A Report compiled in Ontario[37] in 1964 as the culmination of a study of child welfare administration noted[38] that standards of service vary widely among societies, and that the abilities of persons sitting as directors is equally and disconcertingly inconsistent.[39] Being independent corporations, each society has its policies established by its own board of directors. As the providers of the most extensive guardianship services yet in existence, the societies merit very great interest.

Several provinces limit temporary commitment to a period of twelve months, with provision for continuance after another hearing. The total commitment time is limited by some of the statutes.[40] In Newfoundland the temporary commitment may be extended beyond the age of sixteen until the ward is eighteen years old or, with the approval of the Minister, twenty-one. This provision is particularly interesting in view of the fact that at sixteen one is not a juvenile in Newfoundland, but may yet have total authority over one's disposition vested in an agency.

During the temporary commitment, the judge in all provinces but Newfoundland may order parents to contribute to the cost of care of the child. An investigation of the parents will first be held. In New Brunswick, imprisonment is provided for the parents if they do not attend at the hearing to disclose their assets.

Being required to contribute financially may be inconvenient for the parents, and disclosing their assets at a hearing may be uncomfortable, but the legislatures will not allow a parent to totally evade responsibility for his child.

During the time that the child is committed, decisions will have to be made about his future, his training, his conduct or his placement. These are matters normally decided by parents but, as full guardians, the Director or societies alone resolve all questions for their wards. New "parents" have been appointed and the old ones cannot intervene.

The guardianship may be of the person, of property, or of both. The committing judge must determine the mandate of the agency to whom he commits the child.

A temporary wardship terminates when the commitment period expires, when the child dies, or in Alberta and Ontario when he reaches eighteen years of age.

iv Permanent commitment

At the hearing, the judge may decide that a temporary commitment does not adequately protect the child. An order for permanent guardianship would then follow. The effect of such an order is the total severance of parent and child.

The definition of "neglect" or "in need of protection" must actually be made out. The Court of Appeal for Saskatchewan has held[41] that the prime considerations in child welfare cases must be the welfare of the child and the rights of the natural parents. Should these interests conflict, the child must take precedence at all times. However, the fact that the public authorities have made more advantageous arrangements for the child than a parent is able to offer must not influence the court unduly. A parent must have a full opportunity to assert his rights and have the merits of the neglect allegation adjudicated at the hearing.

The fundamental issue involved is a balancing of the needs of the child. Is the need for protection so great as to outweigh the presumption that a child is best reared in the security of his family? In some cases there is no love or security in the family, or the special needs of the child are beyond the ability of even well-intentioned parents to provide. In those cases, the decision of the judge is, relatively, not difficult.

During or at the end of a temporary commitment, the guardian may apply before the judge to have the wardship made permanent. A hearing, with notice to the parents, must be held to determine whether return to his parents or permanent commitment is in the best interests of the ward.

As for temporary commitment, the provinces vary in the authority – Director of Welfare or a society or both – competent to receive permanent wards. Ontario is unique in making children permanent wards of the Crown but giving their care, custody and placement to a society in all cases. Nova Scotia requires that no permanent commitment be made to a society without the consent of the Director. It should be borne in mind that, upon assumption of full guardianship, the Crown or a society are empowered and indeed have a duty to, seek to place the child in adoption. Natural parents are not normally informed of the details of any such placement.

Provisions regulating termination of permanent wardships are essentially similar across the country. Only Newfoundland and Quebec do not set up an upper age limit beyond which the wardship cannot extend. In the other provinces, this limit is commonly twenty-one, although only eighteen in three jurisdictions. Of the provinces with a limit set at eighteen, Ontario and Prince Edward Island authorize judicial extension of the wardship to age twenty-one. New Brunswick is, then, the only province in which the commitment must terminate when the ward become eighteen years of age.

There are a few miscellaneous provisions. Alberta, New Brunswick and Prince Edward Island expressly end a wardship upon adoption of the child. Marriage has that effect expressly in British Columbia alone, and there only if the ward is a female. Only Alberta lists death of the ward as a determinant. Interestingly, Alberta, British Columbia, Manitoba, Saskatchewan and Nova Scotia vest an authority in the Lieutenant-Governor in Council to end any wardship.

v Commitment to a training school

In New Brunswick, the judge at the hearing may order a child to a training school if the child has been engaging in misconduct. The child is a ward of the Director. In Newfoundland, the Director himself is authorized to commit a child placed with him over to a training school. If the child is not twelve years old, a foster home for him must first be sought.

The sending of a child to an institution of criminal detention does not perhaps jibe well with earlier defining the child as "neglected" or "in need of protection". A somewhat analogous procedure was recently established in British Columbia.[42] If a parent, guardian, Superintendent or probation officer signs a complaint in writing that a child is "beyond control", a judge is to hold a hearing to determine if the complaint can be established. The court has all of the options of section 20 of the *Juvenile Delinquents Act*[43] of Canada: adjournment, fine, committal to a probation officer with conditions, committal to a society or the Superintendent of Welfare, or placement in a foster home.

Alternatives to a seizure or public institution of proceedings are not unavailable. Alberta, Newfoundland and Saskatchewan include in their statutes provision for a temporary surrender of a child by a parent. The parent in Saskatchewan must be in need of help, and indicate recognition of the power of the Director to accept the

143

child and then take it before a judge for a commitment order. Alberta goes further and permits a permanent surrender of the child, by which the parent waives all rights, to a hearing or otherwise, or to any voice in the future of the child.

Parental "surrender" of a child may indicate either awareness of inability or an attempt to escape a responsibility. In Ontario and Prince Edward Island, a parental bringing of a child to the authorities to be dealt with pursuant to child welfare legislation it itself a ground for finding the child to be "neglected". Upon such a finding a commitment order permits a judgment against the parents for contribution to the maintenance of the child. New Brunswick is currently adding such a section to its statute.[44]

Provisions requiring reporting to the authorities of any instance of child neglect deserve attention. Alberta, British Columbia and Ontario have such provisions, with Ontario requiring that any person knowing of a neglected child *shall* report the matter. The other two provinces used the word *may*. All three provinces protect the informant from civil liability, even (in Alberta and Ontario) if the information reported is privileged. Lawyers may – in Ontario must – disclose confidences received by them as solicitors and, in that respect, must conduct themselves in the same manner as all other persons.

An issue of great concern to parents, whatever the nature of the disposition of their child, is whether they can ever get him back. Only Newfoundland, Quebec and Saskatchewan do not provide for such return. Elsewhere, the parents may apply to the court, and at a hearing attempt to satisfy the judge of such a new-found parental fitness as to justify varying the previous order and disrupting arrangements made for the child.[45] The onus upon the parents is very heavy.

A crucial element in any statute is the right of appeal. Not all of the child welfare statutes provide for an appeal, but neither do they prohibit one. It is probably fair to say that the right of appeal exists in all provinces, although in New Brunswick appeal is a privilege limited to the Director of Welfare alone.

An estimate of the efficiency and merit of the guardianship system established by the statutes described would be justified only after further massive investigation. However, the consensus of the many communications on this issue received from lawyers and social workers is the complaint that the scheme terminates at best upon the ward reaching age twenty-one. The universal concern is the plight of wards, particularly the mentally retarded ones, who "graduate" from the guardianship protection into a very difficult world where no one is empowered by law to help.

State guardianship by court order

One of the world's best known guardianship plans is currently in operation in the State of Minnesota. The appointment of guardians is a function of the courts, and because of the comprehensive nature of the scheme it will be used as the example of the court order option.

The framework of the present Minnesota program is to be found in the Probate Code of 1961.[46] The appointment of a guardian is dependent upon a judicial finding that the proposed ward is "mentally deficient". A "mentally deficient person" is defined as anyone

> "other than a mentally ill person, so mentally defective as to require supervision, control, or care for his own or the public welfare."[47]

The proceedings may be instituted by a relative or any reputable person resident in the same county as the proposed ward.[48] In rural counties, the hearing will be held by the judge of the local probate court. In urban counties, the hearing will be conducted by a specially designated official who may be a referee appointed by the probate judge or a "court commissioner" who is a special constitutionally created judicial official.[49]

Before the hearing is held, the county welfare board must investigate the case and prepare a report for the use of those presiding at the hearing.[50] The commissioner of public welfare receives notice of all hearings.

At the hearing, a "guardian *ad litem*" is appointed to represent the proposed ward and protect his interests.

During the hearing, the proposed ward is examined by a board which must include two medical doctors.[51] A psychologist may be added to this board by the court. A significant point is that findings must be made jointly by the examiners and the court.[52] Appeal is at the instance of the commissioner or any aggrieved person.[53] If the proposed ward is found to be "mentally deficient", the court is required to do no more than

> "appoint the commissioner guardian of his person and commit him to the care and custody of such commissioner."[54]

While the commissioner is guardian, his responsibilities are actually fulfilled by the county welfare boards and their social workers. It is part of the duties of these boards to "supervise wards of the commissioner".[55] The commissioner is not guardian of the estate.

It is the duty of the commissioner to ensure that all of the resources of the community and state are applied to the needs of the retarded ward. A major advantage of the guardian being a public official is that a continuity of services and approaches may be assured. A system such as the Minnesota one which utilizes a delegation of administrative responsibility requires that the local welfare boards are properly staffed and have access to all essential services and resources. The local boards do not themselves provide medical, rehabilitative, and legal services, but act only to ensure their utilization.

After commitment to him of a ward, the commissioner has the option of placing the ward in an appropriate home, hospital or institution, or of exercising his authority over a ward retained in the community.[56]

Whether the ward is institutionalized or not, the commissioner has all the powers of the traditional private guardian of the person. The legislation specifically enumerates some of those powers. The commissioner must consent to the adoption of the ward.[57] Marriage is a matter for his concern.

> "Mentally deficient persons committed to the guardianship of the commissioner of public welfare may marry on receipt of written consent of the commissioner. The commissioner may grant such consent if it appears from his investigation that such marriage is for the best interest of the ward and the public. The clerk of the district court where the application for a license is made by such ward shall not issue the license unless and until he has received a signed copy of the consent of the commissioner of public welfare."[58]

In certain circumstances the commissioner may arrange for the sterilization of the ward.

> "When any person has lawfully been committed as mentally deficient to the guardianship of the commissioner of public welfare, the commissioner of public welfare, after consultation with the superintendent of the state school for the mentally deficient, a reputable physician, and a psychologist selected by the commissioner of public welfare, and after a careful investigation of all the circum-

stances of the case may, with the written consent of the spouse or nearest kin of such mentally deficient person, cause such person to be sterilized by the operation of vasectomy or tubectomy. If no spouse or near relative can be found, the commissioner of public welfare, as the legal guardian of such mentally deficient person, may give his consent."[59]

Levy notes[60] that the incidence of sterilizations pursuant to this section has steadily decreased since its passage in 1925, but is still at times utilized.

Although the commissioner is not guardian of the estate of a ward, the probate court may authorize him to take possession of the estate of the ward, liquidate it, and hold the proceeds in trust for the ward.[61]

All such estates taken over by the commissioner or held by local boards in trust for wards, are merged into a single fund known as the "Social Welfare Fund".[62] The commissioner may pay out such amounts as he deems proper for the support, maintenance, or other legal benefit of a ward, providing that the sums expended do not in the aggregate exceed the principal amount previously received for the benefit of the ward plus appropriate interest.[63] If the ward dies or is discharged from guardianship, any funds previously in the estate of the ward, and as yet unexpended, are returned to the person entitled at law to receive them. All use of monies must be accounted for. All funds received are deposited in the State Treasury rather than being kept by the commissioner.

An incident of guardianship is that the Minnesota constitution disenfranchises any ward.[64]

A person subject to guardianship may be released on either of two grounds: "restoration to capacity" or by "discharge". Any reputable person or the commissioner may petition the court for a "restoration" order. The order must be made if the ward is found not to be mentally deficient.[65] Any person may contest this petition. An order seeking "discharge" may be sought only by the commissioner, where it appears to him that the ward is not in need of further supervision.[66]

The commissioner of public welfare who is the guardian seeking services for his ward is also the public official charged with providing services to the handicapped. This dual role may ensure care for the ward or it may cause an unfortunate conflict of interest. Perhaps an independent guardian would be a more zealous advocate for the retarded. It would be appropriate at this point to note that the commissioner has responsibilities to many more persons than would be comprised in the list of retarded wards. There is inevitably competition for funds and personnel among many needy and deserving groups.

The Probate Code does not provide for any judicial review of decisions of the commissioner following the guardianship order. Institutionalization might, in certain circumstances, be challenged by a writ of *habeas corpus*, but some sophistication is required – in the absence of a guardian interested in doing so – to seek out the legal process and meet its costs.

Levy[67] conducted an exhaustive analysis of the practice of guardianship in Minnesota. His findings demonstrate serious flaws in the scheme which may have led to its abuse. A great number of wards were immediately institutionalized rather than integrated into the community. Discharge, available only on the motion of the commissioner, was often delayed for years. More rigorous standards of deficiency were applied by the boards when considering discharge than when the issue was commitment.

The commissioner does not seek out retardates in need of a guardian, so only a fraction are actually supervised. The county welfare boards are the crucial link, for they see the people, advise them, and initiate action, as well as fulfill the commissioner's guardianship responsibilities. It would appear that these boards require more supervision and review than is forthcoming.

The great conflict which Levy found was between the concept of "normalization" – said by him to be the policy of the commissioner's staff – and the conservative theories of the local boards which move for guardianship and subsequent institutionalization at almost every opportunity.[68]

The commissioner has no power to compel acceptance of his policy. The intention of a local board to establish guardianship is usually brought to his attention only when the probate court serves notice of a hearing. The commissioner's staff has little opportunity to review or evaluate the decision of the local board. City boards do not even send referral histories to the commissioner.[69] Levy also notes that once guardianship has been established, the commissioner is sometimes threatened with opposition by the county attorney on any restoration petition.[70] The institutionalization of wards is to the financial advantage of the counties.

Certain aspects of the Minnesota plan are clear. Whatever its ostensible nature, it is in fact a program of guardianship by local welfare boards. These boards do not function in the light of advancing scientific awareness. Review and supervision of their policies and decisions is inadequate.

The concepts followed by State officials would appear to be consistent with modern thought.

"In view of changing concepts of mental retardation and the development of more specialized services for the retarded, I believe that some changes in the administration of our guardianship law may be indicated. At the time that a static concept of mental retardation existed in which many of the retarded were thought to be 'hopeless', and when the only service available was the state school and hospital, the tendency developed for the families and counties to abrogate their responsibilities to the retarded. Today, with our belief that basic responsibility for a family member rests with the family, and also because we realize that for many of the retarded the prognosis of a satisfactory adjustment within the community is very likely, we are de-emphasizing guardianship."[71]

State guardianship by contract

We noted earlier that one method of operating a guardianship system was the use of the contract as the means of appointment. The State of California has adopted that method, and we have chosen its system for describing the contract approach.

Recognizing the need for diagnostic and counselling assistance to families of the retarded, the California State Assembly established a network of Regional Centers to provide these services.[72] These Centers are a community-based alternative to hospitalization.

The services a Regional Center may provide or cause to be provided include
1 diagnosis
2 counselling
3 providing state funds to vendors of services to the retarded when failure to provide such services could result in state hospitalization
4 calling attention, through community organization activity and participation, to the unmet needs in the community and assisting in the development of needed services
5 maintaining appropriate records and a registry of clients
6 assisting when appropriate in state hospital placement
7 assisting in upgrading of programs and services for the mentally retarded.[73]

The Centers are financed by State funds but operate as a private agency with independent personnel policies established by municipal Aid Retarded Children associations. Services are provided where possible through existing health, education and welfare programs. The Center may terminate its responsibility only on a client's death, institutionalization, or his moving to another area.

Clients come to the Centers on their own initiative. Each, if accepted as needing assistance, has an individual program tailored to his own difficulties. If necessary, the Center has the financial resources available to participate in securing residential or dental care for a client. No means test is used, nor accounts kept. Voluntary reimbursement from client-families often occurs but is not required.

Once a program is established and found appropriate, the Center must remain in close contact with the client, his family, and the various social agencies to ensure that the program is carried out. Regular review of the program is a function of staff consultations. The basic concept is one of the Center "purchasing" a program for the client from social agencies, and working to keep the contract fulfilled.

The advantage of this system have been described by Pye.[74]

> "In this partnership between the State government and a private agency, a model is developing that can be used to assist us with other social and medical problems. The private agency can move swiftly and flexibly, be intolerant of systems that impede services, be freer of political pressure and influence, can be closer to the client and the problems that he faces. This makes the private agency a logical partner to carry out responsibilities heretofore assumed solely by public agencies."

It may be seen that the Centers are actually acting as "guardians" without any official proceedings and consequent social interdicting of individuals.

California took the further step of providing a formal, but limited guardianship service. Sections 416 through 416.24 of the *Health and Safety Code,* enacted in 1968, establish rules for the nomination and appointment of the Director of Public Health as guardian of the person and estate, or person or estate of any eligible retardate. To qualify for guardianship, the retardate must be either eligible for the services of a Regional Center, or a patient in a state hospital admitted from a county served by a Regional Center.[75]

The scheme would seem to be an admirable one. There is much less scope than in other plans for abuse or inconsistency at the local level. There is no inherent pressure to institutionalization, and indeed strong admonition against such a practice. A guardianship to take effect only after death of the parents is contemplated. Close contact, normalization, and personal interest are required. Provision is made for review. The Regional Centers, which have strict duties imposed by their own legislation and are private agencies, ensure the provision of actual services. There is neither conflict of interest, nor inclination to be less than zealous in demanding services for the ward.

The material sections of the California statute are self-explanatory and provide an exemplary legislative model. The *Guardianship Act* and the *Conservatorship Act* referred to in section 416.8 contain codes of judicial procedure for hearings.

> "CHAPTER 1099   . . .
>
> 416. The Director of Public Health may be appointed as either guardian or conservator of the person and estate, or person or estate, of any mentally retarded person, who is either of the following: (1) Eligible for the services of a regional center. (2) A patient in any state hospital, and who was admitted or committed to such hospital from a county served by a regional center.
>
>   . . .

416.2. The Mental Retardation Program and Standards Advisory Board shall adopt policy guidelines for the guidance of the Director of Public Health in performing his duties under this article. The Director of Public Health shall adopt rules and regulations for the interpretation and implementation of this article. Such rules and regulations shall be consistent with any policy guidelines adopted by the board whenever such guidelines exist.

• • •

416.3. The director may accept and expend grants, gifts, and legacies of money and, with the consent of the Department of Finance, may accept, manage, and expend grants, gifts and legacies of other property, in furtherance of the purposes of this article.

• • •

416.4. The director may enter into agreements with any person, agency, corporation, foundation, or other legal entity to carry out the purposes of this article.

• • •

416.5. The director may be nominated by any one of the following to act as guardian or conservator for any mentally retarded person (1) who is or may become eligible for the services of a regional center, or (2) who is a patient in any state hospital, and who was admitted or committed to such hospital from a county served by a regional center:

(a) A parent, relative or friend.

(b) The guardian or conservator of the person or estate, or person and estate, of the mentally retarded person to act as his successor.

(c) The mentally retarded person.

Such nomination shall be in writing and may provide that the authority of the director is to take effect at some date or occurrence in the future that may be fixed in the nomination.

The director shall promptly accept or reject such nomination in writing. His acceptance shall be binding upon him and his successors. Any nomination to take effect in the future may be withdrawn by the nominator before its effective date.

• • •

416.6 In every case in which he has agreed to do so, the director may petition for his appointment to act as conservator or guardian of the alleged mentally retarded person and his estate or his person or estate in the superior court of the county where the main administrative office of the regional center serving such mentally retarded person is located.

• • •

416.7. If the alleged mentally retarded person is within the state and is able to attend, he shall be present at the hearing. If he is unable to attend by reason of physical or other inability, such inability shall be evidenced by the affidavit or certificate of a duly licensed medical practitioner as provided in Section 1461 of the Probate Code, in the case of a guardianship petition, or in Section 1754 of the Probate Code, in the case of conservatorship proceeding. Such affidavit or certificate shall be filed no later than 10 days prior to the time of the hearing.

• • •

416.8. In addition to the requirements of the Guardianship Act or the Conservatorship Act, as the case may be, the court shall be provided by the regional center with a complete evaluation of the mentally retarded person for whose protection the appointment is sought. The report shall include a current diagnosis of his physical condition prepared under the direction of a licensed medical practitioner and a report of his current mental condition and social adjustment prepared by a licensed and qualified social worker or psychologist. The evaluation report required by this section shall not be made part of the public record of the guardianship or conservatorship proceedings and shall be open to inspection only by court personnel, the person who is the subject of the proceeding, his parents, guardian or conservator, the attorneys for such parties, and such other persons as may be designated by the court. If an affidavit or certificate has been filed as provided in Section 416.7 evidencing the inability of the alleged mentally retarded person to be present at the hearing, the psychologist or social worker who assists in preparing the report shall visit the alleged mentally retarded person and be prepared to testify as to his present condition.

• • •

416.9. The court may appoint the Director of Public Health as guardian or conservator of the person and estate or person or estate of a minor or adult mentally retarded person. The preferences established in Probate Code Section 1753 for appointment of a conservator shall not apply. An appointment of the Director of Public Health as conservator shall not constitute a judicial finding that the mentally retarded person is legally incompetent.

• • •

416.10. No appointment of both the Director of Public Health and a private guardian or conservator shall be made for the same person and estate, or person or estate. The Director of Public Health may be appointed as provided in this article to succeed an existing guardian or conservator upon the death, resignation or removal of such guardian or conservator.

• • •

416.12. The Director of Public Health shall file an official bond in no event less than twenty-five thousand dollars ($25,000); which bond shall inure to the joint benefit of the several guardianship or conservatorship estates and the State of California, and the Director of Public Health shall not be required to file bonds in individual cases.

• • •

416.13. The appointment by the court of the Director of Public Health as conservator or guardian shall be by the title of his office. The authority of the Director of Public Health as conservator or guardian shall cease upon the termination of his terms of office as such Director of Public Health and his authority shall vest in his successor or successors in office without further court proceedings. The Director of Public Health shall not resign as conservator or guardian unless his resignation is approved by the court.

• • •

416.14. The Director of Public Health shall consult with mentally retarded persons and their families with respect to the services he offers, and, in addition, shall:

(a) Act as adviser for those mentally retarded persons who request his advice and guidance or for whose benefit it is requested.

(b) Accept appointment as conservator of the person and estate, or person or estate, of those mentally retarded persons who need his assistance and protection, but who have not been judicially determined to be legally incompetent. Such appointment shall not constitute a finding that the mentally retarded person is legally incompetent.

(c) Accept appointment as guardian of the person and estate, or person or estate of those mentally retarded persons who are or have been judicially determined to be legally incompetent.

• • •

416.15. The Director of Public Health, when acting as adviser, may provide advice and guidance to the mentally retarded person without prior appointment by a court. The provision for such services shall not be dependent upon a finding of incompetency, nor shall it abrogate any civil right otherwise possessed by the mentally retarded person.

• • •

416.17. It is the intent of this article that the director when acting as guardian or conservator of the person of a mentally retarded person through the regional center as provided in Section 416.19 of this article, shall maintain close contact with the mentally retarded person no matter where such person is living in this state; shall act as a wise parent would act in caring for his mentally retarded child; and shall permit and encourage maximum self-reliance on the part of the mentally retarded person under his protection.

. . .

416.18. The director shall provide for at least an annual review in writing of the physical, mental and social condition of each mentally retarded person for whom he has been appointed conservator or guardian, or for whom he is otherwise acting in his official capacity under this article. These records shall be confidential but may be made available to persons approved by the director or the court.

. . .

416.19. The services to be rendered by the director as adviser or as guardian or conservator of the person shall be performed solely through the regional centers.

. . .

416.20. The director shall receive such reasonable fees for his services as guardian or conservator of the estate as the court allows and such fees shall be paid into the General Fund of the State Treasury.

. . .

416.23. This article does not authorize the care, treatment, or supervision or any control over any mentally retarded person without the written consent of his parent or guardian.

. . .

416.24. The agency operating a regional center may enter into agreements with parents, guardians, persons responsible for the care of the mentally retarded, or estates of mentally retarded persons, to use such amounts as they may be able to pay toward the cost of services for such mentally retarded persons. In no event, however, shall there be any charge for diagnosis or counseling."

An amending Bill was introduced into the California Legislature in 1969, the main thrust of which was a proposed decentralization of administrative authority to area boards.[76] On the merit of this amendment reference should be had to the Minnesota experience.

Local authority guardianship

When new legislation in the mental health field came in England in 1959, it brought with it extensive provisions dealing with guardianship.

Under the *Mental Health Act, 1959*,[77] compulsory admission to hospital and guardianship are dealt with in Part IV. A patient may be received into guardianship in pursuance of what is known as a "guardianship application".

A guardianship application may be made in respect of a patient on the grounds:

"(a) that he is suffering from mental disorder, being
    (i) in the case of a patient of any age, mental illness or severe subnormality;
    (ii) in the case of a patient under the age of twenty-one years, psychopathic disorder or subnormality;
    and that his disorder is of a nature or degree which warrants the reception of the patient into guardianship . . .; and
(b) that it is necessary in the interests of the patient or for the protection of other persons that the patient should be so received."[78]

In order better to appreciate the application of this provision, it is desirable to recite the germane definitions contained in the Act, as follows:

151   LOCAL AUTHORITY GUARDIANSHIP

"mental disorder"

"mental illness, arrested or incomplete development of mind, psychopathic disorder, and any other disorder or disability of mind; . . . ."[79]

"severe subnormality"

"a state of arrested or incomplete development of mind which includes subnormality of intelligence and is of such a nature or degree that the patient is incapable of living an independent life or of guarding himself against serious exploitation, or will be so incapable when of an age to do so."[80]

"psychopathic disorder"

"a persistent disorder or disability of mind (whether or not including subnormality of intelligence) which results in abnormally aggressive or seriously irresponsible conduct on the part of the patient, and requires or is susceptible to medical treatment."[81]

"subnormality"

"a state of arrested or incomplete development of mind (not amounting to severe subnormality) which includes subnormality of intelligence and is of a nature or degree which requires or is susceptible to medical treatment or other special care or training of the patient."[82]

The person named as guardian in a guardianship application may be either a local health authority or any other person, but a guardianship application in which a person other than a local health authority is named as guardian is of no effect unless it is accepted on behalf of that person by the local health authority for the area in which he resides.[83] The applicant himself may also be named as guardian in the application. Every such application is to be forwarded to the local health authority which is named therein as guardian, or, as the case may be, to the local authority for the area in which the person named as guardian resides. Unless the individual named as guardian is the local health authority, the application must be accompanied by a statement in writing by the person named as guardian that he is willing to act in that capacity.[84]

An application for admission to guardianship must be founded on the written recommendations in the prescribed form of two medical practitioners. In each case, it must include a statement that, in the opinion of the practitioner, the individual is suffering from mental disorder of a specified kind, that the disorder is of a nature or degree which warrants his reception into guardianship, and that it is necessary in the interests of the patient or for the protection of other persons that the patient should be so received. Certain other particulars must also be included in the written recommendations of the medical practitioners.[85] One of the medical recommendations must be from a practitioner approved for the purpose by a local health authority as having special experience in the diagnosis or treatment of mental disorder. Unless that practitioner has previous acquaintance with the individual, the other medical recommendation must, if practicable, be given by a medical practitioner who has such a previous acquaintance.[86] The medical recommendations can be given separately or can be the joint recommendation of two medical practitioners.[87]

The application itself may be made by the nearest relative or by a mental welfare officer.[88] The mental welfare officer may not make it if the nearest relative has notified him or the local health authority by whom the officer is appointed that he objects to the application being made. At any rate, the mental welfare officer can make an application only after consultation with the person, if any, who appears to be the nearest relative, unless it appears to the officer that in the circumstances such consultation is not reasonably practicable or would involve unreasonable delay.[89] No matter who is the applicant, he must personally have seen the subject of the application within the previous fourteen days.[90]

A guardianship application has a "life" for being accepted of fourteen days beginning with the date on which the patient was last examined by a medical practitioner before giving a medical recommendation for the purposes of the application.[91]

Where a guardianship application is accepted by the local health authority, the application has the effect of conferring on the authority or person named therein as guardian, to the exclusion of any other person, "all such powers as would be exerciseable by them or him in relation to the patient if they or he were the father of the patient and the patient were under the age of fourteen years."[92]

A patient placed under guardianship may be kept under guardianship for a period not exceeding one year beginning with the day on which the guardianship application was accepted, but cannot be kept any longer unless the authority for his guardianship is renewed.[93] Renewal periods are respectively for a further period of one year and successive periods of two years at a time.[94] The renewal procedure involves a medical examination and the preparation of a report in advance of the expiry of the prevalent period of guardianship. Within the period of two months ending with the day on which the guardianship would cease, it is the duty of the "responsible medical officer" (where the guardian is the local health authority) or the "nominated medical attendant" (in any other case) to examine the patient. If it appears to the examining physician that it is necessary in the interests of the patient or for the protection of other persons that the patient should remain under guardianship, he is required to furnish to the guardian, and to the local health authority (where it is not the guardian), a report to that effect in the prescribed form.[95] The furnishing of the report constitutes the renewal of the period of guardianship.[96]

Where a patient is sixteen years of age or over, he has a right to dispute reception into guardianship,[97] or a renewal thereof,[98] by applying to a Mental Health Review Tribunal.[99]

In the case of a patient who is subject to guardianship by virtue of a guardianship application as a psychopathic or subnormal patient, the guardianship must cease when he reaches the age of twenty-five years.[100]

The Act contains a number of additional provisions dealing with guardianship, including the transfer of a detained hospital patient into guardianship, the transfer of guardianship to another authority or person, and the transfer of a patient subject to guardianship to a hospital.[101]

The local health authority is the council of a county or county borough. Every local health authority is required to establish a Health Committee and all matters relating to the discharge of the functions of the authority stand referred to that Committee. The exercise of powers and duties relating to mental health may be referred to a Mental Health Subcommittee by the Health Committee, subject to any restrictions imposed by the local health authority.[102]

Insight into the workings of a guardianship arrangement may be obtained from a reading of the following statutory regulations[103] made under the Act.

"*General powers and duties of guardians*

6.–(1) The guardian shall, so far as is practicable, make arrangements for the occupation, training or employment of the patient and for his recreation and general welfare and shall ensure that everything practicable is done for the promotion of his physical and mental health.

(2) Subject to the provisions of paragraph (3) of this regulation and to any direction given under regulation 10 of these regulations, the guardian may restrict to such extent as he thinks necessary the making of visits to the patient and may prohibit visits by any person who the guardian has reason to believe may have an adverse effect on the patient.

(3) Nothing in this regulation shall operate to restrict the visits of any person authorised in that behalf by the responsible local health authority or the Minister.

Visits to patients on behalf of the responsible local health authority

7. The responsible local health authority shall arrange for every patient who is subject to guardianship to be visited at such intervals as the authority may decide, but in any case at intervals of not more than three months and at least one such visit in any year shall be made by a medical practitioner approved for the purposes of section 28 of the Act.

Duties of guardians other than local health authorities

8. The provisions of the four succeeding regulations shall apply in relation to a patient who is subject to the guardianship of a person other than a local health authority.

Appointment of nominated medical attendant

9.–(1) The guardian shall appoint a medical practitioner to act as the nominated medical attendant of the patient for the purposes of the Act and shall notify the responsible local health authority of the name and address of the medical practitioner for the time being so appointed.

(2) The nominated medical attendant appointed under the last foregoing paragraph may be a medical practitioner employed by a local health authority.

Directions of, and reports to, responsible local health authority

10. The guardian shall, in exercising the powers and duties conferred or imposed on him by the Act or these regulations, comply with such directions as the responsible local health authority think it appropriate at any time to give, and the guardian shall furnish to that authority all such reports or other information with regard to the patient (in addition to the information mentioned in the two succeeding regulations) as the authority may from time to time require.

Notification of residence

11.–(1) On the reception of a patient into guardianship the guardian shall notify to the responsible local health authority the place of his residence and that of the patient and on any permanent change in either place of residence he shall notify to that authority the new place of residence either before, or not later than 7 days after, the change takes place.

(2) If the new place of residence of the guardian is in the area of a different local health authority, the notification required by the last foregoing paragraph shall be sent to that authority and shall include the name and address of the medical practitioner for the time being appointed as the patient's nominated medical attendant under regulation 9 of these regulations and a copy of the notification shall also be sent to the local health authority of the former place of residence.

Notification of death or discharge

12. In the event of the death of the patient or the termination of the guardianship by discharge, transfer or otherwise the guardian shall as soon as may be notify the responsible local health authority."

A patient subject to guardianship will, of course, no longer be so subject when the authorized period has expired and no renewal has been effected. Guardianship may also be terminated at any time by positive action through a written order discharging him from guardianship – an "order for discharge".[104] Such an order may be made by the responsible medical officer, by the responsible local health authority, or by the nearest relative of the patient.[105]

The manner in which the Act provides for the continuity of a satisfactory guardian is sound. Where any person (other than the local health authority) having the guardianship of a patient dies or gives written notice to the local health authority that he desires to relinquish the functions of guardian, the guardianship thereupon vests in the local health authority ,but without prejudice to any power to transfer the patient into the guardianship of another person.[106] Should the guardian be incapacitated by illness or any other cause from performing his functions as such, those functions may – during his incapacity – be performed on his behalf by the local health authority or by any other person approved for the purpose by that authority.[107] If it appears to the county court, upon application made by a mental welfare officer, that any guardian other than a local health authority has performed his functions negligently or in a manner contrary to the interests of the patient, the court may order that the guardianship be transferred to the local health authority or to any other person approved for the purpose by that authority.[108]

On the practical side, it is said to be usually the mental welfare officer who applies for guardianship, often at the request of the relatives.[109] It is normally the local health authority which is the guardian. Instances where the guardian is an individual are rare. While the local authority sometimes arranges for the retardate to live with a private individual paid by them, the local authority generally retains control.[110]

Statistical data show a marked decline in the use of guardianship proceedings. In 1961, there were 220 admissions to guardianship, compared with 47 in 1968.[111] Of those admitted in 1961, 37 were subnormal (one under 16 years of age), and 171 were severely subnormal (5 under 16 years of age). The corresponding numbers in 1968 were 15 subnormal (none under 16 years of age) and 20 severely subnormal (2 under 16 years of age).

Looking at the cumulative numbers of persons under guardianship, there was a dwindling from 1,089 at the end of 1960 to 284 at the end of 1968. (The figure of 1,089 represents not only persons under guardianship pursuant to the *Mental Health Act, 1959*, but also those under guardianship in pursuance of earlier legislation.) Of the 284 persons under guardianship at the end of 1968, 56 were subnormal (one under 16 years of age) and 213 were severely subnormal (six under 16 years of age). The local health authority was the guardian in 246 of the 284 cases.

The striking decline in guardianship utilization has been attributed to the dramatic diminution of compulsion in mental health services and the development of programs for the retarded.

It is felt that the need for guardianship is present where there is no family or the family situation is adverse. The significant thing is to gain "control", especially to protect the individual from third parties. A weakness is said to be that the only real sanction is admission of the individual to hospital.

The sharp decrease in the number of persons kept under guardianship in England does not, in our view, take away from the need for guardianship protection. If, in a given jurisdiction, protective support can be found for most in means short of formal guardianship, so much the better. That the machinery is available to be used in those cases where legal guardianship is indicated is the important factor.

There is much to be said for statutory guardianship provisions in England. Many of the ingredients of their scheme are worthy of consideration for adoption in Canada.

Supervisory guardianship

An example of a guardianship system with strong emphasis on judicial supervision is found in the *Capacity and Guardianship Law* of Israel, passed by the Knesset (Parliament) on August 7, 1962. As a generality, the Law provides[112] that every person is capable of performing all legal acts unless he has been deprived of that capacity or it has been restricted by law or by the judgment of a court.

It is provided that a person found by a court to be legally incompetent can engage in no legal act without the consent of his parents or appointed guardian.[113] Any legal obligation assumed without such consent may be avoided unless the other party was unaware of the legal incompetence. However even should the other party be so unaware, the legal act may be avoided if substantial harm to the incompetent or his property would otherwise ensue.[114]

A finding of legal incompetence may be made by a court upon the application of a spouse, any relative or the Attorney-General. The test applied to the individual subject of the application is whether he is by reason of mental illness or a defect of mind incapable of looking after his affairs. The individual involved, or his representative, must be heard by the court.[115] After a finding of incompetence, the spouse or any person with the status to apply for such a finding may, at any time, make a further application for revocation of the declaration of incompetence.[116]

A guardian may be appointed by the court for a legally incompetent person; for any person temporarily or permanently unable to look after his affairs and lacking anyone to do so for him; for a minor who is orphaned or whose parents have been found legally incompetent; or for a child *en ventre sa mere*.[117]

The Law declares that parents are to be the natural guardians of their minor children,[118] but a guardian may be appointed to displace the parents.[119] If one parent dies, a guardian may be appointed to lend assistance in such manner as the court specifies.[120] The same applies if one parent is found legally incompetent, is deprived by the courts of his guardianship, deserts the family, or is unknown. The extra guardian is not to be appointed unless the court sees special reason for doing so and the surviving parent is allowed to be heard in argument.

The Law provides the court with three options when the identity of a guardian for appointment is considered: an individual, a body corporate, or the Administrator-General.[121] If a corporation is appointed, the court may designate an individual to carry out the duties of a guardian for the corporation.

Various conditions relating to the identity of the guardian must be met. The proposed guardian must consent to the appointment and the views of the ward must be considered provided he is capable of understanding the matter and his views can be ascertained. In any event:

> "The court shall appoint as guardian the person who in the circumstances of the case seems to be the most suitable one in the best interests of the ward."[122]

The statute, in a general way, declares the functions of a guardian: to "take care of the needs" of the ward, including his education, studies, vocational and occupational training and work; to preserve, manage and develop his property; to maintain custody of the ward and determine his place of residence; and to act on his behalf in legal matters.[123]

The standard of performance of guardianship functions is declared to be action in the best interest of the ward in such manner as a devoted person would act in the circumstances.[124] The guardian must consider the views of the ward provided he is capable of understanding the matter and his views can be ascertained.[125] Presumably, it is the guardian himself who, in deciding whether the views of the ward have merit, determines whether the ward actually understands the matter in issue. The status of the ward is simply that he must comply with the directions of the guardian in guardianship matters.[126]

Several guardians for any one ward may be appointed for special reasons.[127] Upon making such an appointment, the court will either impose the duties of guardianship jointly upon the guardians or divide those duties between them. Where a joint guardianship is established, the Law provides[128] that any and all acts of one guardian require the consent of all the others, and that in the event of disagreement, reference must be had to the court which will decide. In any matter that admits of no delay, any guardian may act on his own. All guardians are jointly and severally responsible to the ward for the manner in which they exercise their functions.

Directing itself to problems of temporary duration, the statute vests the court with authority to appoint a temporary guardian or guardian *ad litem*. That order may follow an application by the Attorney-General or any interested party, or, interestingly, the court may intervene in any situation on its own initiative.

This last power of the court – personal intervention – is unique among guardianship schemes, and is a further aspect of the distinguishing characteristic of the Israeli system: close judicial supervision.

At all stages of the guardianship, from appointment to termination, the court maintains an active role. As a general principle, the court may at any time on application of the Attorney-General, an interested party, the guardian, *or of its own motion*, issue directions to the guardian in any matter relating to the carrying out of his duties.[129]

The guardian is not allowed merely to accept such judicial direction as may be given. He must seek out the consent or advice of the court in any matter possibly involving a conflict of interest for him as guardian.[130] He is not allowed, without the prior approval of the court, to act on behalf of the ward in the sale, charging, partition or winding-up of any economic unit or house; in any lease matter; in the registration of any matter requiring registration; the giving of any guarantee; or any other act which the court may specify as requiring approval.[131]

Further, the guardian must provide the court with inventories of the property of the ward, valuations of his property, and accounts of all financial transactions and investments at any times the court may demand them.[132]

The guardian is liable to the ward for damage caused by him to the ward or his property. However the court's role extends to an authority to relieve him of the whole or any part of his liability provided he "acted in good faith and paid proper regard to the interests of the ward".[133] No liability attaches to the guardian for any act for which he obtained the approval of the court. To ensure that the guardian conducts himself properly, the court may, upon appointment or later, require the posting of security by property charge or a guarantee. The amount of the security may be increased, decreased or released by the court as any time.[134]

It is provided that a guardian is not responsible for the maintenance of his ward.[135] Reasonable expenses incurred in carrying out guardianship duties are to be borne by the ward, and the guardian may reimburse himself for them out of the property of the ward.[136] Finally, the court may fix a remuneration for the guardian if it deems it justified. The remuneration is borne by the ward and the guardian takes it out of his property.[137]

A guardianship terminates upon the resignation of the guardian if the resignation is approved by the court;[138] or upon the dismissal of the guardian by the court for any reason it sees fit to do so;[139] or upon the revocation of the legal incompetence of the ward by the court.[140]

Seen in perspective, the Israeli system of close judicial supervision of guardian appears most commendably concerned with protection of the ward. Depending upon the vigor and resources of the courts, guardians could become mere agents of the courts which might almost themselves be the guardians. It seems neither practical nor necessary, unless the operation is small indeed, to convert what is probably supposed to be the check on guardians into the actual performer of guardianship functions.

Special trust arrangements

Various voluntary associations involved with the mentally retarded have devised "group-trust" formulae, as an alternative or supplement to the individual trust technique and other options available to parents seeking to provide for the future of their retarded children. The trust concept – giving a sum of money to a guardian or corporation to be used for the benefit of the handicapped person – is of long standing. The plans which are based upon a group trust involving many parents are primarily of two varieties: the "retardate trust" and the insurance assignment.

In the retardate trust concept, a sum of money is left in trust with an organization which undertakes to provide various services to the retardate beneficiary. The structure of the trustee organization, the services promised and the amount of money involved are variables and matters to be determined in particular trust agreements. This trust idea should not be confused with the leaving of funds with a guardian in trust for the care of a child.

Perhaps the best known attempt in this vein is the Maryland Retardate Trust.[141] The members of the Board of Trustees are appointed by the Executive Committee of the State Association for Retarded Children. The Association sets policies for the Trust.

The particular agreement used for that Trust grants very wide powers to the trustees in relation to their use of funds and excludes most conceivable checks on that power. The general responsibility to the Association is not excluded.

Contributions are made to a Trust in the name of the retardate beneficiary. Under the Maryland plan one subscribes a retardate child by donating $1,000.00 in cash or $2,000.00 in a will or by insurance. Upon the parent's death, the Trust adds the retarded child to the list for active service.

A feature of the program is that no money donated is set aside for any particular child. All moneys become part of the general fund, expended for all or any of the children as the trustees in their absolute discretion see fit. Income derived from the contribution accrues to the general fund, not to the account of the child of the donor.

The agreements make explicit that the Trust does not provide financial security. The Maryland agreement promises only that it will provide ". . . based on the needs of the retardate and the ability of the Trust funds, those 'creature comforts', such as small gifts, cosmetics, shaving supplies, etc., that can put some joy and happiness in the life of a retardate."[142]

In addition to the small tangible items, the Trust Fund programs promise services to the retardate. The Maryland agreement describes its services as follows.

"It will provide a continuing interest in the well-being of the retardate for the rest of his life. Where the retardate is an institution, visits will be made periodically; where the retardate is in a private home, constant touch will be maintained. In both instances, the Trustees, or their employees, will be available for expert and understanding advice and guidance. When there are a sufficient number of participating retardates, the Trust will retain social workers and use the services of professionals. In the meantime, it will have all the knowledge, services and advice of the State Association and the many contacts which this Association now has."[143]

Commonly, the appointed Trustees are persons of public renown and evelated social position. It is clear that such persons are far too busy to be visiting retardates and buying them cigarettes and cosmetics. Staff of the Trust will be charged with this responsibility. Much of the funds available will go to administration and staff costs. Only a percentage of an original contribution will actually reach the retardate. The redeeming feature is that once enrolled, a retardate is to benefit all his life from the Trust, even though more than the original contribution may be spent on him. The plan is similar to an insurance policy, in which benefit paid out may exceed premiums paid in.

Questions do arise. No guarantees are given of the amount that will be expended on any child. The extent of the fund is the limit. Many donations other than those made in the name of the beneficiary would appear essential if all retardates enrolled are to receive the benefit of at least their parent's contribution.

The point that must be noted is that the Trust concept as utilized in Maryland is merely a supplement to, and not a substitute for a major care program: institutionalization or guardianship. Some parents may feel that their money is better left to the guardian or hospital, who presumably are chosen with an interest in the retardate in mind.

In assessing the Retardate Trust idea, the factor of visits by the Trustees can probably be discounted. The decision whether to enrol in such a program should be made by weighing the advantage element – the insurance effect – against the negative factor of duplication of efforts and services. It should be borne in mind that the actual advantages to the retardate will be limited to minor amenities. A further concern is that a guardian may assume that visits, personal contact and other amenities are not to be considered part of his responsibility, since the parents provided for these services otherwise. Such contact is essential to the proper discharge of the role of the guardian.

There is also a Retarded Trust Plan functioning in the State of Massachusetts. It is in most respects identical to the Maryland scheme. Enrolment is by the same method, the trustees are similarly well-known busy persons, and the powers of the trustees are equally extensive and unchecked. An additional feature of the Massachusetts Trust is that one may enrol as a member by donating $10,000.00. Unlike the $1,000.00 and $2,000.00 donation rules, the large amount may be designated for the benefit of one particular retardate. Upon the death of that retardate, any residue of the $10,000.00 accrues to the general fund.

Materials explaining the Massachusetts plan also make clear that the Trust is not a substitute for family or guardian. As will be seen from the following excerpt, the Trust Fund may not be utilized by the trustees for the benefits of a retardate until *all* of his family is gone.

Each local Association within the State chooses a "Guardianship Representative" from among its members. These persons act as a link between the trustees and local needs and events.

The following is an open letter published by the trustees.

"March, 1966
Dear Parents and Friends of Retarded Children:

On May 1, 1966, the MARC Guardianship Plan will have been in effect for five years. It is filling a need for the 30 participants of the plan and their families. It is also filling a need for the Mutual Members in the MARC Member Organizations for they have the assurance of continuing care through the MARC Retardate Trust.

Our thirty participants became eligible for the benefits because their father or mother was a Mutual Member when he or she died. The trustees are beginning to feel acquainted with the participants and their families although in most cases we have not actually met them. But we feel that we do know them, because of the reports that our Social Worker, Miss Alice Boyden, brings back after her visits. In just under two years with us she has become loved and respected for herself, her counsel and the support which the trustees try to give her.

Right now, in every case there is a member or members of the family who care for each participant. The main purpose of the Trust thus becomes one of helping the family where we can and to become acquainted with them and the participants so we can step in later and be even more useful after there is no family remaining. In addition we attempt to conserve the assets of the trust to give assurance that funds will be available later when the need will be greater.

Thus trustees have enjoyed being hosts to the Guardianship Representatives at two of our regular meetings. These were arranged so that the Guardianship Representatives would become better acquainted with the trustees and the work of the Trust and also so that we might have their ideas and suggestions.

The income, expenses, and assets of the Trust have been as follows for each year. On Jan. 17, 1966 our assets were $18,835.16.

Year	Income Including Interest	Expenses	Assets at end of Year
1961-62	$3,881	None	$3,881
1962-63	4,245	None	8,126
1963-64	3,357	$ 695	10,788
1964-65	5,620	1,172	15,236
1965-66	4,486	887	18,835 (Through 1/17/66)"

A statement of the aims of the Retardate Trust in Massachusetts has been provided[144] by one of the trustees.

"The MARC Retardate Trust exists for only one purpose – that is to serve the mentally retarded. When a mutual member dies it is the duty – and the desire – of the trustees to replace the mutual member in the life of the retardate to whatever degree possible, but particularly to be concerned with his happiness and welfare. When a mutual member dies a trustee or a representative of the trustees, visits the family of the deceased. The visitor is seeking to cooperate with the family and make the services of the MARC Retardate Trust available. In the majority of cases when the parents have been close to the retardate, a vast change in the life of the retardate results. No matter what planning may have been done, the problem of readjustment is severe. No degree of planning can foresee the future and control the judgment or circumstances of other survivors.

No amount of planning can provide a substitution for parental love and care. It is rare that the family interest and concern for the welfare and happiness of the loved one surviving has been exhibited in the same degree by other relatives. In many cases the healthy survivors have families and responsibilities which prevent them from devoting the time and attention which they might want to give. Sometimes the break in family ties comes quickly, sometimes gradually, but in any event in most all cases the innocent retardate has lost something irreplaceable and needs the care and interest which has been lost with death.

This purpose of the MARC Retardate Trust can be expressed in many ways. It is expressed by a visit from an understanding person to show interest, attention, to comfort, and to learn the needs and problems o fthe retardate.

It can be expressed by a gift on a birthday or Christmas.

It can be expressed by making certain that medical care is obtained if needed.

It may be expressed by a pretty dress representing the difference between the drab utilitarian garb furnished in state residential centers and the retardate's very own clothing.

It can mean training and guidance to develop the full capacity or latent ability, which could make it possible for a younger retardate to take his place in the outside world.

It could be the difference between the survivor existing, unhappy, not properly cared for in the wrong facility or being placed where he can be happy and properly cared for.

It could be the difference between being an 'unwanted' in a home or community, or being guided into the care of properly trained persons equipped to cope with the problems of the retarded.

It could be making certain that the funds planned to insure proper care and happiness for the retardates are properly administered for the sole benefit of the survivor. Even the best intentioned and devoted persons, if not trained or experienced in the handling of funds can make serious errors of judgment which could be financially disastrous for the retardate.

But the MARC Retardate Trustees, who serve without remuneration, have only one goal – to insure as much happiness and protection as humanly possible for the participants of the MARC Retardate Trust."

Another of the trustees has explained the program of visitations and personal contact.

The Trustees employ a social worker to carry out many of their responsibilities.

Although each local association has the responsibility of notifying the trustees of the death of a mutual member and indicating any problems that have arisen, it is the trustees' responsibility to ascertain in what ways they may be of assistance to the retardate. The social worker, therefore, visits the family, or if there is no family, the person who has been appointed guardian, to find if there are needs for which the trustees should assume responsibility. If there are none, the social worker indicates that she is available for consultation should any new situation arise. At least yearly she gets in touch with the family to be sure everything is working out satisfactorily. If, however, the death of the mutual member causes complications in the continued care of the retardate, the social worker with her knowledge of community resources is able to suggest various possibilities and helps the remaining family determine which is the best solution for their particular problem. Again, a brother who has agreed to be the guardian for his retarded sister might be overwhelmed when he has the full responsibility and would welcome the opportunity to discuss his anxiety with the social worker and be reassured.

If the retardate is in one of the State Residential Centers, the social worker obtains the family's permission to visit him and also to discuss his case with the social worker at the Residential Center in order to learn whether there are ways in which the trustees could be of assistance. This visit also alerts other personnel to the trustees' interest in the retardate and their readiness to be of help.

The social worker is responsible to the trustees, and, after each visit to the retardate and his family reports her findings to the Board and carries out their recommendations.[145]

SPECIAL TRUST ARRANGEMENTS

The British Columbia Association for Retarded Children did attempt to establish a "retardate trust" plan in that Province. The scheme, which was to be known as "The Lifetime Friend Plan", was devised to provide, after the death of his parents, consistent, friendly supervision to the retarded child for his lifetime. In addition to the visitation and regular contact features of the Maryland and Massachusetts plans, the "Lifetime Friend" was to ensure, in co-operation with the proper authorities, that the retardate received proper care, treatment and respect for his civil rights.

The Plan was to be administered by the Association which would provide suitable field and supervisory personnel.

The entry fee for coverage by the Plan was set at $5,000 per child. It was anticipated that parents would provide for this fee by purchasing a life insurance policy in that amount with the proceeds going to the Association. Provision was made for the enry fee being paid by means of a bequest in the parents' will, or through a trust fund administered by a trust company.

The British Columbia plan did not commence operation. To be able to operate successfully, 100 or more subscribers were necessary, and attempts to secure them did not succeed.

Various plans have been formulated to provide for the purchase by parents of life insurance policies which upon the death of the insured parent, creates a fund of money for the benefit of a retarded child. Parents may, of course, purchase such a policy on their own, either naming their child as beneficiary or establishing a trust fund to receive and administer the money. Certain Associations for the Mentally Retarded have formulated insurance schemes on a group basis to secure lower premium rates, with a common proceeds-administering body.

Although these insurance plans are very similar in conception and operation to the "retardate trust", there is a crucial distinction in rationale. The "retardate trust", in essence, sees a minimum amount of money paid to an Association – sometimes in the form of insurance policy proceeds – to purchase certain "friendship" services for the retardate. The insurance schemes are directed to providing, not services, but rather a sum of money, to the retardate.

The best-known of the group life insurance schemes – the NARC Protection Plan – is operated by the National Association for Retarded Children in the United States, and is designed to supplement Social Security benefits for the retardate. A parent may purchase insurance through the Plan if he or his spouse is a member of a local or State unit of the National Association, and is earning income. Annual premiums are in the $60.00 range. The amount of insurance benefits payable for that premium vary from the age at death of the insured parent from $15,000 at 40 years of age or under to $1,250 at age 65 or over. The decreasing benefit rate is explained as a function of need.

> "As the parent grows older, so does the retarded person. Therefore, the older the parent at the time of death, the shorter the period for which the retarded person will need financial support. A pattern of decreasing benefits follows this declining need and makes it possible to offer the plan at a low premium rate."[146]

The Ontario Association for the Mentally Retarded has recently attempted to establish an insurance scheme for its membership. A group life assurance contract was negotiated with a commercial insurance company, with all members who were not yet a certain age and were parents or guardians of retarded children eligible. The offered policy had a face value of $10,000, for which annual premiums set at rates varying with the age of the insuring parent were required. The premium ranged from $24.00 per year for a parent under 35 years old to $336.00 per year for a parent at age 65. The increasing annual premium obviated the necessity of the decreasing-benefit feature of the NARC Plan.

It was recommended to parents urged to subscribe to the Ontario plan that they not name their retarded child as the beneficiary of the insurance, because of the legal complications. Parents were advised to make arrangments in their wills for a trustee to accept the $10,000 and administer it for the retardate.

Thirty-five hundred subscriptions were needed to implement the plan for Ontario, and because less than 200 were received, the insurance company cancelled the contract in 1969.

Neither the "retardate trust" nor the insurance plans seem to have found much favor in Canada. Enrolment requires a significant expenditure of money that is not clearly justified by the benefits returned.

The staff working for the "retardate trust" have no special legal status with respect to the retarded person. They have no authority to take part in any decision affecting his disposition or treatment. Should they intervene in any manner, their duties and liabilities raise troublesome questions of law that cannot be resolved in a contract or agreement. The result must be – and in fact for most "retardate trusts" no more is promised – that the subscription to the scheme will purchase only very limited services of an insubstantial nature. For parents with money to spare, and who believe that the infrequent visits and small gifts would meet a need likely to be unmet by those charged with the care of their child, the investment might recommend itself. The concept is not, however, the appropriate direction for the expenditure of money or remedial efforts so long as major needs of the retarded remain unmet, and so long as many could not join even if the plans were useful.

The insurance purchase would seem a relatively less difficult way – providing one has the money – to build an estate and create a trust for a handicapped child. There are, however, problems with the idea. Those plans which merely purchase services such as infrequent visits do not offer a great deal. Those which actually establish a fund of money for distribution to the retardate may merely duplicate – or indeed pay for – care that is inherent in government services in this field. It would seem to be true that a trust fund could be of considerable assistance to a retardate who will be living in the community. Where insurance is concerned, whether in a group-trust plan or by individual purchase, parents must assess their own case. Benefits are clearly attainable, but not in all cases, and each must be judged carefully on its own merits before any commitment of resources is made.

Citizen advocacy

Voluntary efforts by private individuals are from time to time espoused as the ideal vehicle for assistance to the retarded. Basic to this view is a discounting of the ability of service agencies to provide assistance of other than limited scope.

Considerable professional standing is accorded some of the leading exponents of the voluntary, individualized schemes. Perhaps the most extensively thought-out of these schemes is the "citizen advocacy" concept, and an exploration of its ramifications is merited.

Specific criticisms of the prevailing services are directed primarily to impersonality of service, uninspired and uninspiring administration, conflicts of interest or loyalty, a scarcity of options and efforts, and impractical arrangements.[147]

The most important criticism is that alleging impersonal service. From it, the others follow.

Wolfensberger posits[148] two types of support needed by impaired persons: instrumental, meaning a dealing with the routines of life; and expressive, connoting signs of personal interest, individual thoughtfulness, and shows of affection. To persons of the citizen advocate persuasion, agencies are able to provide merely one-quarter of the support needed by the handicapped.

> "Social service-type agencies are suited to set up arrangements under which instrumental functions are accomplished on a routine basis . . . , but rarely on a direct or emergency basis. . . . Agencies are even less suited to meet a person's expressive needs. Although agency personnel, on an individual basis, may occasionally play expressive functions, the point is that they often will not, cannot, and cannot be expected to."[149]

Even those members of agency staffs who do attempt a personal approach to their caseload create problems when any particular case is assumed by another worker.

Because they cannot involve themselves in personal relationships of any significant intensity, an awareness of the real needs of an individual is seen as usually lacking in agency staffs. The result is that other services are not brought into play. Further, the existence of any one agency may forestall an awareness of need for any additional organized efforts.

The contention is made that agencies, particularly public ones, may often have interests at variance with those of an individual being served. In such a case, the handicapped person has no one to speak for him.

> "Professionals whose career interests, reward systems, and social system ties lie within agencies – as is commonly the case – cannot be expected to provide impaired persons with the loud, loyal, consistent, unwavering voice they need."[150]

Finally, agencies are categorized as having an administration that is uninspired, bureaucratic, and rigid.

> "They administer rather than lead, and far from providing inspiration and positive challenges to the citizenry, they typically are themselves difficult to inspire, resistant to change and dynamism, and often resentful of voluntary citizen self-help action."[151]

The solution to the poor service resultant from the above agency deficiencies is, according to Wolfensberger and his supporters, a citizen advocacy scheme. Such a program was first established in the State of Nebraska, and indications from its founders are that it has met with considerable success.

Wolfensberger, who directed the Nebraska scheme, has defined citizen advocacy to consist of

> "a mature, competent citizen representing, as if they were his own, the interests of another citizen who is impaired in his instrumental competency, or who has major expressive needs which are unmet and which are likely to remain unmet without special intervention."[152]

The essence of the matter is that advocates are not to be agencies, nor professionals, but competent citizens only.

Wolfensberger concedes[153] three potential criticisms of his concept: a lack of motivated and inspired advocates, the practical difficulty of implementation, and the likelihood of very poor review and supervision of advocates, who may be incompetent, misguided, undisciplined or taking advantage of their position.

The delineation of the characteristics of a good advocate merits being set out here. Serious consideration of these criteria is in order.

"First of all, it is important that the advocate has the type of community stability which makes it likely that his relationship to the protégé can be a sustained one. Mobile business executives and armed forces personnel usually lack the continuity of residence that is almost essential for most advocacy functions.

Secondly, the advocate must be willing to undergo orientation and preparation. This preparation need not be lengthy or formal; it may consist of a single workshop, or a few interviews. However, it is likely to screen out many persons who volunteered impulsively but lack perseverance.

Thirdly, the advocate needs to understand his specific advocacy mission.

Fourthly, the advocate must have competence in whatever advocacy role or task he chooses to assume. Because of the wide range of such roles and tasks, incompetence in one must not be judged to imply incompetence in another, and vice versa.

Fifthly, the advocate needs to make a commitment to this mission.

Sixthly, whatever mission the advocate selects, he should display what the community would judge to be 'good moral character.'

These six characteristics appear to be rather basic. In addition, it would be highly desirable if the advocate would consider joining the action group in his community that is concerned with his protégé's impairment."[154]

The functions seen for the citizen advocate are in the main those outlined for a guardian in this book: friend, advisor, guide, protector, and spokesman. The citizen advocate, however, has no legal status. Great stress is placed, accordingly, upon his aggressiveness, persistence, and militancy to persuade authorities of the merits his involvement and demands in any situation.

"It is more important that citizen advocates be vigorous and dedicated than that they be always right. In balance, and in the long run, it is better that they represent their protégés' interests vociferously even if sometimes also irrationally. The mere fact that a person has a spokesman will often assure adaptive agency responses, even if the spokesman's demands are neither reasonable nor met. Thus, agency personnel must be extremely cautious in assessing the quality of an advocacy relationship, and in interpreting their own responses. In agency work, a professional may be apt to belittle the advocate who is 'a pain in the neck' – yet this advocate may well be the one who is effective!"[155]

In the citizen advocacy scheme, the problems noted – scarcity of volunteers, administrative difficulties, and the clear need for supervision and review – are not left without an attempt at resolution. The answer is proposed in the form of an "advocacy office," which would have as its functions –

"1 Planning and budgeting

2 Dissemination of the advocacy concept, in order to: make it a familiar concept in our society generally; draw attention to new options for citizens in search of a human service role; and spread knowledge about the availability of this service to those who may need it.

3 Further definition of desirable advocacy roles

4 Clarification of desirable advocate characteristics

5 Recruitment of citizens for advocacy roles: such recruitment can often be accomplished during the dissemination process. Thus, talks to church groups, civic and service clubs, college classes, etc., can be coupled with challenges to accept an advocacy role.

6 Screening of potential advocates

7 Establishment of guidelines for the conduct of advocates

8 Orientation and education for advocate candidates: however, care should be taken that the professional advocacy office staff – who may come from an agency background – do not yield to the temptation to 'professionalize' the advocacy role. Professionalization or formality would probably destroy the heart and guts of advocacy: a citizen acting to protect the interests of another citizen, as if they were his own, utilizing such means and ways which are *typical of everyday citizenship functioning, rather than everyday professional or agency functioning.*

9 Arranging specific advocacy relationships: this involves development of a file of names of persons in need of advocacy, a determination of the advocacy needs in each case, selection of suitable advocate candidates for a case, bringing the advocate candidate and the impaired person together, and eventually sanctioning the relationship if it appears to be a well-matched one.

10 Supporting advocacy, relationships by means of legal, administrative and professional assistance: this will be discussed further in the section on staffing of advocacy offices.

11 Conducting periodic reviews of advocacy relationships: most advocacy relationships that exist in everyday life are either not subject to legal review at all, or only under unusual circumstances. For instance, parenthood is only reviewed after allegations of gross neglect, abuses, or failure. Similarly, many informal advocacies that might be arranged by an advocacy office might lose their cultural meaning if they were subject to legal or excessive review."[156]

Three functions of the "advocacy office" seem of prime importance. Recruitment is basic. Training would appear in the scheme to be very light, and deliberately so. This need not cause great concern if adequate supervision and assistance is provided to advocates, both as review of conduct and expert counsel. Unfortunately little stress seems to be placed upon review and supervision of advocates.

Wolfensberger notes that the "office" should be staffed by persons with administrative, casework, and public relations skills. Back-up legal and medical advice should be immediately available. (This apparatus is not, of course, to become bureaucratic.) However, once an advocacy pairing is made

"One staff member could probably conduct supervision, review, and follow-up for several hundred established relationships."[157]

To some critics of services to the handicapped, this last arrangement would seem dangerously impersonal.

One could consider that proponents of citizen advocacy are unduly optimistic in not expecting any great need to protect the impaired from the advocate, or alternatively naïve in thinking that very limited review will accomplish that protection. No such criticism would be valid. Wolfensberger would seem quite aware of the possibilities for harm to the impaired.

"An important point to remember is that the advocacy office usually will not exercise any direct advocacy functions, and cannot be held responsible for the actions of the advocates it has 'set up in business'."[158]

Dr. G. Allen Roeher, Director of the National Institute on Mental Retardation has recently stated

". . . the Canadian Association for the Mentally Retarded and the National Association for Retarded Children in the USA have examined the concept of citizen advocacy and appear to be moving forward in exploring its value with a view to implementation into practice."

It is too early to assess the implications of citizen advocacy in a manner similar to that in which we have assessed other helping schemes.

Legal Aid

Of undoubted value to any system of administering justice is the scheme for providing the means of retaining legal counsel to those lacking in financial resources. Again, however, the retardate is the least likely to benefit from a program of legal aid.

To take advantage of the opportunity of such assistance, one would require

a an awareness and understanding of one's legal rights, the nature of a violation of them or the need for protection at law;
b an awareness of the existence of the legal aid plan, its meaning and the location of its officers;
c the ability to explain the facts of the case and one's resources to the assessment officers; and
d the ability to instruct counsel should one be acquired.

The point need not be belabored that the retardate will have difficulty in using the opportunities made available to him. He needs close contact with a person who is able to counsel him in all respects of living in the community.

Legal aid plans make no special provisions for those with mental disabilities. The jailed or hospitalized retardate will probably have someone who will advise him that legal counsel is needed and how to obtain it. The retardate who is not incarcerated may be completely adrift.

Ombudsman

Recent decades have seen the development of massive governmental structures and great bureaucracies. A further trend has been the delegation to boards and tribunals of much of the administrative authority of popularly-elected legislative bodies. Social complexity and technological advancement have made it essential that semi-autonomous tribunals and employees of government departments make a great many of the decisions that most intimately affect daily life. Legislatures are concerned with such matters as licences, taxation and compensation payments only at a general policy level.

The delegation of administrative authority carries with it a potential for mistakes and abuses, the correction of which are beyond the capacity of the ordinary citizen. Administrative agencies are given a wide discretion within which to make their decisions. The discretion is essential because a continual reference to the legislature for guidance is not possible.

The law has developed a set of rules determining how administrative discretion is to be exercised. These rules are not concerned with the correctness of a decision made, but rather only with the manner in which it is made. If procedural rules of fair play are not observed, a citizen may appeal to the courts. If those rules are correctly applied, then the discretion granted will support an incorrect decision of a question before a board or civil servant. The seeking of appeal court review, of course, involves an extensive and complex operation. Recognition of the relative helplessness of the citizen has lent great popularity to the concept of the ombudsman – "people's man". That official is appointed by the legislature, but functions independently without governmental restraint. It is his function to investigate complaints made to him alleging an abuse of, or mistake in, the exercise of administrative authority. Designed to be a cost-free advocate for the citizen, the ombudsman is vested with investigative, reporting and pressuring powers so that he may see to the correction of a poor decision.

Sweden, Denmark and New Zealand have had the longest experience with the ombudsman role. In Canada , the Provinces of Alberta, New Brunswick and Quebec have made the scheme part of their administrative structure.

The concept of the ombudsman is not universally held in esteem. The chief argument against it maintains that an ombudsman is an unnecessary duplication of the function of members of the legislature in acting for their constituents. It is not within the scope of this book to assess the merits of the ombudsman concept. It can at least be said that a public official so constituted would not be a detriment to the public interest.

Special concerns of retardates would appear particularly conducive to a useful role for an ombudsman. More so than for most social groups, the lives of the retarded are affected by the decisions of public servants. Commitment, institutional care, social benefits, rehabilitation and property management are all matters of great moment aptly suited to the efforts of the ombudsman.

The critical point is, that however helpful the concept under discussion could potentially be to the retarded, the same problem arises as under a plan of legal aid. Before an ombudsman could assist a retardate, the retardate would have to understand that he has a problem, know that help is available and how to obtain it. Counselling and close personal contact is an essential service that must be provided to the retardate.

References

1. R.S.M. 1970, c. M110.
2. See Chapter 4, section entitled "Mental Incompetency Proceedings".
3. In the Act, "supervision" is defined to mean ". . . the caring for, assisting, guiding, protecting, or overseeing of mental retardates not in institutions, by any person or agency with the approval of the minister under such terms and conditions as he may prescribe. The Director of Psychiatric Services in the Department of Health is empowered to place under supervision, as he may consider necessary, any person whom he believes, upon the receipt of a certificate from a physician, to be mentally disordered.
4. R.S.P.E.I. 1951, c. 21, as amended.
5. *Ibid.*, s. 1.
6. S.P.E.I. 1968, c. 37.
7. *Ibid.*, s. 2(o).
8. *Ibid.*, ss. 54 and 55.
9. *Ibid.*, s. 59(o).
10. That legislation is analyzed and discussed later under the heading of extension of child protection laws.
11. Alberta, British Columbia, Ontario and Saskatchewan.
12. *The Infants Act*, R.S.A. 1970, c. 185.
13. *The Infants Act*, R.S.O. 1960, c. 187, ss. 4-15.
14. *The Infants Act*, R.S.S., c. 342, ss. 9-20.
15. R.S.O. 1960, c. 187, s. 16(1).
16. *Ibid.*, s. 16(2).
17. R.S.S. 1965, c. 342, ss. 21 and 25.
18. R.S.O. 1960, c. 187, s. 20.
19. R.S.S. 1965, c. 342, s. 28.
20. *Equal Guardianship of Infants Act*, R.S.B.C. 1960, c. 130.
21. *Ibid.*, s. 6.
22. *Ibid.*, s. 7.
23. R.S.S. 1965, c. 342, ss. 3 and 22.
24. R.S.B.C. 1960, c. 130, s. 15.
25. See the *Equal Guardianship of Infants Act*, R.S.B.C. 1960, c. 130, s. 6 and *The Infants Act*, R.S.S. 1965, c. 342, ss. 3 and 22. These statutes are analyzed and their usefulness considered elsewhere in this book as legislation concerning infants.
26. *The Child Welfare Act*, R.S.A. 1970, c. 45.
   Protection of Children Act, R.S.B.C. 1960, c. 303.
   The Child Welfare Act, R.S.M. 1970, c. C 80.
   Child Welfare Act, S.N.B. 1966, c. 3.
   The Child Welfare Act, 1964, S.N. 1964, c. 45.

    Child Welfare Act, R.S.N.S. 1967, c. 31.
    The Child Welfare Act, 1965, S.O. 1965, c. 14.
    The Childrens' Protection Act, 1961, S.P.E.I. 1961, c. 3.
    Youth Protection Act, R.S.Q. 1964, c. 220.
    The Child Welfare Act, R.S.S. 1965, c. 268.

27 *Martin et al* v. *Duffel*, [1950] 4 D.L.R. 1 (S.C.C.).
    Mugford v. *C.A.S. of Ottawa* (1969), 4 D.L.R. (3d) 274 (S.C.C.).
28 Mr. Justice Rand in *Hepton* v. *Maat*, [1957] S.C.R. 606 at 607.
29 British Columbia deals with the medical care issue in an indirect manner by permitting the authority who seizes a child to obtain necessary treatment. The actual seizure itself would have to proceed on some other ground of neglect.
30 The section numbers in each Act which relate to procedure will not be noted. In all of the statutes, these sections follow immediately upon the list of grounds for intervention.
31 Nova Scotia, Prince Edward Island and Quebec.
32 (1955-56), 17 WW..R. 628, 5 D.L.R. (2d) 275.
33 Alberta, British Columbia, Manitoba, Newfoundland, Prince Edward Island and Quebec.
34 Alberta, Nova Scotia and Saskatchewan.
35 The provision of the Alberta, New Brunswick and Saskatchewan statutes.
36 The Ontario situation.
37 Report of the Advisory Committee on Child Welfare to the Minister of Public Welfare, 1964, Toronto.
38 *Ibid.*, page v.
39 *Ibid.*, page 11.
40 Those of Alberta (36 months), and Ontario and Prince Edward Island (each 24 months).
41 *L.M.* v. *Director of Child Welfare* (1968), 64 W.W.R. 216, 68 D.L.R. (2d) 187 (Sask.). Similar principles are expressed by the Supreme Court of Canada in *Hepton* v. *Maat*, [1957] S.C.R. 606.
42 *An Act to Amend the Protection of Children Act*, S.B.C. 1969, c. 27, s. 5.
43 R.S.C. 1952, c. 160.
44 Bill No. 9 of New Brunswick 1970.
45 *Mugford* v. *C.A.S. of Ottawa (1969)*, 4 D.L.R. (3d) 274 (S.C.C.).
46 MINN. STAT. 525.749 (1961).
47 MINN. STAT. 525.749 (6) (1961).
48 MINN. STAT. 525.741 (1) (1961).
49 Levy, *Protecting the Mentally Retarded: An Empirical Survey and Evaluation of the Establishment of State Guardianship in Minnesota*, 49 MINNESOTA LAW REVIEW 821,828 (1965).
50 MINN. STAT. 525.752 (1) (1961).
51 MINN. STAT. 525.752 (1) (1961).
52 2 Patton, *Minnesota Probate Law and Practice* 554 (1955) cited by Levy, *op. cit.* 829.
53 MINN. STAT. 525.79 (1961).
54 MINN. STAT. 525.753 (2) (1961).
55 MINN. STAT. 393.07 (1a), (2), (1961).
56 MINN. STAT. 525.762 (2) (1961).
57 MINN. STAT. 259.24 (1) (1961).
58 MINN. STAT. ANN. 517.03 (Supp. 1964).
59 MINN. STAT. 256.07 (1961).
60 *Op. cit.*, page 830, fn. 45.
61 MINN. STAT. 256.93 (1961).
62 MINN. STAT. 256.88 (1961).
63 MINN. STAT. 256. 91 (1961).
64 MINN. CONST. art. 7, 2.
65 MINN. STAT. 525.78 (1961).
66 MINN. STAT. 525-611 (1961).
67 *Op. cit.*
68 *Ibid.*, at p. 837-39.
69 *Ibid.*, at p. 840.
70 *Ibid.*
71 Ames, Frances C. *The Minnesota Experience*, page 9. (Mrs. Ames is the Supervisor of the Section on Mental Retardation of the Minnesota Department of Public Welfare.).
72 Assembly Bill 691 of 1965.
73 Pye, California's Regional Centers, page 5 (pamphlet).
74 *Op. cit.*, page 13.
75 Health and Safety Code, section 416.
76 Assembly Bill No. 225, [Chapter 1594].
77 7 & 8 Eliz. 2, c. 72 (U.K.).
78 *Ibid.*, s. 33(2).

79 *Ibid.*, s. 4(1).
80 *Ibid.*, s. 4(2).
81 *Ibid.*, s. 4(4).
82 *Ibid.*, s. 4(3).
83 *Ibid.*, s. 33(3).
84 *Ibid.*, s. 33(4).
85 *Ibid.*, s. 26.
86 *Ibid.*, s. 28(2).
87 *Ibid.*, s. 27(4).
88 *Ibid.*, s. 27(1).
89 *Ibid.*, s. 27(2). See s. 54 in respect of the duty of a mental welfare officer to make an application.
90 *Ibid.*, s. 27(3).
91 *Ibid.*, s. 34(2).
92 *Ibid.*, s. 34(1).
93 *Ibid.*, s. 43(1).
94 *Ibid.*, s. 43(2).
95 *Ibid.*, s. 43(4). According to s. 59: "the responsible medical officer" means the medical officer of health of the responsible local health authority or any other medical officer authorized by that authority to act (either generally or in any particular case or for any particular purpose) as the responsible medical officer; "the nominated medical attendant" means the person duly appointed to act as the medical attendant of the patient.
96 *Ibid.*, s. 43(5).
97 *Ibid.*, s. 34(5).
98 *Ibid.*, s. 43(6).
99 Such tribunals and their operation are discussed and assessed in a scholarly fashion in GREENLAND, MENTAL ILLNESS AND CIVIL LIBERTY (1970).
100 7 & 8 Eliz. 2, c. 72, s. 44(1).
101 *Ibid.*, s. 41.
102 A full consideration of the local health authority services concerned with mental health administration is contained in EDWARDS, MENTAL HEALTH SERVICES 60 (3rd ed., 1961). ed., 1961).
103 The Mental Health (Hospital and Guardianship) Regulations, 1960, Part III (Guardianship), Statutory Instrument No. 1241 (1960).
104 7 & 8 Eliz. 2, c. 72, s. 47(1).
105 *Ibid.*, s. 47(2)(*c*).
106 *Ibid.*, s. 42(1).
107 *Ibid.*, s. 42(2).
108 *Ibid.*, s. 42(3).
109 Interview with Mr. H. R. Green, Solicitor, Department of Health and Social Security, London, June 10, 1969.
110 *Ibid.*
111 These and subsequent figures and notions obtained during interview with: Mrs. W. M. Curzon, Advisory Officer, Department of Health and Social Security; Mrs. P. Roberts, Children's Department, Home Office; and Mr. J. S. Heap, a senior mental health officer of the London Borough of Croydon: London, June 11, 1969.
112 s. 2.
113 ss. 9, 4, and 80.
114 ss. 5 and 6.
115 s. 8.
116 s. 10.
117 s. 33.
118 s. 14.
119 s. 26.
120 s. 28.
121 s. 34.
122 s. 35.
123 s. 38.
124 s. 41.
125 s. 42.
126 s. 43.
127 s. 45.
128 s. 46.
129 s. 44.
130 s. 48.
131 s. 47.
132 ss. 50 to 51 both inclusive.
133 s. 57.

134 s. 58.
135 s. 40.
136 s. 55.
137 s. 56.
138 s. 60.
139 s. 61.
140 s. 62.
141 Maryland Association for Retarded Children, *Maryland Retardate Trust* (available from the Association at 1514 Reiserstown Road, Pikesville, Maryland 21208).
142 *Ibid.*, p. i.
143 *Ibid.*
144 Holland, When a Mutual Member Dies, in "To Keep on Caring", a pamphlet publication of M.A.R.C., at pp. 7 and 8.
145 Barus, the Social Worker, in "To Keep on Caring", *ibid.*, at p. 9.
146 "How to Provide for Their Future", a pamphlet publication of N.A.R.C. (1968).
147 Wolfensberger, Toward Citizen Advocacy for the Handicapped, Impaired, and Disadvantaged (Revised Edition, January 15, 1971) (mimeo'd).
148 *Ibid.*, p. 4.
149 *Ibid.*
150 *Ibid.*, p. 5.
151 *Ibid.*, p. 4.
152 *Ibid.*, p. 6.
153 *Ibid.*, footnote 147, p. 17.
154 *Ibid.*, p. 20.
155 *Ibid.*, p. 25.
156 *Ibid.*, p. 18.
157 *Ibid.*, p. 19.
158 *Ibid.*

others
and yet
others

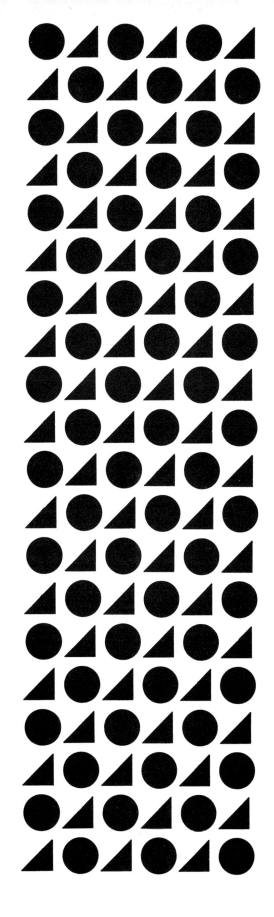

others and yet others

Introduction

Elderly persons

Native Canadians

New Canadians

General protection

References

Introduction

The general introduction of this book took note of the difficulties in defining "retardation". Even such definitions as have been formulated are not totally satisfying instruments with which to work in assessing issues and problems. The "gray areas", "borderline groups" and "degrees of disability" controversies will not be resolved, nor are they restated here.

Of the various approaches to defining retardation, the wider and more general approach deals with retardation in terms of social functioning. This approach carries with it the notion that intellectual capability is merely one factor in assessing a disability. Adopting this reasoning, the analysis and considerations contained in this book could be extended to encompass groups of individuals who are not, in the popular sense, labelled retarded.

In this chapter, we briefly explore the manner in which the problems of the retarded are also the problems of the elderly, the native and the new Canadian. Needless to say, our remarks do no more than sketch an outline.

Others considered and with respect to whom there may be some parallel include the physically handicapped, the narcotic addict, the alcoholic, the probationer and the parolee. All of these groups are the subjects of agencies and organizations the purpose of which is to serve them. We have not dealt with these groups here.

We also discuss what we see as a general trend to the protection of all members of the society.

Elderly persons

The observation is common that people are, in our society, living to a greater age in greater numbers than ever before. General advances in medical knowledge have permitted and abetted this consequence of improved social conditions. That the field of geriatrics is growing by leaps and bounds must be evident to all.

Many elderly persons manifest problems of social adaptation similar to those of the retarded. These problems may be a consequence of physical deterioration. A great many other difficulties are effects of the social status of the aged, rather than of a physical condition.

Senility – or more properly "chronic brain syndrome associated with senile brain disease" – is ascribed to an individual manifesting certain behaviors.

> "These cases vary from mild organic brain syndrome with self-centering of interest, difficulty in assimilating new experiences, and 'childish' emotionality, up to and including those so severely affected by senile brain disease as to require institutional care. Deterioration may be minimal or it may progress to a state of vegetative existence, with or without superimposed psychotic, neurotic, or behavioral reactions."[1]
>
> "Other behaviors reportedly associated with senility include lessened alertness, intolerance of change in routine, memory impairment for recent events, and preoccupation with bodily functions such as eating and excretion."[2]

It is important to note that senility is a pattern of behavior, not a physical condition. Although cerebral "degeneration" or cerebral arteriosclerosis are often present, neither is a determinant. Experts cite various studies which show that behavior may be markedly "senile" when only minor organic damage has occurred, and conversely that major physical impairment may be found in persons with no observable behavior pathology whatsoever.[3]

References for Others and yet others are on page 181.

Cerebral degeneration which impairs intellectual ability will clearly affect competence to manage many facets of one's life. The problem which first springs to mind relates to basic physiological needs. One frequently reads of aged persons found dead or near death in conditions of appalling meanness, at times even with great wealth or resources available. Severe mental disorder is often apparent, but seldom discovered by anyone with help to offer.

On a less immediately striking level, mental degeneration is sometimes coupled with the failure to seek out available social resources such as financial or medical assistance.

Various legal issues arise. How often are the senile victimized by being pressured into contracts they are unable to understand for goods or services they cannot use or do not need? When are the senile so incapacitated that they, like many retardates, are legally incompetent to contract? Do the senile, and may they, vote? To what extent are they responsible in tort for their behavior? Do they retain the capacity in law to enforce their rights in the courts, and are they able to understand that their rights are being abused? Are they competent to make a will? Who protects their property from dissipation by themselves or persons with undue influence over them?

It is becoming increasingly clear that, for anyone whose behavior manifests senility, very serious consideration must be given to the provision of assistance similar to that needed by the retarded. Many protective devices such as mental incompetency proceedings, mental hospitals legislation, social benefit programs and legal assistance plans exist and apply to the elderly. Each of these devices has been examined in relation to the retarded and found inadequate as a comprehensive solution. Either the schemes are not completely appropriate to special needs, or their utilization is often beyond the capacities of those who are intellectually deficient, socially unaware or socially unskilled.

An added dimension of the problem of senility is that its effects are apparently not irreversible. The evidence is persuasive that the prime cause of senile behavior is social.[4] Sudden upheavals in the life of a person seem more likely to account for the psychoses associated with old age than are organic changes. Vulnerability to life stresses and inability to compensate for frustration induce erratic behavior and inattention to "normal" activities which no longer produce pleasure and satisfaction. The result is a degeneration to disorientation, hostility and disinterest in life.

Treatment programs in institutions which have sought to reintroduce social pleasures and personal gratification in meeting increased social expectations are reported to have been very successful.[5] Merely providing aged persons with a life in which to participate has reversed the degeneration of age and returned the elderly to a state of alertness and social competency.

Our remarks have isolated the problem of senility for discussion because it is a problem in itself and because it is the end of a process which can be prevented.

The problems of the elderly are said basically to be lack of money, ill-health, lack of strength and mobility, and loneliness and lack of usefulness or employment.[6]

Poverty is common among the aged sector of our citizenry and, to a very great extent, is the underlying cause of many of their other difficulties. The poor ones cannot afford a proper and balanced diet, often live in squalor, and cannot participate in activities that maintain the crucial interest in life. Loneliness and uselessness combine to shut the elderly off from the rest of the world and lead them to care little more for themselves than they think society apparently does. A trip to the doctor may be "too much trouble".

The issues involved in the care of the old are complex and for most people they are not very interesting. Initiatives by governments in the fields of reducing the poverty and improving the housing of the old are being taken: many feel at an unreasonably slow pace. Other care, while it may be available, is not really being delivered. Still other care for them seems hardly developed.

A number of programs have been aimed at benefitting the elderly. Old Age Security, reduced or free coverage for medical and hospital care, regulation of standards for homes for the aged, and legislation geared to outlawing discrimination against a prson because of age, are examples. Reduced realty taxes and travel and transit fares are others. More and more, our senior citizens are being recognized as a special group with special needs.

Some extremely serious implications can be drawn from a recent newspaper column written in a light vein.[7]

"What to do with old ladies

In jailing that 69-year-old widow for defrauding the welfare out of $1,127, Judge P. J. Bolsby was only doing what we would expect any sensible law officer to do. That's how we feel about 69-year-old widows and old people in general.

Of course when some doctors were found gypping OHSIP out of hundreds of thousands by making false claims, not only were they not charged with anything, their names were kept out of the papers.

It's all a question of images. Doctors have a great image. They're healers, counselors, hand-holders, performers of miracles and dispensers of all-day suckers to little children. That's the image and you don't mess around with it.

Old people have a lousy image. First of all, they're old, and everybody knows that's bad. Old people don't look so hot. They're stooped over and their skin has a liverish look. Old women have stringy hair and mustaches and wear funny-looking clothes. They really turn you off.

Not only that, old people are not with it. They're always harking back to the good old days and griping about how things aren't what they used to be. They don't dig the new sound. Every little noise, like a transistor or a mini-motorcycle gets them all hot and bothered. They call the cops and so on.

If you're shopping or something these old people always get in the way. They move slow and look surprised at everything. And they frown and mutter if you just bump them a bit going through a door. It really gets you down.

Old men are the worst. They sit on benches and stare at all the girls going by in hot pants. I mean, you'd think by the time a guy got old he'd be past that sort of thing. Real creepy. No wonder people say so-and-so's a dirty old man.

So what are we going to do with all these old people?

The Trudeau Government's idea of starving them out isn't bad; but these old cats are tough and the more you squeeze them down the more they keep coming on. Some of them can live for months on end on nothing but bread and margarine. It's really depressing.

The image is the real problem. If there was only some way we could give them a new image we might be able to tolerate them. It's going to be hard, though; trying to pretty up the old dollies with permanents and sharp make-up has been tried but the results are poor. You know, the make-up sort of cakes. Not nice.

And old guys in bell bottoms and safari jackets isn't going to work, either. In fact, any kind of mod clothes on old people only comes out as some sort of satire on the young. And the young have enough to put up with now. Especially from the old. They know the old don't like them.

Maybe the Government's right, maybe the only thing to do is go on starving the oldies. Really give it to them good; like, when it comes time to hand them their annual 2 per cent cost-of-living increase on their pensions this year, why, find some excuse to postpone payment. Then just forget it. Or their income tax could be raised, on the excuse they're unproductive and therefore should pay more.

They're only human. They can't take that kind of pressure indefinitely."

Native Canadians

There are a host of complex social, political and legal issues bearing upon the position in Canadian society of Indian, Eskimo and Métis peoples. Our immediate concern is the sketching of certain parallels between their situation and that of the mentally handicapped in relation to the understanding of rights and the utilization of resources.

The difficulties of native Canadians within the overall social framework must be assessed from two viewpoints: that of the group and that of the individual.

Few people remain unconvinced that the Indian, Eskimo or Métis populations are disadvantaged groups within Canadian society. They do not have available to them the quality of educational and medical resources taken for granted by all but the most poverty-stricken of Canadians. Their communities are in almost all instances isolated – both in terms of geography and social participation, from the mainstream of Canadian life.

The historical approach to the provision of services to native populations – as opposed to other Canadians – has been to dispense social assistance payments at the subsistence level, and to virtually ignore the responsibility to provide the economic and social development opportunities considered essential for everyone else. The result has usually been, by default, the creation of a dependency cycle and an absence of the means of development to self-sufficiency and independence. Unemployment and receipt of welfare are often at epidemic levels, the consequences of discrimination and inadequate services.

Native peoples have very much been treated by their governments as second-class citizens. For other citizens, governmental functions are assigned to different levels of government and different departments within governments. The native peoples as an entire group have been assigned to a department of government at both federal and provincial levels. They have, in effect, become a function of government like taxes, roads or defence. Hence the *Indian Act*,[8] which encompasses within it almost the full range of governmental concerns, with those concerns directed for particular application to one segment of the population to the exclusion of other laws of general application on any subject covered by the Act.

It must be noted that the *Indian Act* does not merely consolidate provision for various governmental functions into one document for one group. It also provides special restrictions and limitations upon that group which do not apply to any other citizen: Cabinet authority to determine whether Indian moneys are being used properly; Cabinet prescription of the manner of election of Indian band officials and the rules for conduct of meetings; authority in the Minister of Indian Affairs and Northern Development rather than in the courts to determine all questions respecting testamentary dispositions of Indians; authority in the Minister to control the sale or barter of produce by Indians; and a prohibition against the possession by an Indian of an intoxicant while off his home reservation.

The *Indian Act* would seem clearly based upon a view of the Indian as a person basically incompetent to manage his affairs, and quite unable to participate in Canadian life in any normal fashion. Indeed, the Act makes provision for the Minister enfranchising an Indian if, in his opinion, the Indian ". . . is capable of assuming the duties and responsibilities of citizenship". However, a person who meets the criteria, and becomes enfranchised, is deemed to no longer be an Indian within the meaning of the Act, and the Act no longer applies to him. The assumption of the same legal status as that of other Canadians requires the Indian to give up his special protective umbrella.

Arguments have raged for a long time over the question whether treating native peoples as a group separate and apart was a measure adopted with the intent of securing better services for them. Whether that was the intent or not, treating them as a group separate from the rest of the population has certainly been accompanied by the phenomenon of two very different levels of service: one level for the general population and one for the special group. A great differential in the quality of service at the two levels has persisted.

As has been noted, inferior social services for native peoples have been accompanied by a lack of developmental opportunities. In recent years, governments have started to provide the resources and counsel necessary for the development of locally-controlled business ventures. Concomitant with concentration in that direction has grown the recognition of a lack of training and experience in business management among the indigenous people. Programs to fill that void are coming into operation, with the best-known perhaps being the entrepreneurial courses developed by Saskatchewan NewStart Incorporated for experimentation in the Prince Albert district.

The courts have of late broken new ground in the application of the laws of Canada to native populations. The Supreme Court of Canada held in *Regina* v. *Drybones*[9] that the *Indian Act*, in applying special penalties respecting intoxication in a public place to Indians, was in violation of the guarantee of freedom from discrimination on racial grounds contained in the *Canadian Bill of Rights*. The *Indian Act* is, therefore, to that extent inoperative, and Indians are recognized as being entitled to equality with all others in respect of any legislation of the Parliament of Canada.

On a somewhat different tack, the courts of the Northwest Territories have deemed it appropriate to take account of local customs and native sensibilities in matters of marriage, criminal procedure and the imposition of sentence in criminal matters.[10]

The most promising development is the growth of self-awareness among native populations, and their determination to unite to secure the same opportunities available to other Canadians. Poverty and neglect still dominate native communities, but the time would appear to have arrived when the people are prepared to demand and assume independence. That the process should appear to involve a running battle with government is inevitable, as the transition takes place. Although conditions are still poor, it is probably fair to say that the native Canadian among his own people is advancing to a social participation and economic status long overdue. Success is now attainable – as a people.

The native Canadian who seeks to live away from his own community and make his way in the mainstream of economic life will often face appalling hardship. Particularly is this true for those who move to large urban centres without education and skill training, and a familiarity with the highly-organized, complex, and intensely competitive structure of city life.

All of the ingredients of "culture shock" – loneliness, fear, discrimination and bewilderment with rules and institutions – may be felt by the individual in the alien and impersonal social structure with which he must cope. Unawareness of support or assistance services may well be coupled with an ignorance of legal rights and responsibilities. Extreme poverty, exploitation, and brushes with the law often occur. In such situations, the individual often will not know his rights, or will lack the aggressiveness to assert them and break the mould of dependency and acceptance of whatever white society does to him. At the least, the individual is unlikely to seek out and take full advantage of the educational and personal advancement opportunities available – if, of course, they are in fact open to him.

The difficulties of native Canadians attempting to cope in mainline society without the requisite resources has led to the establishment of counselling and referral centres by indigenous peoples, and, of late, stirrings of government action in the direction of special services. An example of such a special service in this line is the appointment in Manitoba of "court communicators", natives themselves with court and social work experience, to assist Indians in communicating with lawyers, obtaining legal aid, explaining court procedures, and acting as liaison with the probation service. This sort of role would seem likely to be very helpful in other areas of social coping as well, such as those relating to employment, education, social benefits, health care, housing and personal involvement in the general Canadian society.

New Canadians

In many respects, the immigrant to Canada is at a disadvantage. The degree of disadvantage will vary according to the person. There is the "culture shock" which often occurs when an individual comes to a new country. In more tangible terms, he may not be able to speak the language, not be aware of social programs available to assist him, nor understand the legal system. Government and its agencies may be looked upon with fear rather than as vehicles of support.

There is little doubt that many of these people need protection. A number of ethnic organizations exist to help them through the period of transition which may be basically a learning process. Individuals of similar ethnic origin who have successfully bridged the gap often help "their own".

The needs of new Canadians for supportive measures leading to adequate social functioning are, in many ways, similar to those of the retarded. New Canadians are easy victims for the predators of society. Not knowing what help is there nor where to find it, they may be the last to seek it. They may wrongly feel that their status in Canada would be placed in jeopardy should they contact the authorities. Where the system of government in their native land was oppressive to them, it may cause them to believe that the Canadian way is no different.

For most immigrants, the protection required is of a temporary nature and the needs will diminish with time. Their children will not, as a rule, inherit the problems.

General protection

We have noted, on a number of occasions, various new approaches and priorities in governmental activities. In fact, much of the current thrust of government is aimed towards the provision of more and more direct social services and protective schemes.

One need think only of the recent growth in consumer protection legislation. Used car dealer registration and the requirement of mechanical fitness certificates for used cars, mortgage broker registration, the cost-of-credit-buying disclosure laws, provision for cancellation of contracts with itinerant salesmen, and potential easier bankruptcy rules, are examples of governmental intervention into the marketplace on behalf of the citizen.

Employment standards legislation is also in an expansion period. Labor safety standards, minimum wage rules, workman's compensation, fair practices requirements, upgrading and training programs, broader unemployment insurance coverage, equal opportunities for women laws, and active government advocacy on behalf of employees who receive unfair treatment, will ease the lot of disadvantaged workers.

On the general level, there are the *Canadian Bill of Rights* and various provincial human rights codes directed at the prevention of discrimination.

In the area of social and health care, improved social assistance and rehabilitation programs, new institutions and approaches, and more comprehensive medical and hospital care and insurance coverage, are in the offing.

On the legal side, the development of legal aid schemes, greater court awareness of the needs of particular classes of persons, and the appointment of officials such as the ombudsman, are measures that will protect individuals and make possible the redress of their grievances.

The trend to legislative programs designed to protect citizens from exploitation and to actively assist their successful social integration may suggest to some that the need of the handicapped for special attention is lessened. We believe the contrary to be true.

Continual improvement and expansion of social services are essential. Such services do, however, make life more complex with the addition of new rules and bureaucracies. Greater social awareness, competence and self-confidence will be needed to know about, seek out and to secure delivery of available assistance. On a continuing basis, some expertise is vital to ensuring that an appropriate form and quality of service is received by an individual "client". There is always, too, the concern that abuse or repression may result from an inappropriate application of social service resources.

References

1 ULLMAN and KRASNER, A PSYCHOLOGICAL APPROACH TO ABNORMAL BEHAVIOR 580 (1969), quoting DSM-1.
2 *Ibid.*, at p. 581.
3 *Ibid.*
4 *Ibid.*, and the studies cited therein.
5 Kastenbaum, *Wine and Fellowship in Aging: An Exploratory Action Program*, 13 JOURNAL OF HUMAN RELATIONS 266 (1965). See, also, Volpe and Kastenbaum, *Beer and TLC*, 67 AMERICAN JOURNAL OF NURSING 100 (1967).
6 Waife, *The Aged Poor*, contained in MCIVER (ed.), THE ASSAULT ON POVERTY 41 (1965).
7 Dennis Braithwaite, writing in the *Toronto Telegram*, Wednesday, July 28, 1971, at p. 16.
8 R.S.C. 1952, c. 149.
9 [1970] 9 D.L.R. (3d) 473.
10 See, for example, Tierney, *"Mr. Justice" in the North,* THE CANADIAN BAR JOURNAL 1, (July, 1971).

guardians
and
guardianship

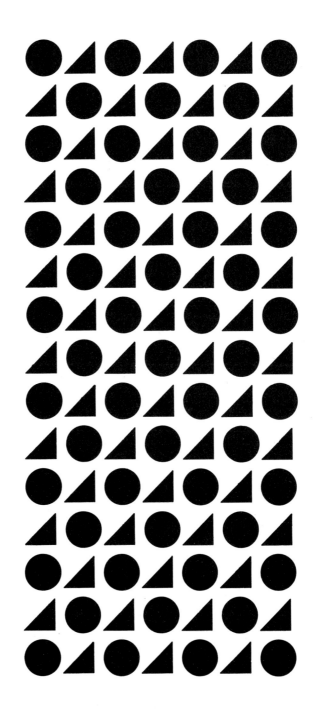

guardians and guardianship

Introduction

In the Conclusions of the Stockholm Symposium of the International League of Societies for the Mentally Handicapped (1967), the statement is found that "A retarded person, whether he is an adult or a child who is an orphan or abandoned, and who has a general inability to manage his life has a right to have a guardian who is legally and actually qualified to protect his interests and promote his personal welfare."[1]

Article V of the Declaration of General and Special Rights of the Mentally Retarded holds that "The mentally retarded person has a right to a qualified guardian when this is required to protect his personal well-being and interest."[2]

Looking at existing legal systems, it is clear that there is already protection afforded to children or minors, no matter why that protection is required. It follows, therefore, that there is existing protection available to the mentally retarded who have not yet attained a specified chronological age. The real need for any guardianship system, if it is intended to fill a vacuum, relates to adult retardates or those who have passed the age embraced by child protection statutes. Nonetheless, in propounding a scheme, as is done here, it may be that – in contemplation of a future need – something can be done in the way of guardianship protection at an early age apart from child protection laws. Continuity of service is a factor.

One of the points made in this chapter is the relatively little attention paid in the past, and even now, to matters of protecting the person as opposed to his property. The scheme of guardianship recommended relates essentially, as a result, to the personal aspects. This is not to suggest that less attention should be paid to the management of property, nor that property aspects are currently dealt with in such a manner that they cannot stand improvement. Indeed, the conservation of the property of a mentally incompetent person remains a real need. The possibility of having separate procedures – one for the protection of the person, the other for the protection of the estate – should be seen. Combined procedures should be considered as well. Also, the unification in one guardian of protecting both the person and the estate should be seen as a workable pattern, as should a dichotomy of these matters into a guardian of each – one of the person, and the other of the estate – with respect to the same ward.

The presentation of subtopics within this chapter has not been without difficulties. There are, of necessity, overlapping matters which spill over from one section to another. The entire chapter must be read to appreciate its full significance.

It would not be surprising if the system proposed did not fit all jurisdictions: indeed, it might not. Certain legal concepts, traditions or institutions have, in a given province, become entrenched. It might be just as well, or perhaps even better, not to disturb certain of these within their context. Rather, the principles and spirit of the system are advocated. The incorporation of even part of the proposals may have the desired effect.

No doubt exists, however, that there would, in any province, be fresh legislation required to implement a system of guardianship. The nature and extent of the legislation indicated would depend upon the existing statute law in the province and, of course, the form which the government intends the guardianship system to take.

Merely because a retarded person is in need of various forms of assistance does not *ipso facto* mean that he needs a guardian. There are innumerable ways in

References on Guardians and guardianship are on page 210.

185

which he may be helped short of guardianship. We must be careful, if there is to be a formal guardianship system, that it is not used (rather abused) to the extent that other forms of help fall into disuse. On the contrary, current forms of help should be augmented, even to the extent which excludes guardianship arrangements wherever possible. The following statement from the Conclusions of the San Sebastian Symposium on Guardianship of the Mentally Retarded is to the point.

> "Guardianship has in some cases been used too much and in other cases (more frequent) used too little. There is a danger whenever one social institution is improved that it will become overburdened with responsibilities which should properly be assigned to a parallel service or agency. The participants in the Symposium, believing firmly in the need for extended and improved guardianship services in all countries, also expressed their conviction that the need for guardianship can and should be prevented in many individual cases. Certainly, the development and application of a comprehensive system of services for training and rehabilitation of retarded children and adults with various degrees of handicap can contribute to the growth of retarded persons' potential for self management. However, the participants also believe that, in addition to the institution of formal guardianship, a parallel service of personal counselling is required, available to mentally handicapped persons who, if they receive appropriate guidance and advice on a continuing basis from a counsellor who has earned their confidence, may not require formal guardianship. For this reason recommendations have been included looking toward the development of such a service along with the renovation of the theory and practice of guardianship itself."[3]

If all that is required in the particular case is help on a voluntary basis involving friendship and support, consideration should be given to the further development of programs offering these features, through voluntary and service organizations.

When, however, the protection required involves the exercise of legal rights, powers, duties and responsibilities, one must look to a formalized system of guardianship having its derivation in statutory enactment. It is a matter far more serious than simple friendship and support for which, it makes sense, no laws should be required.

The creation of a new or extension of an existing agency to deal in guardianship matters is herein proposed. This agency should be known as the "Guardianship Authority".

Protecting the person

The law has, for centuries, provided the means whereby the financial interests of the mentally handicapped have been protected. This has not, for the most part, been true of the personal interests involved. Surely the need for personal protection is just as great, if not greater, than that for financial protection?

The imbalance involved was recognized in the United States by the Task Force on Law of the President's Panel on Mental Retardation.

> "Guardianship is a mechanism through which the court, acting for society, 'guards' the rights and liberties of a retarded person when he cannot guard them for himself. It accomplishes this by transferring the legal power of choice in certain personal (or financial) matters from the retarded person to another who is able and willing to exercise it. In the past the law has seemed to place more emphasis on the protection of property rights of the retarded than on the protection of their personal rights. Both are important and we would seek to redress the balance."[4]

The protection of property aspects can to an extent, provide some measure of personal protection. However, it stands to reason that those without any property are at a greater disadvantage, since they would not even receive that protection. The deficiency in law of protection on the personal side seems to be almost universal, a point made in the Conclusions of the Symposium on Guardianship of the Mentally Retarded held in San Sebastian, Spain in 1969.

> "Although the laws of almost all countries provide for the appointment of guardians for persons who cannot adequately protect their own interests, it is a fact that in many countries these appointments are only made when the person has property which has to be administered. Since it is customary in many countries to give guardians a percentage of the property they administer, there is often difficulty in recruiting guardians (other than family members) for wards who are not wealthy. Since most of the mentally retarded have little property they have seldom enjoyed the benefits of guardianship.
>
> Even when guardians are appointed, both they and the appointing courts view their function as primarily one of managing the funds, conserving them for the ward's benefit and representing the ward in contracting with others, so that these others may be protected in the contractual relationship. In these cases insufficient attention is usually paid to the importance of decisions affecting the ward's personal life."[5]

A study of the laws and practices in Canada indicate that the situation falls within that of most other countries. Too little attention in law is paid to the protection of the personal aspects. This is not to say that no attention whatsoever is paid to these aspects. Indeed, there are all kinds of persons, agencies and organizations which, in many ways, help the mentally handicapped on the personal side. However, these and many others who would like to help are restricted. There is a limit as to what help can be given when the helper has no special legal status. Some would prefer to bolster existing agencies and forget about a system of guardianship. They say that there is *de facto* guardianship now. While this may be true, the level of guardianship available in this sense falls far short of what is actually needed. Our social worker correspondents cite numerous instances of adult retardates floating helplessly despite the existence of the current help available.

Criteria for guardianship

Throughout this book, the guardian is seen as both a "shield" against exploitation and misjudgment, and a "guide" or teacher to successful social adaptation. The analysis later in this chapter of the functions of a guardian explores the manner in which such assistance may be provided. The most crucial issue must be to demarcate the class of persons to whom guardianship should be applied. The general answer will be that it should be applied to those who need it because they are not now functioning adequately on their own.

It may be that certain persons who are not well adapted socially will grow in ability in the process of muddling through the problems of life. This learning process is generally assumed for everyone. There are clearly a great many persons, however, who appear manifestly unable to learn to cope for themselves. Whether this inability is a consequence of an innate defect or the nature of the experiences to which they have been subjected, such persons undergo often inordinate misfortune. It is for their benefit that the guardianship scheme has been conceived and formulated.

What, then, should be taken as indications of the need for, or the likelihood of benefit from, the provision of guardianship?

　　　　　　　　CRITERIA FOR GUARDIANSHIP

One point is very clear. Mere intellectual ability is an inadequate determinant. Intelligence is whatever a test measures when used as the definition of intelligence.

Performance on intelligence tests does not necessarily correspond to social adaptation. Further, grave doubts are conceded by professionals in the use of these tests as to the actual accuracy of any of them in measuring intelligence.

Determination of the need for guardianship must be a process considering intelligence but persuaded by functioning ability.

> "A person who is managing to adjust in society, who supports himself, stays out of trouble with the law, and does not squander his money is 'normal', and such overt social behaviour should take precedence over any measurement on a psychological test."[6]

The decision to appoint a guardian should not, then, be a function of examinations of psychological or medical conditions. It is behavior which is the crucial determinant.

The integrity of the social scientist and the legislator force an awareness that official standards of behavior in our society are essentially those of the middle-class. Evidence has been noted earlier in this book that much of the retardation of social abilities may be traced to conditions of poverty and cultural deprivation. It would appear that as much as three-fourths of retardation is not attributable to any known cause.

The devising of standards indicating a need for guardianship involves deciding whether to permit a ward to develop to a successful and happy coping with life that is consonant with the values of a lower socio-economic class.

Certain standards may be postulated as "absolutes". Illness, victimization, criminality, danger, poverty and a debilitating lack of education are most certainly not in any sense desirable for anyone. Existence in any of these conditions *without the apparent ability to so manage oneself or one's affairs as to alleviate the problem* is strong evidence of need for guardianship services.

Evidence that a retardate is foolishly dissipating or squandering his assets, and will suffer thereby, may be an indication for guardianship – albeit perhaps restricted – that could as well be categorized as an "absolute" standard. It is in essence the foregoing category of conditions upon which child welfare statutes base a finding of "need for protection". Expansion and specification of these conditions may be very usefully seen by reference to the examination of those statutes included in this book.

It should be restated that guardianship involves such a deprivation of independence and rights that serious civil liberties issues must not be forgotten. In that context, the extension of the criteria for guardianship beyond the realm of basic standards for a reasonable life may very well be out of the question. Advanced education, marked social grace and skills, and affluence are not goals which would justify the imposition of guardianship. Lack of such advantages should not be included in any formulation of criteria. If the ward's successful integration into the community is the *raison d'être* of the guardianship proposal, beyond the achievement of that goal, the scheme should attempt no more than to secure the opportunity of advancement for the ward *if he seeks out that social betterment*.

In assessing the meaning of any indications for guardianship, it would be well for the court to be provided with multi-disciplinary advice. The social circumstances of the individual, his organic disabilities if any, and his intellectual standing will be factors vitally important to an understanding of the reasons for the overt behavior and the apparent capacity to change it alone.

Reference must be made to certain aspects of the environment of proposed wards. Many, while adults, and most, while children, have parents able to provide some care and natural guardianship. The existence of parents should not however be considered a contradiction for appointment of a guardian. Either as assistance for parents or reserve held in abeyance, the appointment should follow meeting of the statutory criteria. Similarly the existence of agencies or friends rendering advice or assistance should not be a bar to guardianship. Finally, the fact of reception of special services training, or institutionalization should not militate against guardianship. Neither, of course, should the latter factors be considered a reason for guardianship unless relevant as evidence of the general standard of social dysfunction.

The last point to be made – and a crucial one – is that a guardianship order should extend no further than supported by evidence of dysfunction. Many disabled persons are competent to handle certain matters and for those in that position it would be a serious mistake to impose a guardianship unlimited in scope.

Procedures for determination

Having accepted the need for a system of guardianship and settled upon the criteria for the purpose, it now should be considered how and in what form the determination would best be made. In this regard, there are innumerable possibilities. Essentially, the issue is whether the determination should be made in a court or outside the court system.

Some have presumed that the system should follow that employed in the system of admission to mental hospitals in the particular country. The Expert Committee on Mental Health of the World Health Organization made no specific recommendation in this regard, but did state: "In countries where compulsory admission to a mental hospital is dependent on a judicial order, the establishing of extramural supervision would presumably be a judicial function. In others, where compulsory admission to a mental hospital depends on the next of kin and the psychiatrist, the same procedure would presumably be followed in establishing extramural supervision."[7] As an example, the *Mental Health Act, 1959*[8] in England observes the thoughts of the Expert Commitee since, for the purpose of a guardianship application, it prescribes a procedure analogous to that to be used in an application for admission to hospital for treatment which requires the support of medical recommendation. In the case of a guardianship application, the application must be forwarded with medical recommendations to the local health authority, rather than to the hospital as with the application for admission to hospital. To follow this plan in Canada, where compulsory admission to a psychiatric facility is based upon medical documentation, would see the use of a system outside the courts. All matters considered, the conclusion reached in this book is that guardianship proceedings should be a matter for the courts. Court proceedings are required before a child is found to be in need of protection under child welfare legislation and an individual who is the subject of guardianship proceedings should have the same rights as a child in such case. Medical certification as a measure of compulsory mental hospitalization may be appropriate for compulsory mental hospital admission since, under forward-looking mental health legislation in Canada, there seems to be a tendency to require a situation of immediacy as a condition precedent to hospitalization against the will of the proposed patient. Even though some might say that civil rights are not as well protected under a system of medical certification to hospital, such an avenue of approach may be necessary under the emergency circumstances that might exist. On the other hand, the question of guardianship has more the character of long term planning. Needless to say, a physician is not as well equipped to determine the need for guardianship as he is for hospitalization. A court would much better be able to weigh all of the evidence adduced. Even if the forum is a court, medical and other expert opinion could and should be part of the evidence which the court takes into account. There is no doubt but that multi-disciplinary resources are required to assist in the decision and, accordingly, it could be a board of expert professionals outside the court system. Yet, fears have been expressed that without a court system a possible result – particularly in borderline cases – would be harsh and oppressive interference with individual rights. Some refer to the appointment of a guardian, especially if the ward would rather decline, as a questionable imposition with implications so serious that the full process of the courts is necessary to ensure that guardianship is a measure of protection rather than something which an individual should be protected from. Although it may be considered an artificial point, there seems to be a great deal of merit in the suggestion that a guardian appointed by a court of law might feel a deeper sense of responsibility than if appointed otherwise.

The Task Force on Law in the United States does not see the matter as an issue and simply presumes that the matter will be dealt with by a court.[9]

At the international level, the participants at the San Sebastian Symposium, while allowing some room for flexibility, clearly showed a court preference, as may be seen from the following excerpt of the Symposium Conclusions.

> "The tribunal or decision-making body should be a court. However, consistent with national law, an administrative body acting judicially might be used. If the latter is used, it should not be part of an agency which renders services to the retarded, and there should be provisions for appeal to the courts. The judge or chairman of the decision-making body should be a lawyer, preferably one with a knowledge of the mentally retarded and special competence in dealing with their needs."[10]

Having decided that the appropriate forum will be a court, there is the question, of course, whether it should be an existing court or a special type of court to be created for this purpose. Mental incompetency proceedings in Canada, described earlier in this book, are now within the jurisdiction (with minor exceptions) of the Supreme Court of a province. This may be most suitable with respect to the protection of the estate of the individual, for which such proceedings are almost exclusively used, but hardly so when personal protection is being considered. Supreme Courts do not have social service staff attached to them. Such a staff could represent an essential ingredient in assisting the court in arriving at sound decisions in matters of guardianship.

There are already in existence suitable courts which could, without major difficulty, accommodate guardianship proceedings. Reference is made to Juvenile and Family Courts which now have jurisdiction with respect to, amongst other matters, children in need of protection under child welfare legislation. These courts are known by different names in the various provinces and, during recent years, have undergone in a number of jurisdictions a certain evolution which seems yet to be completed. With the various professionals who are either part of the staff of these courts or at their disposal, it becomes increasingly clear that the Juvenile and Family Courts should be invested with jurisdiction in guardianship proceedings. Other positive factors in selecting these courts include their built-in capacity for the holding of informal proceedings and the greater degree of confidentiality associated with them as opposed to the situation in adult courts. Ample support for selecting these courts is found in the statement of the San Sebastian Conclusions to the effect that if the decision-making body is to be a court, "consideration should be given to conferring jurisdiction upon a special court, as for example, a family or children's court."[11]

While the advantages of a system of guardianship for those who truly need it are evident, to apply it to those who could manage without it would be most unwise and unfair. For this reason, individual civil rights should play a crucial role in the proceedings.

The initiation of proceedings should be upon application to a judge of the court by an interested party, including a relative or friend of the individual, or an officer of the guardianship agency (referred to later in this chapter). On this score, the San Sebastian Conclusions note that it should be possible for a person on his own application to secure the appointment of a guardian with specified duties "where it is found to be in the best interests of the applicant and of the community",[12] and this makes good sense. Where there is no one else to take guardianship proceedings which are indicated, it should be the duty of the guardianship agency to do so.

Notice of a hearing should be given to all concerned, including the potential ward, the person then having his charge, if any, and the guardianship agency which should, as a matter of law, be a necessary party to the proceedings. The notice should be in simple language and explain the rights involved. Conceivably, it will be clear that the potential ward would not comprehend such a notice and, in such case, the judge should be able to dispense with notice to him. Dispensing with such notice should not be done lightly since it is, of course, begging the question.

At the hearing itself, the potential ward should have to be present unless, for good reason, the judge dispenses with the need for this attendance. According to the Task Force on Law, when this happens "the judge should see the retarded person, and the reason for non-attendance should be specified in the record."[13] The Conclusions of the San Sebastian Symposium indicate that if the individual is incapable of being present, "the decision-making tribunal has a duty to visit him at the place where he is."[14]

As to the conduct of the hearing, it should be informal. However, it should be a full evidentiary hearing. The Task Force on Law believes that the hearings "should not generally take place in open court but should be held in the judge's chambers or another private place agreeable to all concerned."[15]

Not only should the individual who is the subject of the proceedings have a right to legal representation, it should be mandatory. This point is recognized both by the Task Force on Law and the San Sebastian Conclusions.[16] Without question, the legal aid plans of the various provinces should embrace guardianship proceedings within the scope of the legal aid services which they provide.

Considering the costs of the proceedings, the San Sebastian Symposium noted that the establishment of the need for guardianship and the appointment of a guardian when necessary is in the public interest and, in this regard, had the following to say.

"Because it is desirable that there be no significant deterrent to the initiation of appropriate proceedings, it is recommended that the parties themselves not be required to bear the costs of the proceedings, including representation. If, within the framework of a particular jurisdiction, costs must be assessed, they should be minimal with liberal provisions for waiver. In such cases, attorney as well as members of the tribunal, are to receive salaries or other compensation from other appropriate sources."[17]

According to the San Sebastian Conclusions, guardianship proceedings should be "as informal as possible consistent with fairness and the preservation of civil rights."[18] The Task Force on Law of the President's Panel on Mental Retardation was of the view that the rights of the retarded person would not be adequately protected unless the hearing is used as an instrument of genuine cooperation and exchange of ideas between the court and representatives of the care-taking professions. It went on to say that the court "must have at its command a comprehensive clinical evaluation covering medical, psychological, educational and social factors.[19] On this score, the San Sebastian Symposium was of the view that the decision-making body should have the recommendation of a multi-professional and interdisciplinary team with respect to the issues to be decided: in particular, the decision-making body "should be required by statute to avail itself of the expertise of behavioral scientists or, in the alternative, such expertise should be represented in the membership of the decision-making body."[20] In the context of this book it would make good sense for the guardianship agency (referred to later in this chapter) to present to the court a documented assessment prepared by the agency. This agency would have the multi-professional resources at its disposal for the purpose.

Although it is to be hoped that guardianship proceedings will not be contentious, that possibility cannot be precluded. Indeed, the potential ward should always be consulted as to his wishes. In the event that he does not wish to become a ward, then through his legal representative, there should be full opportunity to oppose any declaration that he is in need of guardianship and to present evidence – professional or otherwise – to that effect.

Should the judge find that the individual is not in need of guardianship, the matter would end there.

Should the judge find the individual to be in need of guardianship as defined by statute, he should declare him to be so. The judge should then select and appoint a guardian, having regard to the available resources and the particular needs of the ward. Guidance as to the selection of the guardian should be offered by the guardianship agency. In the case where there is no suitable person or body willing to act, the judge should automatically appoint the guardianship agency to serve in that capacity.

While the general powers and responsibilities of a guardian would be prescribed within a legislative framework, the judge should have the power to impose any conditions of guardianship which he deems in the best interests of the ward. In other words, the court should tailor-make a scheme which is to be followed in the guardianship arrangement. In this regard, the Task Force on Law of the President's Panel on Mental Retardation had the following to report.

> "But where legal guardianship of any kind is required, it should be carefully adapted to the specific requirements of the case. For some, of course, a comprehensive guardianship will be needed. But we urge that, as far as possible, mentally retarded adults be allowed freedom – even freedom to make their own mistakes. We suggest the development of limited guardianships of the adult person, with the scope of the guardianship specified in the judicial order. For example, the guardian's discretion to arrange for care for the retarded person in a foster home, boarding home, or other day or residential care facility should be defined in the court's order.

Plenary guardianship should be reserved for those who are judicially determined to be incapable of undertaking routine day-to day decisions and who are found to be incapable of basic self-management. Where this is the case, discretion or even objection on the part of the ward can have no relevant meaning. It follows that his liberty to choose place of residence and regimen of care must be removed by the court. But the court is properly concerned with the generic need for protection and care, not with its substantive details. This is where the duties of the guardian begin. The law may properly leave to him the decision whether to arrange for family care or select some sort of private or public institutional care for his charge.

In the case of a retarded adult whose disabilities do not preclude the conduct of everyday affairs but are sufficiently severe to make unlikely the prudent management of substantial business or financial interests, we recommend the institution of a conservatorship, handling property problems only. Indeed, even when the person must be placed under guardianship, the handling of any substantial amount of property might well be vested in a conservator especially qualified to handle the particular kind of assets involved rather than in the personal guardian. We do not suggest any general rule since this is an area where the significant factors will vary from case to case, but the two functions should be severable when the occasion warrants."[21]

In San Sebastian, the difficulties involved where the guardianship could not be tailor-made to the needs of the ward were described as follows.

"Although it is possible in most countries to establish guardianship of property without invoking guardianship of person, this distinction does not really reflect the character of the guardianship most appropriate for the protection of the mentally retarded whose faculties are only partially impaired. The result of this deficiency in the legal system has been twofold: on the one hand there has been a reluctance to invoke guardianship on behalf of a person who needs only moderate protection, since to do so would clearly place him under greater legal incapacity than necessary; on the other hand, where the need for protection is pressing but not complete, it has often been considered necessary to place a seriously retarded person under plenary guardianship when a more limited form would have been sufficient, if it had been available."[22]

It follows, therefore, that the court should make a careful assessment of the particular guardianship arrangement so that the level of guardianship ordered will best suit all concerned. The court could, in addition, include a requirement that the guardian report to the court at stipulated intervals.

The guardianship order should remain in force until terminated by further court order for which an application might be made by any person who has an interest including the ward, the guardian or the guardianship agency. There should be an appeal from any order of the court in guardianship matters to a higher court, depending upon the court system in the particular province.

If, during the force of a guardianship order, the guardian dies, becomes incapacitated from performing his functions or is unwilling to continue as guardian, the guardianship agency should automatically, and without further court order, become guardian until such time as another guardian is available. In such case, the guardianship agency should investigate the possibilities of obtaining another guardian and, at such time as it has found what it considers a suitable one, it should make application to the court to replace itself with a new guardian. Where the guardianship agency is of the opinion that a guardian is not exercising his duties properly, it should be its duty to move the court for a change of guardian. In emergency circumstances, the guardianship agency should have the power to intervene and assume guardianship of a person who is a ward on the condition that, within a prescribed period of time, it apply to the court for ratification of this step.

Timing of proceedings

An individual may require a guardian for most or all of his life or at a particular stage during it. Some might be in a position that they would, but not for the protection they are currently receiving, otherwise need a guardian. The latter situation is demonstrated by the case of a retarded person who is under the care of his parents and faring well. Should his parents become incapable of looking after him or die, the situation would be entirely different. The fact is that, in many instances, a person can be identified as one who is in need of guardianship which, in a sense, is already being fulfilled.

In the event that this fulfilment suddenly collapses, the crisis is created. This is the concern expressed by the parents of the retarded who say: "What will happen to my retarded son or daughter when I die?" There are a number of reasons, consequently, why proceedings in advance of the actual need should be permitted and perhaps even encouraged by law.

From a practical point of view, there is the question of identification. While the parents are alive, who knows better than they that their child is one who is in need of special protection. There should be provision for them to identify, in a legal fashion, their child as one who, in the future, may very well need a guardian.

Significant justification for taking proceedings in advance of actual need is reflected in the wisdom of proper planning. If a person were declared one in need of guardianship, then when the actual need did arise, much of the groundwork would have already been laid. Parents could, in a number of ways, acquaint the retardate with what may be in store for him. Indeed, the parent of a child would surely feel much better if his child was swimming in the absence of the parent, had the parent earlier taught the child how to swim. Where it is contemplated that the immediate guardian, when the guardianship commences, will be an agency, there would be good cause for the parent to familiarize the retardate with the workings of the agency. Conversely, the staff at the agency could become familiar with the retardate. In this way, the necessary confidence of the retardate in his potential guardian could be built and a smoother transitional period can be expected.

Moreover, the advance proceedings make it possible for the "machine" to be "ready to roll" at the critical time. Indeed, the initial period – one of adjustment, one of resettlement and probably one just following tragedy – is the crucial one. Certainly during that period, if ever, the services of a guardian can be a significant determinant in the future course of the ward's life.

All of the above is not even to mention a positive factor associated with the type of early planning contemplated – "peace of mind". How reassuring it would be to parents of the retarded to be able to sit back and say we have just prearranged the future of our son or daughter. Indeed, the law regulates the prearrangement of funerals in many jurisdictions.[23] The person can safely die knowing with confidence that the final arrangements will be conducted according to his wishes. Prearranging the future care and supervision of a retarded person is a matter which should be within the present grasp of every one who is now charged with this responsibility.

It follows, therefore, that where the known need is clear for guardianship, the need should be capable of establishment at an early stage. To have a person declared in need of guardianship who does not currently require a guardian is a form of insurance which would fill a sorrowful vacuum.

Identity of guardian

The Expert Committee on Mental Health of the World Health Organization some years ago considered the matter of guardianship, but they did "not wish to make specific recommendations regarding the type of body which should have such a supervisory function . . . since this must depend on the situation in any given country". With this we would agree. In Canada, matters of "Property and Civil Rights" are, according to the *British North America Act, 1867*,[24] within the exclusive legislative jurisdiction of each province. It follows, therefore, that there is a strong argument for stating that in our country the answer to the question of who or what bodies may be appropriate guardians must depend on the situation in any given province. Nonetheless, there are basic principles which should be respected universally. If these principles are respected, it is conceivable that their translation into practice will resemble an entirely different form from one jurisdiction to another, but this is not to be seen as a disadvantage. Indeed, what we are seeking is full utilization of resources within the existing or projected framework of a given province.

The identity of the guardian being such a crucial matter, it is considered important here to recite the relevant text of the Report of the Task Force on Law of the President's Panel on Mental Retardation.

> "In appointing guardians, courts should look first to parents and other close relatives, but not necessarily in the order of formal kinship. The person most able, best situated and most motivated for the task should be sought. The guardian should express in his will his advice as to his successor.
>
> Guardians would be encouraged to fulfill their obligations if they were upheld and assisted by community organizations. In addition to the present voluntary associations, considerable support could come from the establishment of a state protective service for the retarded. Such a service could provide consultation and referral for the retarded and their families, for employers and other persons interested in working with the retarded.
>
> The protection of guardianship should not be denied where there is no suitable relative available, or where the retarded person's financial assets are too small adequately to compensate a private person serving as guardian. Studies should be made to consider how best to deal with this problem. One possible solution is the establishment, perhaps through a state protective service, of a program of public guardianship of the person. Although guardianship might then be formally vested in a state agency, duties would actually be carried out by individual staff members, emphasizing the personal nature of the guardianship.
>
> We do not wish to preclude the possibility that a private non-profit agency or group might be instrumental in providing the personal attention, stability and continuity which gives vitality to guardianship of the retarded. Such bodies are found in Europe and there are a few of them in the United States. We recommend, however, that only those expressly chartered for this purpose and licensed by a state protective agency be looked to by the courts as sources of personal guardians."[25]

On the question of who should be the guardian, the following is an excerpt from the Conclusions of the San Sebastian Symposium.

> "If the retarded person has parents who are willing and able to act as guardians there will naturally be a preference for appointing them for this function, but this

preference should not preclude another choice when there is evidence that this would be in the best interests of the retarded person. As for relative other than parents, it was recognized that other family members frequently make excellent guardians, but there was no general support for the idea that any presumptive preference be accorded to them.

The crux of the problem, in many cases is to find another suitable guardian when there is no appropriate family member available. Parents may give valuable assistance to the appointing authorities by recommending (in their wills or otherwise) persons whom they consider suitable successor guardians, but, again, this recommendation should not be considered binding, since additional factors may have to be considered by the appointing authority at the time. As always, the best interests of the retarded person must be given priority.

There are some persons who should not be considered as guardians because of the possibility of conflict of interest. These include a person who is performing some professional or other remunerated service for the ward – as physician, teacher, landlady, superintendent of an institution, attorney, etc. or who is employed in one of the service systems in which the ward is enrolled.

Among the factors to be considered in the selection of a guardian is accessibility. It is not possible to say with precision how often the guardian should see his ward of how much time he should spend attending to his ward's affairs, since these will vary from situation to situation, but it is clear that if he is to give the necessary time and maintain direct contact, he cannot live too far away or to be too busy with other responsibilities. Much will also depend on whether the guardianship is plenary or limited. Even if he is a full time professional guardian, he should not have too many wards. In addition, the issue of continuity has to be considered. The person appointed should, on the face of it, be one who is likely to be able to serve for a significant period of time; another factor is the preference of the ward himself, if it can be determined.

Because of the importance attached to continuity, serious consideration was given in the deliberations of the Symposium to the possible role of voluntary associations, and more particularly parents associations, as guardians. There is some precedent for this approach, in the child welfare field and also in recent legislation pertaining to the retarded adult, such as that enacted in 1968 in France. There is also precedent for permitting that appointment of an official who holds a certain position in a public or private organization, such as the head of a society for the protection of children, or an official public guardian, as in the Canton of Geneva. This official in turn has the responsibility and duty to delegate his actual guardianship function with respect to each ward to another suitable person who can, in a practical sense, carry it out. Neither of these models was universally acceptable to the participants, however. Strong preference was expressed for vesting guardianship in an individual person, rather than in a board, or a corporation, or an office, and also for having that person directly appointed by and responsible to the tribunal which adjudicates guardianship matters, rather than being merely the delegate of the person named. The element of accountability entered into these discussions."[26]

To present in a meaningful manner suggestions made as to who or what bodies could serve as guardians on the Canadian scene is to enter in what might be considered by many as an exercise in utter confusion. The documentation of the suggestions which follows may, however, provide some insight.

Parents are said to be the natural persons to serve as guardians for their retarded offspring, but sometimes they overprotect and are unsuitable. In some instances, under the guise of protection of a retarded child from competition or social expectations of the community, parents may unwittingly exploit the child so that he becomes the family drudge and is isolated from normal social contacts when he becomes an adult. Other family members or special friends are put forward as potential guardians because of their apparent close relationship. This relationship may not exist in fact and, accordingly, they could be poor guardians: moreover, a conflict of interest could exist.

Particular classes of persons have been the subject of recommendation as appropriate guardians: a new classification of foster parents trained in the care and supervision of adult retardates; or married couples who have had happy homes and whose children have grown and married; or parents of the retarded who do or have properly cared for their retarded children, and who could be good guardians for other retarded children because of the similar circumstances involved; or persons involved with the operation of group homes who could act as parent substitutes.

Other suggestions refer to professionals and non-professionals: for example, thoroughly qualified social workers; or intelligent lay persons trained by a panel of professionals as consultants. The responsibility of a guardian is great and some believe that a guardian should be more than one individual: others that guardianship should be on a one-to-one basis. With respect to those guardians who bear no special relationship to the ward, remuneration is felt by many to be an essential ingredient.

Looking away from the individual and to the agency (public or private), it is felt an important fact that an agency can live forever. Continuity can be guaranteed by a dossier and staff members who read it. As to whether it should be an existing or projected agency, the concern of adding to the load of already existing agencies is voiced, thereby pointing to the possibility of creating a new agency. In response to this, it is claimed that there are too many agencies now. A new agency could serve to coordinate existing services and draw on them.

As to whether the responsibility should lie within the public or private sector, it is said that it should fall upon provincial governments because guardianship appears to be a long term need. Some feel the government should look after financing and standard setting, but not provide the direct service: a voluntary agency should be designated as agent for the purpose; or an agency should provide the service on a "fee-for-service" basis. Others feel that government funds mean loss of freedom to act.

Particular suggestions include provincial departments of welfare, because of their responsibility for screening adults now regarding disability payments. District welfare offices or local welfare departments are put forward because their administrative structures and field staff resources are suitable.

Additional suggestions include provincial departments of health; or mental health divisions of those departments, since they already administer institutions for the retarded; or institutions for the retarded themselves, since they are already multi-disciplinary and could utilize their out-patient services; or medical rehabilitation branches of the departments of health; or local health departments; or public health nurses.

Provincial agencies involved with correctional services; or probation services have also been suggested as appropriate guardians.

We have already dealt with officials known as the Public Trustee, Official Guardian, Public Curator and their counterparts. While they have been suggested as suitable guardians, it is pointed out that generally their services are costly, and they act in a slow and cumbersome fashion. They are, hardly without exception, committees of the estate and not of the person: they are not guardians of the "person", but of the "purse". Personal matters are considered only insofar as they affect the estate. Their offices do not have the social service staff without which they could not perform even a small degree of personal supervision of the type which would be required in a guardianship arrangement. While the possibility that these offices could become equipped to offer a scheme of guardianship of the person cannot be excluded, it seems to be the consensus of opinion of the officials in charge of them that they are opposed to accepting such a responsibility. In a brief prepared on behalf of the Government of Ontario for the Federal-Provincial Conference on Retardation held in Ottawa in October, 1964, it was stated that the "need for personal guardianship beyond that provided by the Public Trustee or Official Guardian is now widely recognized as an essential part of a comprehensive service for the mentally retarded."

Because basic human rights are involved, human rights commissions of the various provinces have been mentioned as potential guardians. So have local juvenile and family courts, systems of legal aid and ombudsman.

Private and voluntary agencies have been the subject of suggestion for assuming the responsibilities of guardianship. The Canadian Association for the Mentally Retarded at the national, provincial and local levels is one of them. They are said to have the commitment and the sensitivity to needs and could promote national uniformity. On the local level, only some of these bodies have the resources necessary.

Other existing bodies, the names of which have been brought to the attention of this Project, include the Canadian Mental Health Association at the national, provincial and local levels; Big Brothers; Big Sisters; and the John Howard Society. Rehabilitation societies, settlement houses, social planning councils, university women's clubs and churches have, as well, been mentioned.

By far the most significant possibility of an existing agency which might be suitable is the child protection agency, often called the "children's aid society". The type of services contemplated in the guardianship program are, in many respects, now provided to children under child protection laws by these agencies. It would be a logical extension of their services to assume responsibility for the mentally retarded of all ages. They have or should have the structure, experience and expertise indicated. Their staff are well aware of the problems and repeatedly express vital concern about their retarded wards whose wardship is about to terminate because of the maximum age having been attained under the child welfare laws. It has been said that parents do not die when a child reaches 18 or 21: why should the child protection agency die? There is a good argument, in some cases, against termination upon the reaching of the statutory age. Certainly, the extension of the services of these agencies would make good sense from the point of view of continuity. Whether or not these agencies have the inclination for such an extension is something which has not been measured in this book. Our correspondents close to or part of these agencies have been both for and against. Of course, if they are currently burdened and perhaps greatly overburdened with problems now within their jurisdictional scope, it stands to reason that additional responsibilities would not be welcomed with open arms. All the while, however, the provision to them of additional funds to bolster their staffs and other resources might help to change the attitudes of those who might be considered opposed. At a Panel held in Toronto in 1965, it was a recommendation "that the Acts governing Children's Aid Societies be extended to allow them to take on more staff and to take responsibility for personal guardianship of the mentally retarded regardless of age."[27]

In the final analysis, it is difficult to make any clear recommendations as to who should be guardian. The fact is that suitable guardians may come from a number of sources. It is simply a matter of matching the needs of the ward with the resources in the particular community. What those resources are can be determined only by feasibility studies in that community. For example, an agency in a given community might be eminently suitable to provide services in a guardianship arrangement, whereas its counterpart in another community may be wholly unsuitable. Patterns of community social services vary greatly. Not only is this so, but these patterns are constantly changing. Accordingly, studies on feasibility must take into account what will be the picture of the community social service programs in the future. The creation of a new division within an existing agency might hold the answer. Pilot projects on a limited scale may point the way.

There must be a guardian for every person received into guardianship. Furthermore, there must be a way whereby there is continuity of guardianship so that during the period of wardship the ward is never without a guardian. In only one manner can these conditions be fully met: through the extension or creation of an agency to carry responsibilities in this field. An agency can live forever. Given the appropriate statutory powers and duties, it could ensure the provision of the required services.

The type of agency contemplated would have essentially a *residual* character, exercising authority and performing duties only where needed. It would, however, be bound to act where there is no one else to act. In particular ,it would have the following basic duties:

1 to identify persons who appear to be in need of guardianship where no one else has done so;
2 to take guardianship proceedings where no one else is suitable, available or willing to do so, and where the person appears to be in need of protection;
3 to assume the role of guardian where no one else is willing and appropriate to serve in that capacity;
4 to take proceedings to displace a guardian by substituting another guardian (itself if necessary) to rectify a situation where the existing guardian is not discharging his duties properly;
5 to assume the role of guardian (which would automatically fall upon the agency) when a guardian dies, becomes unwilling or incapacitated.

Even where the guardian is an agency, it will of course, have to work through individuals in the particular guardianship arrangement. It is essential that the agency be equipped to operate effectively at the local level. There is no doubt that the individual guardian, whether or not he has a connection with an agency, must possess certain qualifications and qualities.

"The primary consideration in the selection of a guardian for a particular ward must be the best interests of the ward himself."[28] This is the principle stated in the Report of the Conclusions of the San Sebastian Symposium. It went on to state that he should be a "capable person who has interest in advancing the welfare of the retarded person whose life he is to guide; he should have an understanding of the nature of his ward's particular disability, his potential and actual strengths and weaknesses . . . . a person who understands the social environment, and, in particular should know how to find and use the full range of general and special services and opportunities which can be exploited for the benefit of the retarded . . . . a warm human being, well motivated toward his ward."[29]

Needless to say, the guardian must be one who is flexible and has the ability to sense the need for change. He must be readily accessible to the ward and be prepared to act swiftly in an emergency. He must be a person whom the ward recognizes and trusts. He should have a strong and ever-present concern for the fundamental rights of all human beings and acknowledge that the needs of his ward are not to be subordinated to his (the guardian's) personal judgment.

There is no doubt but that it will be difficult to find good guardians. Without guardians, there can be no system of guardianship: indeed the enactment of a statutory framework for the purpose would represent an exercise in futility. The difficulty of securing the services of appropriate people was expressed as a very great concern at San Sebastian. It was concluded there that those who lack the motivation and long experience of close relatives should at least have training for the task. The development of a "professional guardianship service" was, therefore, foreseen: "the growth of a cadre of qualified persons who will devote part or all of their time to exercising the function of guardianship with respect to a certain limited number of retarded wards."[30] In order to recruit and train sufficient numbers of guardians, it was recognized as necessary to demonstrate the demand. Moreover, it was made clear that for their professional service, guardians would have to receive remuneration. The cost of remuneration could be derived from the ward if he had ample funds available, but it was generally felt that it should come from public funds. There may be scope for voluntary guardians to serve without remuneration. It was felt further that parents' associations must press, "within the voluntary sector" for the development of a "new agency" which would bring together the following elements:

1 provision of counselling services to retarded adults, as well as to family and other individual guardians having a retarded ward (child or adult);
2 development of a training program for prospective guardians (including parents);
3 establishment of a roster of qualified guardians from among whom the association or agency can make recommendations to the appointing authorities;
4 retention of a panel of experts who can assist guardians, as needed, with technical decisions (medical, legal, financial, social);
5 management of a communal trust fund in which small amounts of capital belonging to individual retardates can be combined for more economical management.[31]

Responsibility for the tasks enumerated above was not, for stated reasons, felt appropriate for parents' associations, but it was noted that in certain countries some or all of them may be seen as a public responsibility. In this respect, the five elements listed above are seen as necessary support services to the guardianship agency contemplated and, accordingly, should be part of the plan.

Functions of guardian

It need hardly be said that it would be difficult, if not impossible, to function as a guardian if an individual did not know exactly what were his rights and responsibilities when he was to act in that capacity. In so far as possible, these rights and responsibilities should be defined. Not all of them, of course, can be.

Certain rights and responsibilities can, of course, be defined in legislation itself. These are the general matters which will apply to all guardianship arrangements. Other rights and responsibilities can be prescribed by the court which appoints the guardian and here the court can take into account the particular situation before it. The court would be expected, as part of the particular guardianship arrangement, to prescribe the particulars in this regard. Still others, depending upon the circumstances involved, would have to be determined in the light of the interpretation of the general law applicable.

Looking to one example, under the British *Mental Health Act, 1959*,[32] the effect of a guardianship application is to confer upon the guardians or guardian "to the exclusion of any other person, all such powers as would be exercisable by them or him in relation to the patient if they or he were the father of the patient and the patient were under the age of fourteen years."[33] There is some merit in the guardian acting as a good parent. Generally, he could ensure that everything practicable is done to promote the ward's health – both physical and mental, arrange for matters of residence, education, training, occupation and employment, guide the ward in matters of dealing with others, domestic relations, finance and living problems, and oversee the general welfare and recreation of the ward. One of the crucial issues is whether the guardian should be a "substitute parent" or "substitute ward". In this respect, there is a significant statement contained in the Conclusions of the San Sebastian Symposium.

> "The retarded adult, even one who is under guardianship, should not be regarded merely as 'a child who never grew'. He is usually biologically mature; he has the experience of living, even if he has not gained wisdom from it to the fullest extent. Frequently he aspires to an image of himself as grown man (or woman). He has many of the needs of an adult. Although in certain respects he remains childish, to represent him as having exactly the same status as a minor is misleading and may encourage over-protection which is not in his best interest."[34]

As a general rule, services of a guardian should be "offered" to the ward and be "supportive" in character. Unless absolutely essential to do so, they should not be "imposed" nor have an "oppressive" character. Any imposition should be purely a last resort, since the risk is there that it will destroy the guardianship arrangement.

The underlying goal of a guardian would seem to be to phase himself out of existence. In other words, he should do everything possible to help the ward stand on his own feet in all respects. Once having done so, what could be better than knowing that the guardian is not required any longer? At such a stage, being certain that it is not premature, the guardian should, in conjunction with the ward, take whatever steps are necessary to terminate the guardianship arrangement.

Although it is a very lengthy quotation, it is desirable to recite here what was concluded on the subject of the functions and duties of a guardian at the San Sebastian Symposium.

> "Clearly the duties and functions of guardians will vary with the abilities of the ward and with the degree and character of his handicap, and thus, we assume, with the type of restriction of legal capacity which will have been specified in his particular case. The type and adequacy of the needed general and special services which can be marshalled on the ward's behalf will have bearing on the guardian's role, as will many other circumstances. Yet there are certain duties and functions common to all guardianships, some of which apply also to the role of special counsellor, mentioned earlier.
>
> A basic responsibility of all guardians and counsellors is to maintain close contact with the retarded person or persons for whom they are responsible. They should visit them regularly, get to know them as individuals, with their own potentialities, abilities, shortcomings, and needs. The guardian or counsellor should seek to develop an aura of mutual confidence and trust, and make an active effort to see that the retarded person participates as much as is appropriate in the life of his community.
>
> In their relations with the retarded persons for whom they are responsible, both

guardians and counsellors should make it a rule to respect the wishes of the retarded person whenever possible and to allow him to make his own choices when feasible. The guardian who has a mandatory power based on the specific restrictions of legal capacity of the retarded person, should make every attempt to use this power only when it is necessary to help the retarded person in areas where he is particularly handicapped.

Guardians and counsellors have an important role to play in easing the relationships between the retarded and other people, in interpreting their point of view and their needs to neighbours, employers, local shopkeepers, members of the clergy, and persons called on to render professional services.

The guardian has a responsibility to recruit, when necessary, expert services such as those of an attorney or physician. The counsellor should concern himself with the retarded person's own actions in this regard, encouraging him, for example, to visit the dentist regularly.

The guardian or counsellor should also see to it that any civil duties are performed by or on behalf of the ward, such as, for example, securing an identity card or registering for military service or paying any imposts, if these are required. At the same time the guardian will see that the appropriate authorities are informed, to the extent necessary, of the relevant special circumstances arising from the condition of mental retardation.

Conversely, the guardian or counsellor should advise or assist or act for the ward in relation to securing his personal and civil rights. For example, if he is entitled to social security benefits, or other insurance coverage, public or private, the proper steps should be taken at the proper time. The application of fair labour standards to the ward should be assured.

As one of his most important functions, the guardian should select and mobilize appropriate community resources, drawing on both the generic and specialized services for education, rehabilitation, health care, recreation, employment, social services and specialized day or residential care, as needed. To do so he must necessarily familiarize himself with the range of applicable services and programs offered by public, voluntary and proprietary agencies. The task requires initiative and good judgment even in communities with well developed service systems, and will demand even more resourcefulness in less well endowed areas. It is to be hoped that guardians will take an active part, along with natural parents and other interested citizens, in promoting, through public and voluntary effort, the development of needed services where these are lacking.

The counsellor, although not authorized to act on behalf of the retarded adults whom he advises, should have similar information concerning the resources. As appropriate in each case, he should encourage initiative on the part of the retarded adult, complementing this with action of his own, as necessary, to assist the retarded person to secure access to the programs most likely to benefit him. In short, the guardian or counsellor should be a vigorous advocate and spokesman for the retarded person, both in the public and private sectors.

Even when the retarded person is enrolled in a well organized program of daily activity or in a residential facility, public or private, the guardian has a responsibility to keep track of his progress and to review the appropriateness of the placement, to assure himself that the service is as represented, and that the retarded person is not being mistreated or neglected. He should concern himself particularly with the curtailments of personal liberties which often occur in institutions, the use of restraints or corporal punishment, or simple failure to provide the retarded person with opportunity for sufficient activity to maintain his physical and emotional health.

Where the ward is enrolled in a comprehensive service system, the guardian or counsellor should insist on being advised of any significant plans for changing his ward's programme.

Usually the guardian will have responsibility for looking after the ward's finances, as well as guiding his personal decisions. In some instances, this may be his primary function, in which case it is hoped that he will be able and willing to act informally as a counsellor also. The participants of the Symposium felt strongly that, contrary to previous practice, the guardian's role as personal advocate, as outlined above, transcends the fiscal management role, and that where the guardian has aptitude for the role of personal advocate but not for financial management, he can be instructed to use professional fiduciary services, as necessary. Despite their decided preference for consolidating all powers in a single guardian, the participants did not wish to exclude entirely the possibility of recourse to a divided guardianship, separating guardianship of person and estate, where special circumstances justify it. In some countries such co-guardianships are well accepted.

It must be particularly emphasized that the administration of the economic affairs of the retarded person should be based solely on the interest of that person. Property should be maintained and conserved to the extent this is beneficial for the retarded person, but it must not be forgotten that such economic resources as the retarded person may have should be used for his own advantage, and, whenever feasible, according to his own desires."[35]

With respect to residence, the guardian could canvass the resources in the community and ensure that the ward is placed in a setting which best suits his needs and desires, and these should remain always under constant review. The guardian could go a long way in preventing institutionalization. A good number of persons who are now institutionalized probably could remain at home if provided with guardians. Where institutionalization is indicated, the guardian could facilitate it, enabling the admission to occur smoothly. The guardianship should, under no circumstances, terminate upon admission. It was recommended at the Federal-Provincial Conference on Mental Retardation in Canada in 1964 that "the principles of guardianship be studied with regard to [the problem] of . . . continuity (i.e. not discontinued if child enters a hospital school) . . .".[36] Indeed, if a retarded individual is in an institution and does not have a guardian, he should have one. The Task Force on Law of the President's Panel on Mental Retardation had the following to say in this regard.

"We believe that all retarded persons living in institutions, but not admitted on their own application, should have outside guardians who could check on the ward's treatment, care and release possibilities. As elsewhere, the guardian would have responsibility for maintaining contact with the ward wherever he lived or received care, and of reviewing his progress with those who have professional responsibility for him. The guardian should remain throughout the spokesman for his ward, the lay interpreter of his needs, the partisan who watches over him and his interests, his alter ego in the assertion of legal rights."[37]

While the ward is in an institution, the guardian could serve as the "community link" ensuing that the rights of the ward are protected fully. Should there be a need for consent to treatment or surgery, the guardian could, under certain circumstances, provide the required consent. (The same could apply to such consents required for the ward in a general hospital.) In the event that there is some contention about the property of the institutionalization, the guardian could serve as the applicant on behalf of the ward to a statutory review board for the purposes of resolving this issue. The guardian could generally work with the hospital authorities with a view to the discharge of the ward into the community and have the stage set in this regard. The vital support and direction needed in the post-institutional period of resettlement and adjustment could be provided by the guardian.

As an almost daily routine, everyone enters into variety of contracts. By close contact with his ward, the guardian should be aware of any requirements in this respect. Depending upon the conditions of guardianship, the guardian may – under certain circumstances – act as the legal personality of the ward for the purposes of making contracts. This will overcome a difficulty in the past which saw certain third parties reluctant to deal with the retarded person himself. The guardian could also serve in an advisory capacity whenever the ward proposes to enter into a contract on his own or encounters any difficulty or confusion surrounding it. As the term of guardianship progresses, the guardian could become more and more the friendly counsellor, seeing the ward grow in ability to manage his affairs. Where indicated, the guardian could serve in a protective role against exploitation of the ward by ensuring that all laws dealing with the ward as consumer are observed and enforced.

Should the use of a motor vehicle be applicable, the guardian would be able to match the requirements of the law with the capabilities of his ward. He could assist in the process of arranging for the statutory requirement of testing and issuance of a licence. Not the least important ancillary matter, the guardian should ensure that proper liability insurance is arranged.

In connection with the exercising of the right to vote, the guardian should make certain that the ward is enumerated for the purpose if the law permits. The guardian, in a personal matter of this nature, should guard against anyone – including himself – placing an undue influence upon the ward in respect of how the franchise is exercised. Furthermore, the guardian should be able to assist the ward in the mechanics of attending the polling station and concern himself with training the ward in the responsibilities of citizenship.

Although a guardian is probably not responsible for the torts of a ward, it would be important for him to counsel the ward to keep out of trouble and teach him responsible social behavior.

Concerning the possibility of the ward making a will, the guardian would direct his attention to the issue of testamentary capacity. The guardian should seek legal and medical advice on this issue. In the event that the ward is determined to have testamentary capacity, he should discuss with the ward the manner in which his (the ward's) wishes may best be given effect in the will. In this connection, the guardian must never forget the delicacy of his own position. He should be absolutely certain that there is no question of his having placed undue influence upon the ward for any hope of personal gain.

In the field of crime and corrections, the guardian should endeavor to keep the ward out of trouble and away from bad influences through counselling. If the ward is apprehended for some reason by the police, they could properly deal with the guardian and, under certain circumstances, the matter could end there. In the event that the ward is charged with an offence, the guardian could arrange for legal representation and be helpful in securing bail. It would be the duty of the guardian, through defence counsel, if indicated to bring the existence of retardation to the attention of the court. Should there be a conviction, the guardian might be helpful, again through defence counsel, in submitting to the court what would be the appropriate disposition as to sentence. Probation might be facilitated on the basis of certain undertakings which the guardian could give. If a period of imprisonment is necessary, the guardian could endeavor to see that the ward was placed in a rehabilitation program and, through visitation, act as the community link to the ward. The guardian should check to see that the ward is not abused in prison and prepare him for return to the community. Needless to say, it would be an additional responsibility of the guardian to work for an opportunity of early parole from prison which could certainly be enhanced where the guardian is working toward it.

Concerning the possibility of civil litigation, through close contact with his ward, the guardian should do his best to see that there is no cause for the ward to be sued civilly. At the same time, should the rights of the ward be infringed and civil action be the means of redressing the wrong, the guardian should take the appropriate steps with a view to legal action. In either event, he should make certain that a lawyer is retained for the purpose. Through the lawyer, he can see that the existence of retardation is brought to the attention of the court. In the section dealing with being a party to a civil action, the roles of "next friend" (for the plaintiff) and "guardian *ad litem*" (for the defendant) were discussed. The guardian should be considered a ready-made "next friend" or "guardian *ad litem*" and the court should take account of this. Should there be a question of assessing the merits of proposed settlement, monetary or otherwise, the guardian should discuss these with the lawyer and interpret the same to the ward.

Dealing with matters of vocation and employment, the guardian should discuss the capabilities and needs of the ward with experts and match them with the resources available. He should do his utmost to have the ward placed in the best training program suited to his needs and obtain for him all public benefits available for the purpose. Once the ward has received his job training, the guardian possessed with a full knowledge of the employment capabilities of the ward, should assess the labor market to determine at what level the ward could enter it without frustration. If any employment licences are required, the guardian should – of course – assist in obtain them. Once employment is obtained, the guardian should constantly review the performance of the ward to ensure that the employment is satisfactory both to the ward and to the employer. He should ensure that the ward is not in any way exploited or abused, with particular reference to labor standards, minimum wage laws and other regulations and benefits in the field. Should there be an indication that the ward is working at a level either too high or too low, the guardian should take whatever steps are necessary to remedy the situation. Where laws relating to workmen's compensation are applicable, the guardian should ensure that the ward is properly covered. Should he be injured, it would be the additional duty of the guardian to make certain that a claim for such compensation was submitted and, throughout the process, that the full benefits of the compensation scheme were made available to the ward. In instances where unemployment insurance is available, the guardian would be expected to see that the ward is enrolled and, should the ward become unemployed, that the benefits of the unemployment insurance plan were made available to him.

The domestic relations of his ward will confront the guardian with problems of a highly complicated and emotional nature, requiring the utmost in tact and consideration. Only rarely, if at all, should the guardian attempt to act without professional advice. The guardian will be in a position to discuss with his ward the prospects and advisability of marriage and the proposed partner. He should assess the resources available both for the couple and for their assistance, and bear in mind the likely alternatives to the marriage. A great deal of aid would have to be given in the following of legal, medical, social and religious procedures for marriage. Arrangements for the matrimonial residence will have to be made. After the marriage, the guardian might find himself in a more difficult position since the marriage itself will not terminate the guardianship arrangement. He must be prepared to be a close friend capable of resolving marital problems or, if necessary, directing the couple to the appropriate social agencies for that purpose. An assessment of capacity for parental responsibility may sometimes be required. Sometimes arrangements for medical care and childbirth will have to be made. It is conceivable that the guardian may have a role in helping to determine the issue of whether the parents will be allowed to keep their child. Needless to say, the guardian should, wherever necessary, ensure that social agencies are involved in a capacity supportive to the couple. Conversely, the guardian should do his part to see that the ward and his partner are protected from undue efforts by such agencies which would seek to disrupt the family. Decisions may have to be made concerning the possibility of prevention or termination of pregnancies. Here considerations of the widest scope will be involved and the guardian must be available to interpret these to the ward and to make any arrangements required to effect any decision made. Marital problems may require the guardian to assess and receive counsel on, and then to consider with his ward, the possible dissolution of the union. The initiation of such a proceeding, protection of his ward during the process and reconstruction of the life of the ward afterwards will call for a very active role on the part of the guardian.

Some of the more obvious aspects of the guardianship role will be the maintenance of a watch on the assets of the ward and their protection from exploitation or dissipation. Depending upon the terms of the guardianship order, the guardian may, as well, be responsible for administering the estate in whole or in part. The guardian should remember that the needs and wants of his ward may not parallel the standards of the guardian. It will be the crucial issue how far the satisfaction of the values of the ward is consistent with the duty of the guardian to preserve the estate committed to his protection.

Many social assistance programs are available to the retarded. These include pensions, allowances, retraining payments and like benefits. The guardian should ensure that all possible benefits are applied for and received. Consistent with the terms of his appointment, the guardian should assist the ward in the administration of these benefits. The guardian should arrange appropriate insurance (medical, hospital and other) protection for the ward, taking full advantage of any special benefits available to a person in the ward's category.

The obtaining of sound legal advice to determine the position in law of the ward, upon the death of any family member may be very important. It should be made certain that full advantage is taken of all legal protection available to the ward in this respect so that he is not deprived of any rightful share in a family estate. With tact, some effort would be indicated before the death of any close member of the family of the ward, to ascertain whether provision for the ward is made in the will.

With respect to matters such as income taxation, the guardian should assist the ward in completing and submitting the appropriate forms, making sure that all benefits that should accrue to him are sought. In the event that the completion of such forms are too complicated for the guardian himself, then professional advice should be obtained.

Legal aid and ombudsman schemes may be available to, and indicated for the protection and enhancement of the position of the ward. Every effort should be made by the guardian to see that the ward is able to utilize these resources fully.

Central registration

There are examples, in Canada and elsewhere, of registries for handicapped persons. Merits of such a system include identification, research, planning of services and insuring their delivery. On the negative side, there is invasion of privacy involved and generally the branding of a person as different from others. In deciding whether or not to establish such a system, all relevant factors must be carefully considered and weighed.

In this age of computers and human data banks, perhaps we are moving generally in the direction of universal systems of registration for various purposes.

Dealing with the field of the handicapped, the effectiveness of delivery of service and benefit programs looms as an overwhelming factor. Such programs can be the best in the world, yet if they are not delivered to those intended to reap the benefits of them, they are no better than no programs at all.

The establishment of a system of central registration would be a desirable feature to be incorporated in the services of the guardianship agency contemplated. We have already discussed, under the heading of timing of proceedings, the possibility of parents taking guardianship proceedings in advance of the actual need which, in a sense, is registration. The registration system could, however, be broader than that encompassing those who may never need guardianship but could use some assistance outside such a scheme.

The guardianship agency would, no doubt, be very well aware of existing programs for the retarded and keep abreast of new programs as they become available. Were they to know the identity of those in the community who could benefit from or be a part of these programs, the existence of a registry could enable the agency to reach out into the community to ensure that the full benefits were delivered. This service could be part of or apart from any formal guardianship arrangement. In other words, it could see that the benefit accrued to its own wards (as part of its being guardian), to the wards of other guardians (by notifying those guardians), or to individuals not under guardianship (by notifying either the individual himself or the person looking after him). Using computers, the information relating vital statistics, personal characteristics, needs and capabilities of the individuals can constitute the input. When the individual becomes eligible for enrolment or participation in any particular program as, for example, having reached the minimum age, the computer would indicate so and the necessary measures could be taken to see that the benefits are delivered to him.

Position of the ward

Many retarded persons would not want a guardian. The ramifications of the proposal may well infuriate them. Disturbing issues arise that perhaps do not admit of an easy solution.

Criteria for guardianship have been discussed. If these are not met then the individual involved will be left to his own devices. If some of the criteria do exist, an application for a guardianship order may be made by any interested person or agency, and a court will find the individual lacking in social adaptation. The grounds for the appointment of a guardian are laid.

The question then becomes – at the moment of pronouncing the appointment of a guardian – whether the proposed ward wants what he may view a restriction of his freedom. Some may argue that the issue is not so important as it seems: the court has already found the individual to be deficient in social skills and judgment and cannot then rationally allow him to determine whether he needs assistance.

The problem may have another side. Guardianship is proposed for those not capable of full social responsibility. Yet, responsibility is the managing of one's own affairs and the desire to so manage independently. The refusal of a guardian may be a rejection of dependency: the prime indication of social responsibility.

The paradox must be the responsibility of the court dealing with the application. As a practical matter, it may be fair to assume that courts will not commonly refuse to appoint a guardian for a retarded person who has just been found to be in need of protection. The best feasible answer to the problem may be for the courts to ensure that the retardate is provided with the opportunity and assistance to challenge the primary allegation that he is incapable of proper social functioning.

Objections that a ward who has a guardian imposed upon him will be so hostile as to render the appointment almost meaningless have some merit. The ideal close and trusting relationship seen as essential to many functions of a guardian presupposes a desire for the relationship. Even should, however, the guardian require time (or be completely unable) to overcome resentment so that he may be a guide and teacher, the ward will still benefit from efforts on his behalf related to certain matters. Relationships do often improve, and in the interim very important protections are provided. The role of the court in tailoring guardianship plans to individual cases, by limiting restrictions on independence to those necessary, is crucial in alleviating resentment.

The system must recognize that its plan of protection is not complete upon the issuing of a guardianship order. The ward must have recourse to the law to protect his own interests against improper activities of his guardian.

A ward should, of course, have the right of appeal to a higher court against the making of a guardianship order. He should have ready access to persons who will assist him in that appeal.

At the time of appointment, a ward should, so far as is possible, be made aware of the powers, rights, responsibilities and duties of his guardian. There should be informal and considerate access to an officialdom ready to answer queries as to his rights and the conduct of his guardian. Those officials should be at his disposal should he need relief or protection.

The optimistic view of the guardianship proposal is that it will help the ward to grow in ability as well as protecting him. A ward should be able on his own initiative or that of an interested party to apply for a varying or easing, and indeed for termination, of the terms of guardianship. If indicated, a ward or someone on his behalf should be able to apply for an order replacing or displacing his guardian. Counselling and assistance must be seen as his right. A ward would, of course, have legel recourse against a guardian for any damages improperly suffered by him.

Our society is a mobile one. People move to utilize opportunities for finnacial or social advancement. That right should not be denied the ward. Insofar as it is possible, guardianship schemes should be sufficiently flexible to permit movement and change of guardian at least within any province. The move should not be inordinately easy, however. Residential, training and employment arrangements are disrupted by a move. These may be replaced elsewhere, but a whim of the ward should not be permitted to destroy a very effective guardianship arrangement. The first premise of the right to some self-determination must be weighed together with other factors.

The provision of legal rights and protections for the ward are crucial if, for no other reason, than that the ward is a citizen and a human being. Further advantages are the natural consequent discouragement of improper behavior by the guardian, and the encouragement of a seeking out by individuals and families of the benefits available upon the appointment of a guardian.

Supervision of guardianship

With the establishment of guardianship legislation and individual guardianship arrangements under it, this would represent a field in which problems may arise from time to time. Some of these problems may, due to their very nature, reach the attention of those who may be in a position to resolve them. Others, however, may be dormant in nature and without active investigation, a situation which should be remedied in fact goes unnoticed. For this reason, there should be some means whereby guardianship arrangements may be supervised. Reference has already been made to the possibility of the court, when appointing a guardian, requiring that the guardian report to the court at stipulated intervals.

The possibility of court supervision was considered by the Task Force on Law of the President's Panel on Mental Retardation as follows.

"Careful evaluation and expert advice at the time of a formal hearing on the appointment of a guardian for an adult will reveal the probabilities of changes in the subject's condition and capabilities, as well as the significance of future court reviews and their optimum frequency. To require automatic review of every case with equal frequency is to do injustice both to those who need it and those who do not. In this area too there should be a wide range of choices from which the court may draw the most appropriate. Thus, the latest date for the next routine review of the guardianship should be specified in the order. Under reasonable conditions, the ward should be able to appeal to the court on issues involving the guardianship at any time. The court should also be free to act on the advice of third parties. Of course, the court may require a report on the status and condition of the ward from any guardian at any time."[38]

The Conclusions from San Sebastian indicate that the courts will have enough to do in guardianship matters without having to be concerned about supervision of the system. The courts, it was there suggested, should have the support of a well-staffed agency – "public and permanent" – which would have the power and the duty to bring before the courts some of the information upon which court action should be taken. The proposed agency would carry out the following functions.

"Gathering information on the overall system, for the purpose of evaluating its effectiveness and proposing necessary changes.
Reviewing reports filed by guardians (not to the exclusion of judicial review of the same).
Investigating individual cases, either in response to complaints, or on its own initiative, including direct contact with wards on a random sampling basis.
Bringing to the attention of the courts pertinent information on which court action is necessary.
Reviewing the work of professional guardians in relation to the number of wards accepted by each and advising courts relative to limiting the number of wards any one guardian can properly serve.
Identifying persons needing guardianship who might otherwise not have an application made on their behalf.
Initiating the necessary legal action where families or other concerned persons do not do so.
Advising courts on the criteria for selection of guardians.
Providing interim services by assigning a person to act as temporary mentor in emergencies, or while a new guardian is being selected.
Securing competent professional persons to assist the courts as expert witnesses, members of the evaluation teams, etc."[39]

The functions enumerated above should all be incorporated within the structure of the guardianship agency. Indeed, some of these functions have already been stated here in as being appropriately within the scope of that agency.

We recommend that there be established in each province a scheme of guardianship, making provision for the appointment by a court of appropriate guardians to function under the supervision of a guardianship agency for the protection and development of persons who are mentally retarded and who by reason of that mental retardation are substantially deprived of capacity to manage their persons or their property or both, where such appointments are determined to be in the best interests of the retardate and of the community, all the while ensuring the preservation of individual rights.

References

1 Contained in Section on Guardianship (III. 2) of "Legislative Aspects of Mental Retardation", reprinted as Appendix B to INTERNATIONAL LEAGUE OF SOCIETIES FOR THE MENTALLY HANDICAPPED, CONCLUSIONS: SYMPOSIUM ON GUARDIANSHIP OF THE MENTALLY RETARDED (1969) (hereinafter cited as SYMPOSIUM) 31.
2 International League of Societies for the Mentally Handicapped, October 24, 1968.
3 SYMPOSIUM 14.
4 THE PRESIDENT'S PANEL ON MENTAL RETARDATION, REPORT OF THE TASK FORCE ON LAW (1963) (hereinafter cited as TASK FORCE) 24-25.
5 SYMPOSIUM 10.
6 ULLMAN and KRASNER, A PSYCHOLOGICAL APPROACH TO ABNORMAL BEHAVIOR 559 (1969).
7 WORLD HEALTH ORGANIZATION, LEGISLATION AFFECTING PSYCHIATRIC TREATMENT 14-15 (*Wld Helth Org. techn. Rep. Ser.* 1955, 98).
8 7 & 8 Eliz. 2, c. 72.
9 TASK FORCE 25-26.
10 SYMPOSIUM 25.
11 *Ibid.*
12 *Ibid.*
13 TASK FORCE 25.
14 SYMPOSIUM 26.
15 TASK FORCE 25-26.
16 TASK FORCE 26; SYMPOSIUM 26.
17 SYMPOSIUM 26.
18 SYMPOSIUM 24.
19 TASK FORCE 26.
20 SYMPOSIUM 25.
21 TASK FORCE 25.
22 SYMPOSIUM 11.
23 See, for example, in Ontario, *The Prearranged Funeral Services Act, 1961-62*, S.O. 1961-62, c. 108, as amended by S.O. 1968, c. 99.
24 30 & 31 Vict., c. 3 (U.K.); see s. 92, head 13.
25 TASK FORCE 26-27.
26 SYMPOSIUM 22-23.
27 "Legal Aspects of Mental Retardation", held at Toronto Psychiatric Hospital, March 2, 1965, p. 41 (Discussion).
28 SYMPOSIUM 22.
29 *Ibid.*
30 SYMPOSIUM 23.
31 SYMPOSIUM 24.
32 7 & 8 Eliz. 2, c. 72.
33 *Ibid.*, s. 34(1).
34 SYMPOSIUM 19.
35 SYMPOSIUM 20-22.
36 Recommendation of Welfare Group I in DEPARTMENT OF NATIONAL HEALTH AND WELFARE, REPORT (MENTAL RETARDATION IN CANADA) (1965) (reporting Federal-Provincial Conference held in Ottawa, October 19-22, 1964) 286.
37 TASK FORCE 27.
38 TASK FORCE 26.
39 SYMPOSIUM 27-28.

recommendations

APPEARING IN THE TEXT
ARE HERE REPEATED IN
COMPREHENSIVE FORM

one   All laws and practices thereunder should conform to the principle that exclusions or limitations of rights and opportunities should always be construed restrictively: the fact that a person is found "incompetent" or "incapable" to do a particular thing, or in a certain respect, does not necessarily mean that he is incapable or incompetent to do something else, or in another respect.

Living and doing / Introduction p13

two   Where any legislation is enacted dealing with residential care of the retarded, consideration should be given to defining, where possible, the status in law of the residents and those charged with his care.

Living and doing / Residential settings p19

three   Steps should be taken to educate and counsel the mentally handicapped at the "grass roots" level in respect of the making of contracts and their implications in modern society.

Living and doing / Contracts p23

four   The provinces should seriously consider the adoption in their statutes of a provision similar to section 2-302 of the *Uniform Commercial Code* to endow not only the mentally handicapped, but also the general population, with what appears to be a much needed protective mechanism of a remedial nature in matters of contract.

Living and doing / Contracts p23

five   Licensing authorities should recognize that the existence of retardation is not relevant to finding of fitness to drive: what is important is inability to learn to drive safely.

Living and doing / Driving p26

six   A study should be undertaken to gather statistical data relating to retardates who wish to drive, their success rate in obtaining licenses and their driving performance records in comparison to the driver population so that a proper assessment of the significance of these matters in practical terms can be made.

Living and doing / Driving p27

seven   The mentally handicapped should in no case be prohibited from voting so long as they are otherwise qualified and are able to satisfy election officials of the same by compliance with any formalities that the law may require.

Living and doing / Voting p29

eight   Counselling should be made available to retardates who have estates and wish to make wills, concerning the wisdom or otherwise of so doing, and such counselling should, without exception, be based upon legal advice given in the particular case, bearing in mind the delicate issues involved.

Living and doing / Making a will p33

nine   A review should be made of the training and education of the police in identifying and handling mentally handicapped suspects and accused persons to ensure that such training and education are adequate.

Living and doing / Crime and corrections p34

ten	The *Criminal Code* should be amended to make it a statutory duty of the court to appoint a lawyer for an unrepresented accused person where the court has reason to believe that that person has a mental handicap. Living and doing / Crime and corrections p34
eleven	The sections in the *Criminal Code* authorizing remand for observation should be amended to ensure that mental retardation is included within their scope. Living and doing / Crime and corrections p35
twelve	Consideration should be given, in the case of a minor criminal charge, to placing a mentally handicapped accused person in a program of rehabilitation rather than in the criminal process, but only where a decision is then taken to withdraw the charge for all time. Living and doing / Crime and corrections p38
thirteen	Nothing short of a court finding of unfitness to stand trial should stand in the way of a criminal trial on a serious charge. Living and doing / Crime and corrections p38
fourteen	The *Criminal Code* should be amended to allow the court to postpone the fitness to stand trial issue to a later stage than the present law permits. Living and doing / Crime and corrections p38
fifteen	The *Criminal Code* should be amended to permit the advancement of the determination of the fitness to stand trial issue in a proper case to the stage of the preliminary hearing. Living and doing / Crime and corrections p38
sixteen	The full area of criminal responsibility in Canada should be fully reassessed and, in particular, to determine whether the concept of diminshed responsibility should be a part of it. Living and doing / Crime and corrections p39
seventeen	Each province should examine its practices relating to the review of persons detained upon the order of the Lieutenant Governor to ensure that they are effective and fair. Living and doing / Crime and corrections p42
eighteen	Release from custody following a finding of unfitness to stand trial should be considered a possibility in appropriate instances. Living and doing / Crime and corrections p43
nineteen	Following an acquittal by reason of insanity, release from custody should be viewed as a potential disposition. Living and doing / Crime and corrections p43
twenty	Each province should take a hard look at the accommodation, custody and programs for persons detained under the order of the Lieutenant Governor with a view to improving their chances of rehabilitation. Living and doing / Crime and corrections p43
twenty one	A criminal court should be bound to order a pre-sentence report in the case of every person convicted with respect to whom mental handicap is known or suspected. Living and doing / Crime and corrections p44

twenty two	Laws in the correctional field should be amended so that, in appropriate instances, mentally handicapped prisoners may be permitted to take advantage of community resources for them. Living and doing / Crime and corrections p45
twenty three	Laws providing authority for transfers of prisoners from correctional institutions to psychiatric facilities should be amended, where indicated, so as to allow these transfers to take place without delay on the basis of local arrangements. Living and doing / Crime and corrections p46
twenty four	Community agencies for the handicapped should make the existence of their services known to the parole authorities (both federal and provincial) encouraging the use of these services to facilitate parole in appropriate cases. Living and doing / Crime and corrections p46
twenty five	Study should be directed to the possibility of incorporating into our correctional jurisprudence the English legal concepts of the "hospital order" and "guardianship order" in lieu of sentence. Living and doing / Crime and corrections p46
twenty six	Committees such as "The Committee for Representation Through Understanding" should be established at the local level to study and urge improvement in the treatment of mentally retarded persons who find themselves in the criminal or correctional processes. Living and doing / Crime and corrections p47
twenty seven	A committee should be established in each province to examine the rules of civil practice as they relate to the handicapped with a view ultimately to the improvement of these rules if and where indicated. Living and doing / Being a party to a civil action p48
twenty eight	There should be "benefit reduction holidays" for the handicapped during the crucial transitional period. Work and working / Introduction p56
twenty nine	School-leaving age should be sufficiently flexible to accommodate the special requirements of the handicapped. Work and working / Vocational rehabilitation p57
thirty	Provincial and municipal governments, as well as industry and commerce, should follow the exemplary lead taken by the Government of Canada in its policy of hiring on the basis of ability rather than disability. Work and working / Qualification standards p63
thirty one	Occupational licensing and certification bodies should recognize the merit of making their qualification processes more flexible to accommodate the handicapped. Work and working / Qualification standards p63
thirty two	Mandatory employment laws should not be adopted in Canada. Work and working / Mandatory Employment Laws p64

forty four	The staff of the statutory committee should receive special training as to the problems facing institutional professional staff and learn how they (staff of the statutory committee), even though their transactions are limited to property, can assist in the habilitation and rehabilitation of the patient.
	Property and property management / Property management by statutory committee p108
forty five	Institutional professional staff generally, and social service staff particularly, should receive special instruction involving the functions of the statutory committee to learn in what ways they can facilitate his work.
	Property and property management / Property management by statutory committee p108
forty six	The members of the professional staff of an institution in which an individual is a patient should be permitted direct and swift access to information in the hands of the statutory committee.
	Property and property management / Property management by statutory committee p108
forty seven	The statutory committee should consult frequently with the professional staff of an institution, outlining the particular circumstances under which the consultation is made.
	Property and property management / Property management by statutory committee p. 108
forty eight	The professional staff of an institution should be as helpful as possible in assisting the personnel of the statutory committee in the performance of his duties by supplying information relevant and suitable to the character of an inquiry by the office of the statutory committee.
	Property and property management / Property management by statutory committee p108
forty nine	The statutory committee should be encouraged, subject to the advice of the professional staff of the institution in each case, to consult the wishes of the patient through personal interview.
	Property and property management / Property management by statutory committee p109
fifty	The office of the statutory committee should be decentralized as and where required through the establishment of regional or local offices with a view to providing a greater measure of accessibility to affected citizens.
	Property and property management / Property management by statutory committee p109
fifty one	The statutory committee should be permitted (by legislative clarification if necessary) to allow a degree of flexibility, consistent with the potential of the particular patient and in keeping with the protection of his estate, to enable him to manage a portion of his financial affairs.
	Property and property management / Property management by statutory committee p109
fifty two	There should be an on-going assessment of classes of facilities with respect to which patients or residents thereof may fall within the estate administration jurisdiction of the statutory committee.
	Property and property management / Property management by statutory committee p110

fifty three	In the event that the transfer of jurisdiction in mental incompetency proceedings to a lower court would be otherwise appropriate and increase their availability (for example by reducing costs and increasing speed) this should be done.

Property and property management / Mental incompetency
proceedings p113

fifty four	Provision should be made in any legal aid plan so that it embraces mental incompetency proceedings in a manner which would involve an assessment of the means of the person alleged to be mentally incompetent and, where the value of the estate is relatively a small one, the court should not order the costs of the proceedings to be taken out of the estate.

Property and property management / Mental incompetency
proceedings p113

fifty five	Where there is any doubt that a statutory committee has the power to initiate mental incompetency proceedings, he should be given express statutory authority to do so in instances where there is no other suitable person who is willing or able to initiate them.

Property and property management / Mental incompetency
proceedings p113

fifty six	To ensure that there is always a committee available, even for small estates, the statutory committee (where it is not clear that he has authority for the purpose) should be clothed with legislative authority to become committee of the estate of a person who is declared mentally incompetent under mental incompetency proceedings.

Property and property management / Mental incompetency
proceedings p113

fifty seven	Serious consideration should be given to making provision for prepayment on a lifetime or long-term basis as part of social benefit programs which require periodic premium payments.

Property and property management / Social benefits p117

fifty eight	Legislation authorizing the payment over of statutory social benefit to a third person to administer for the benefits of the retardate should be such as to foster and ensure that sound selection of the third person are made.

Property and property management / Social benefits p117

fifty nine	All programs which provide benefits that diminish or disappear as other income is received should be reassessed to determine whether the diminution is such as to negate or destroy altogether any incentive and, in the event that it does, consideration should be given to the establishment of formulae which, under given circumstances, will ease the lessening of benefits to a degree which is consistent with the preservation of the incentive feature.

Property and property management / Social benefits p117

sixty	Extensive study should be conducted to determine whether parents of the retarded and the handicapped generally are put to actual greater cost for that reason and, in the event that they are, this should be recognized and reflected by amendment to the *Income Tax Act* (Canada) to allow special and appropriate deductions, failing which recognition and relief the Provincial Legislatures should be urged to provide such relief through the vehicle of their income tax statutes.

Property and property management / Income tax implications
p124 sixty one There should be established in each province a scheme of guardianship, making provision for the appointment by a court of appropriate guardians to function under the supervision of a guardianship agency for the protection and development of persons who are mentally retarded and who by reason of that mental retardation are substantially deprived of capacity to manage their persons or their property or both, where such appointments are determined to be in the best interests of the retardate and of the community, all the while ensuring the preservation of individual rights.

Guardians and guardianship / Supervision of guardianship p210

appendices

appendix a

DECLARATION

of general and special rights of the mentally retarded

WHEREAS the universal declaration of human rights, adopted by the United Nations, proclaims that all of the human family, without distinction of any kind, have equal and inalienable rights of human dignity and freedom; and

WHEREAS the declaration of the rights of the child, adopted by the United Nations, proclaims the rights of the physically, mentally or socially handicapped child to special treatment, education and care required by his particular condition.

Now therefore

The International League of Societies for the Mentally Handicapped expresses the general and special rights of the mentally retarded as follows:

ARTICLE I: The mentally retarded person has the same basic rights as other citizens of the same country and same age.

ARTICLE II: The mentally retarded person has a right to proper medical care and physical restoration and to such education, training, habilitation and guidance as will enable him to develop his ability and potential to the fullest possible extent, no matter how severe his degree of disability. No mentally handicapped person should be deprived of such services by reason of the costs involved.

ARTICLE III: The mentally retarded person has a right to economic security and to a decent standard of living. He has a right to productive work or to other meaningful occupation.

ARTICLE IV: The mentally retarded person has a right to live with his own family or with fosterparents; to participate in all aspects of community life, and to be provided with appropriate leisure time activities. If care in an institution becomes necessary it should be in surroundings and under circumstances as close to normal living as possible.

ARTICLE V: The mentally retarded person has a right to a qualified guardian when this is required to protect his personal well-being and interest. No person rendering direct services to the mentally retarded should also serve as his guardian.

ARTICLE VI: The mentally retarded person has a right to protection from exploitation, abuse and degrading treatment. If accused, he has a right to a fair trial with full recognition being given to his degree of responsibility.

ARTICLE VII: Some mentally retarded persons may be unable due to the severity of their handicap, to exercise for themselves all of their rights in a meaningful way. For others, modification of some or all of these rights is appropriate. The procedure used for modification or denial of rights must contain legal safeguards against every form of abuse, must be based on an evaluation of the social capability of the mentally retarded person by qualified experts and must be subject to periodic reviews and to the right of appeal to higher authorities.

ABOVE ALL — THE MENTALLY RETARDED PERSON HAS THE RIGHT TO RESPECT.

As adapted by the International League of Societies for the Mentally Handicapped of which the Canadian Association for the Mentally Retarded is the Canadian member.

appendix b

GUARDIANSHIP AND THE LAW

a project of the

Canadian Association for Retarded Children
Association Canadienne Pour Les Enfants Arriérés

Project Address 243 Queen Street West, Toronto, Canada

6th May 1969

Director
B.B. Swadron, LL.B., LL.M.,
of the Ontario and
Prince Edward Island Bars

Consultants
J.D. Morton, Q.C.,
M.A., LL.B., of the
Irish and Ontario Bars

N.D. Starkman, LL.B.,
of the Ontario Bar

Advisory Council
D.E. Zarfas, M.D., C.M.,
D. Psych., C.R.C.P.(C),
F.A.A.M.D., *Chairman*

W.R. Kirk, M.A.

S.J. Koegler, M.D.,
D.C.H. (England),
C.R.C.P.(C)

His Honour Judge
G.H.F. Moore

G.A. Roeher, B.A.,
B.S.W., M.A., Ph.D.

(Miss) W.M. Skelton,
B.A., M.S.W.

(Mrs.) A. Stevenson,
LL.B.

Mr. John C. Doe, Q.C.,
Barrister and Solicitor
123-4th Street
YOURTOWN,
New Brunswick.

Dear Mr. Doe:

With the move away from institutionalization and the changing complexion of services for the
mentally retarded, the adequacy of the current laws as
applied to them emerges as a critical issue.

This Project was established to examine
relevant laws and practices in Canada with a view to
recommending, if indicated, a scheme which would ensure
protection of the rights and welfare of the mentally
retarded and any other classes with parallel needs.
Present thinking is that certain of the retarded could
be afforded this protection only through a statutory
system of guardianship. The guardian, who might be an
individual or agency, would be available to provide
such supervision and assistance as may be required in
any given case. Many details in such a system would,
of course, have to be settled.

So that our study will have a broad and sound
basis, it is essential for us to be aware of any problems
encountered with respect to the mentally retarded under
all fields of law. Perhaps in your professional experience, you have dealt with cases involving retarded
persons and wondered whether the law, as applied to them,
was reasonable and just. I would be grateful if you
could take the time to communicate any pertinent
information and your personal views to me.

Yours sincerely,

Barry Swadron

Barry B. Swadron
Project Director.

BBS/rs

222

appendix c

le 19 août 1969

Director
B.B. Swadron, LL.B., LL.M.,
of the Ontario and
Prince Edward Island Bars

Consultants
J.D. Morton, Q.C.,
M.A., LL.B., of the
Irish and Ontario Bars

N.D. Starkman, LL.B.,
of the Ontario Bar

Advisory Council
D.E. Zarfas, M.D., C.M.,
D. Psych., C.R.C.P.(C),
F.A.A.M.D., *Chairman*

W.R. Kirk, M.A.

S.J. Koegler, M.D.,
D.C.H. (England),
C.R.C.P.(C)

His Honour Judge
G.H.F. Moore

G.A. Roeher, B.A.,
B.S.W., M.A., Ph.D.

(Miss) W.M. Skelton,
B.A., M.S.W.

(Mrs.) A. Stevenson,
LL.B.

M. Louie Phillipe Framboise,
284 rue des Erables,
CHUTE DES OISEAUX,
Quebec.

Cher Maître:

Dans le passé, la plupart des déficients mentaux étaient relégués dans des institutions. Aujourd'hui, on essai autant que possible de les intégrer dans la société. Vu cette évolution, il importe d'examiner si les lois présentement en vigueur sont encore adéquates.

Le but de ce projet est d'étudier les lois applicables et la pratique au Canada en vue de proposer, s'il y a lieu, des mesures destinées à protéger les droits et à assurer le bien-être des déficients mentaux et d'autres groupes de personnes manifestant de semblables besoins. L'on croit généralement aujourd'hui que ce but ne saurait être atteint quant à certains arriérés que par l'institution d'une tutelle statutaire. Le tuteur, qui pourrait être un individu ou un organisme, serait disponible pour fournir la surveillance et l'assistance requises dans chaque cas. Il y aurait évidemment beaucoup de détails à régler.

Pour établir notre étude sur une base large et solide, il est essentiel que nous connaissions tous les problèmes qui se posent par rapport aux arriérés mentaux dans tous les domaines du droit. Dans l'exercice de votre profession, vous avez peut-être rencontré des cas impliquant des personnes arriérées et vous vous êtes peut-être demandé si l'application de la loi à leur égard entraînait des résultats raisonnables et justes. Je vous serais tres reconnaissant si vous pouviez prendre le temps de me communiquer tout renseignement pertinent ainsi que vos impressions personnelles.

Votre bien dévoué,

Barry Swadron

Barry B. Swadron
Directeur de projets

BBS/bp

223

appendix d

GUARDIANSHIP AND THE LAW

a project of the

Canadian Association for Retarded Children
Association Canadienne Pour Les Enfants Arriérés

Project Address 243 Queen Street West, Toronto, Canada

13 August 1969

Director
B.B. Swadron, LL.B., LL.M.,
of the Ontario and
Prince Edward Island Bars

Consultants
J.D. Morton, Q.C.,
M.A., LL.B., of the
Irish and Ontario Bars

N.D. Starkman, LL.B.,
of the Ontario Bar

Advisory Council
D.E. Zarfas, M.D., C.M.,
D. Psych., C.R.C.P.(C),
F.A.A.M.D., *Chairman*

W.R. Kirk, M.A.

S.J. Koegler, M.D.,
D.C.H. (England),
C.R.C.P.(C)

His Honour Judge
G.H.F. Moore

G.A. Roeher, B.A.,
B.S.W., M.A., Ph.D.

(Miss) W.M. Skelton,
B.A., M.S.W.

(Mrs.) A. Stevenson,
LL.B.

Mr. D. W. Good, M.S.W.,
567 - 8th Street,
MEDICINEJAW,
Manitoba.

Dear Mr. Good,

    I am taking the liberty of seeking advice from a selected number of professional people whose work and experience can help us in this special study.

    The Project is examining relevant laws and practices with a view to recommending, if indicated, a scheme which would ensure protection of the rights and welfare of the mentally retarded of all ages and any other classes with parallel needs.

    In order that our study have a sufficiently broad practical foundation, it is important that we be knowledgeable of problems or difficulties encountered at the case level. If you are aware through your professional experience of instances wherein the law has not appeared just or reasonable as applied to retarded persons, we would be grateful if you could take the time to communicate any pertinent information to us.

    Current thinking leads us to believe that certain of the retarded could be afforded the necessary protection only through a system of "guardianship" deriving its force from special legislation designed for the purpose. The guardian, who could be an individual or agency (governmental or otherwise), would be available to provide that degree of supervision and assistance as was required in the particular case. Accordingly, we are also interested in your views concerning what existing agency or agencies within your Province could, by logical extension, offer and deliver to the retarded services of a protective nature.

    Since time is of the essence to this Project, a reply at your early convenience would be appreciated.

Yours sincerely,

Barry B. Swadron
Project Director

BBS/bp

appendix e

Management of Patients' Assets by the Public Trustee

Public Trustee's Authority

1. The Mental Health Act provides for the appointment of the Public Trustee as "Committee" of the estates of some, but not all, patients in certain psychiatric facilities. It further provides that the Public Trustee shall cease to be Committee when a patient is no longer considered to be incompetent, or when a patient is discharged and is considered competent, or dies. "Committee" in this connection means the person duly appointed to take over the patient's assets so that they will be managed in the best interests of the patient and his dependants.

2. The Public Trustee's authority extends to the estates of patients in certain psychiatric facilities, as defined by the regulations to the Mental Health Act, when the attending physician certifies to the Public Trustee that a patient is incapable of managing his own affairs. The Public Trustee has no authority to manage a patient's affairs until a certificate is issued unless a patient appoints the Public Trustee to act for him, nor does the Public Trustee have authority in those cases where a Committee has been appointed by the Court. The status of a patient for whom the Public Trustee does not act may change by the issuance of a certificate of incompetence by the attending physician. It is also possible that the authority of the Public Trustee to act as Committee may cease by virtue of the attending physician issuing a notice cancelling the certificate of incompetence.

Management of Estate

3. The Public Trustee will, in most cases, arrange to get in cash, bank accounts, and securities; he will take charge of all the patient's assets such as chattels (including motor cars), moneys and real estate and will collect moneys owing to a patient in the nature of rents, mortgage payments, wages, pensions, unemployment insurance, disability benefits and any accounts receivable. He will in turn, *insofar as the patient's assets will permit*, pay rent, mortgage payments, taxes, fire, life and disability insurance premiums, instalments on motor cars or furniture. He will also set up an allowance for dependants. With respect to some of these payments such as rent, hydro, telephone and gas, it will usually be expected that the wife, or other dependant, will look after them out of the allowance that is made to her from a patient's estate. *It must be pointed out that the Public Trustee uses only a patient's moneys and other assets for the above mentioned purposes. He has no Government or other funds available for this purpose and if the patient has no or insufficient assets, these payments cannot be made.* The Public Trustee's Office is self-supporting; that is, it is not subsidized by the Government. When services are rendered, the Public Trustee is obliged to make a charge therefor in most cases. This charge will not exceed the amount the Court would allow a Trustee for a similar service and in many cases is nominal. The Public Trustee makes every effort to manage the affairs of a patient so that his assets can be returned to him, when the Public Trustee ceases to act, so far as possible in the same state as they were at the time the Public Trustee assumed management of the estate. Assets may be sold as required to meet the financial needs of a patient or his family or where it appears to be in the patient's best interest.

No Confiscation of Property

4. Management of a patient's estate by the Public Trustee does not mean confiscation of his assets by the Government. All assets under management by the Public Trustee are held by him in trust. The management of an estate is carried on with the intention of protecting the estate and making proper provision for the needs of dependants.

No Authority Vested in Other Persons

5. Once a certificate of incompetence has been issued under the Mental Health Act and until such time as a patient is discharged or the certificate of incompetence is cancelled, no person other than the Public Trustee has any authority to withdraw moneys from a bank, cash cheques, collect debts or payments owing to a patient or deal with his assets in any way even though they may have had a power of attorney to do so prior to the Public Trustee assuming management of an estate. The authority given to the

Public Trustee by the Mental Health Act, therefore, fills a vital gap and affords a quick and inexpensive method of appointing a Committee to deal with matters requiring attention. If the Public Trustee were not authorized by law to manage the estate, delay and expense, in many cases out of all proportion to a patient's assets, would be involved in an application to the Court for the appointment of a Committee. Some delay may occur between the time of issuance of a certificate of incompetence and notice thereof being received by the Public Trustee, but every effort is made to keep the delay to a minimum.

Motor Vehicles

6. Motor vehicles owned by a patient are not to be driven by anyone until written permission is first received from the Public Trustee who will have to be satisfied as to the necessity of another person operating a vehicle and that adequate insurance is in force.

Co-operation Needed

7. The Public Trustee is made Committee of a patient's estate by law to enable him to assist the patient and his family as well and as speedily as circumstances warrant. He endeavours to carry out his responsibilities in this connection to the full extent permitted by good judgment, and insofar as a patient's assets will allow and in accordance with the law, but this cannot be accomplished without the full and prompt co-operation of the officials and staff of the psychiatric facility; any interested social service or welfare organization and a patient's spouse and family. The Public Trustee's actions in managing a patient's affairs and providing assistance to a patient's dependants may be delayed if he is lacking information as to the needs of the patient and his family.

Financial Report

8. Misunderstanding and delay can occur through a lack of information with respect to a patient's assets when the Public Trustee becomes Committee. The Mental Health Act requires the officer-in-charge of the psychiatric facility to obtain a financial statement of a patient's affairs and to forward a copy to the Public Trustee. The information contained in this financial statement is necessary to enable the Public Trustee to act quickly and effectively. It is, therefore, in the best interest of a patient if the officer-in-charge is furnished with as much information as possible by any persons who have knowledge of the patient's affairs. Similarly, the Public Trustee should be informed promptly by anyone having knowledge of the patient's family needing financial assistance.

Communicating with the Public Trustee

9. When writing or phoning the public Trustee, please give the patient's full name and the Public Trustee's file number, or failing that, give some identifying information, such as the patient's former address or the name of the spouse. This will assist in determining who is looking after the estate at the Public Trustee's Office.

Return of Estate

10. Upon the Public Trustee ceasing to be Committee of a patient's estate every attempt is made to return his assets as quickly as possible. However, delay can occur between the time the Public Trustee's authority ends and the time notice thereof is received by the Public Trustee. Necessary adjustments have to be made respecting the estate including the preparation of a detailed Statement of Receipts and Disbursements. If estate funds are required immediately, arrangements can be made, upon request, to have part of the moneys released at once or funds can be made available at the psychiatric facility providing a request is made in sufficient time.

Summary

1. First be sure that the Public Trustee is Committee of the Patient's estate.
2. If he is Committee, it is his desire to act as speedily and as effectively as possible.
3. He then alone has authority to manage and deal with the patient's estate, but there is no confiscation of the patient's property.
4. He can only do these matters efficiently if he is fully and promptly informed as to the assets and requirements of the estate.

5. The patient's spouse and family, the staff of the psychiatric facility and Social and Welfare agencies having information of assets and family needs, should furnish it promptly to the Public Trustee.

6. The spouse and family should assist the staff of the psychiatric facility so that the financial statement may be fully completed and forwarded promptly to the Public Trustee.

7. When contacting the Public Trustee give the patient's full name, the name of the psychiatric facility in which he is confined and the Public Trustee's file number if known.

8. If the file number is not available give some identifying information such as the name of the spouse, the patient's address before admission to the psychiatric facility and the date of admission.

9. Motor vehicles owned by a patient are not to be driven without the written permission of the Public Trustee.

10. The only funds available to the Public Trustee for use on behalf of a patient and his family are from the assets of the patient's estate.

11. If estate funds are urgently required when a patient is resuming management of his own estate, the need should be made known to the Public Trustee.

Issued by the Public Trustee, Department of The Attorney General of Ontario, June 1st, 1968.

Discrétion et efficacité à la curatelle publique

Qu'est-ce que la curatelle publique?

C'est un organisme du gouvernement du Québec qui, sous la direction du ministère des Finances et sous la surveillance de l'inspecteur des compagnies de fidéicommis, administre des biens. Cet organisme existe en vertu de la loi de la curatelle publique, S.R.Q., 1964, chapitre 314 et amendement 14-15 Elizabeth II, chapitre 18 (1966).

Qui bénéficie de ses services?

a) Tout malade non déjà pourvu d'un tuteur ou d'un curateur privé, traité en cure fermée dans un hôpital psychiatrique reconnu par le ministère de la Santé, et déclaré incapable d'administrer ses biens par le surintendant, sur l'avis de son bureau médical.
b) Les parents du malade, ses intimes, ses créanciers, ses débiteurs ou tout autre intéressé dans leurs relations avec l'administré.
c) Toute personne intéressée directement ou indirectement au règlement d'une succession réputée ou déclarée vacante.
d) Tout inéressé à un bien sans maître ou à un bien abandonné par une corporation ou société éteinte.
e) Les créanciers ou héritiers légaux d'un absent au sens du code civil.
f) Les compagnies d'assurance sur la vie, lorsque le ou les bénéficiaires sont introuvables.
g) Le condamné à mort ou à l'emprisonnement à perpétuité.
h) Les dépositaires de valeurs mobilières non réclamées par les héritiers dans les cinq années de l'ouverture de la succession.

Quels sont les services rendus par la curatelle publique?

a) *Enquête:* Une enquête permet d'inventorier, d'évaluer et de recueillir les biens, capitaux et revenus d'un administré, en vue de les conserver et de les faire fructifier.
b) *Comptabilité:* Sous la surveillance des vérificateurs du gouvernement du Québec, un personnel compétent assure la protection de toutes les valeurs mobilières.
c) *Assurances:* Avec les fonds de l'administré, le service des assurances veille au maintien des polices de tous genres et à la réclamation de tous les bénéfices qui y sont prévus.
d) *Sécurité sociale:* Ce service assure la perception des pensions de vieillesse, rentes gouvernementales ou privées et allocations sociales, pensions de retraite de toutes sortes, prestations d'assurance-chômage et autres.
e) *Budget:* Dans le meilleur intérêt de l'administré, ce service voit aux dettes et créances de l'administré, à ses obligations envers ses dépendants; il établit un budget familial, s'il y a lieu.
f) *Immeubles:* Ce service se charge de la gestion des propriétés, de leur entretien ou, au besoin, de leur vente ainsi que du contrôle des hypothèques à payer et à percevoir. Il étudie les titres de propriété et les assurances.
g) *Successions:* Toute succession réputée ou déclarée vacante peut être soumise au curateur public, qui voit à son règlement suivant les stipulations de la loi. Ce service recueille aussi les successions dévolues à ses administrés.
h) *Entreposage:* Un vaste entrepôt moderne sert à la conservation des biens mobiliers et personnels. Les titres mobiliers et autres objets de valeur sont gardés dans les chambres fortes de la banque au sous-sol de l'immeuble, et sont assurés contre toute perte.
i) *Service juridique:* Des juristes étudient tous les problèmes d'ordre juridique et cherchent à les résoudre le plus économiquement et rapidement possible, s'appliquent à protéger et à faire valoir les droits des administrés de la curatelle publique.
j) *Direction générale:* A la direction, le curateur et ses principaux conseillers veillent au bon fonctionnement et à l'efficacité des différents services de la curatelle publique; ils prennent les décisions qui s'imposent dans l'intérêt des personnes dont ils administrent les biens.

Quand cesse l'administration du curateur public?

Les pouvoirs du curateur public cessent lorsque l'une ou l'autre des situations suivantes se présente:

a) Lorsqu'il lui est signifié un jugement nommant un curateur ou un tuteur.

b) Lorsque le surintendant de l'hôpital psychiatrique avise le curateur public que le malade est capable d'administrer ses biens.

c) A l'échéance d'un congé d'essai de six mois non révoqué.

d) Lorsqu'un jugement définitif d'une Cour compétente annule le certificat d'incapacité établi par le surintendant de l'hôpital psychiatrique.

e) Lorsqu'un héritier à une succession réputée vacante comparaît, prouve ses droits à l'héritage et accepte la succession telle qu'elle se trouve.

f) A l'acceptation de la succession d'un exadministré défunt par les légataires, héritiers ou autres ayants droit.

Que coûte l'administration?

Le tarif des honoraires en vigueur est très raisonnable; il est déterminé par un arrêté en conseil, mais le curateur public peut, dans les cas de pauvreté, les réduire ou y renoncer.

Quels avantages procure le curateur public?

a) Les administrés du curateur public profitent des services de spécialistes de diverses disciplines: administration, assurance, budget, comptabilité, finance et placements, science juridique, sécurité sociale, garde et conservation de documents, meubles et autres objets de titres mobiliers. Tout ce personnel est lié par un serment de discrétion et travaille sous la surveillance étroite de l'inspecteur des compagnies de fidéicommis.

b) Dès sa libération définitive, l'administré du curateur public reprend, sans formalités, l'exercice de tous ses droits. Au contraire, le malade qui a été interdit et pourvu d'un curateur privé, ne peut reprendre l'exercice de ses droits sans convoquer à nouveau un conseil de famille et demander à la Cour supérieure de le relever de son interdiction. La personne noninterdite soumise à la curatelle publique ne souffre d'aucune publicité.

c) Dans le cas des successions vacantes, le curateur public protège, recueille et distribue l'actif au bénéfice des créanciers et des autres personnes intéressées.

d) Dès la cessation de ses pouvoirs, le curateur public rend ses comptes à qui de droit.

CURATELLE PUBLIQUE: EFFICACITÉ ET DISCRÉTION

Publié par l'Office d'information et de publicité du Québec

appendix g

THE DEPARTMENT OF SOCIAL AND FAMILY SERVICES

FORM 1
The Family Benefits Act, 1966
APPLICATION FOR AN ALLOWANCE

(1) APPLICATION BY A

PERSON WITH DEPENDENT CHILD(REN) ☐ OR SINGLE PERSON ☐ OR MARRIED PERSON ☐

WHO IS: WHO IS: WHO IS:

☐ BLIND	☐ BLIND	☐ BLIND
☐ OTHERWISE DISABLED	☐ OTHERWISE DISABLED	☐ OTHERWISE DISABLED
☐ A DEPENDENT FATHER	☐ AGE 60 - 64	☐ AGE 60 - 64
☐ A MOTHER	☐ AGE 65 OR MORE	☐ AGE 65 OR MORE
☐ A FOSTER MOTHER		

PART I - ALL APPLICANTS

(2) NAME OF APPLICANT

SURNAME	GIVEN NAME(S)	F.W.A.

ADDRESS _____

NUMBER STREET OR RURAL ROUTE

MUNICIPALITY	MUNICIPAL CODE #

CITY, TOWN, VILLAGE OR P.O. TOWNSHIP, COUNTY

PART II - ALL APPLICANTS OTHER THAN FOSTER MOTHERS

(3) PERSONAL DATA
A.

	NAME(S)	BIRTH DATE DAY MONTH YR.	PROOF OF BIRTHDATE	PLACE OF BIRTH	MAIDEN NAME, IF APPLICABLE
APPLICANT					
SPOUSE					
APPLICANT'S MOTHER					
APPLICANT'S FATHER					

B. LEGAL MARITAL STATUS OF APPLICANT

☐ SINGLE ☐ MARRIED ☐ WIDOW(ED) ☐ DIVORCED ☐ SEPARATED ☐ DESERTED

ADDRESS OF SPOUSE, IF DIFFERENT FROM APPLICANT _____

_____

IF APPLICABLE, PROVIDE DETAILS REGARDING DATES, PLACES, PROOFS, AND OTHER PERTINENT INFORMATION

_____

_____

_____

IF APPLICANT OR SPOUSE WAS PREVIOUSLY MARRIED, PROVIDE DETAILS _____

_____

_____

(4)

DEPENDENT CHILDREN – GIVEN NAME(S) AND SURNAME(S) UNDER WHICH BIRTH WAS REGISTERED FOR EACH CHILD	BIRTHDATE DAY MO. YR.	PLACE OF BIRTH	BIRTHDATE PROOF	SEX	SCHOOL	GR.

CHILDREN AWAY FROM HOME	AGE	RELATIONSHIP	OCCUPATION	CONTRIBUTIONS YES	NO

5 RESIDENCE

SHOW APPLICANTS RESIDENCE IN CANADA (A) IMMEDIATELY PRIOR TO APPLICATION

(B) TOTAL RESIDENCE PRIOR TO APPLICATION

	YEARS	MONTHS
(A)		
(B)		

ADDRESS IN AUGUST 1940: _____

IF BORN OUTSIDE CANADA, STATE DATE OF ARRIVAL IN CANADA: _____

6 ASSETS

A. (I) CHECK FOR EACH ITEM HELD BY APPLICANT, SPOUSE OR DEPENDENT CHILDREN AT THE TIME OF APPLICATION.

TYPE	DESCRIPTION	A	S	C	AMOUNT	TYPE	DESCRIPTION	A	S	C	AMOUNT
1. CASH ON HAND						8. LOANS, NOTES					
2. BANK ACCOUNTS						9. ACCOUNTS COLLECTABLE					
3. POSTAL SAVINGS						10. OFFICIAL GUARDIAN					
4. CREDIT UNIONS						OR PUBLIC TRUSTEE					
5. SAFETY DEPOSIT BOX						(MONEY IN TRUST)					
6. BONDS, STOCK SHARES						11. AUTOMOBILE OR TRUCK					
AND OTHER SECURITIES						12. INTEREST IN BUSINESS					
7. MORTGAGE RECEIVABLE						13. OTHER					

(II) ARE ANY FUTURE ASSETS EXPECTED? (SUCH AS UNADJUSTED CLAIMS, INSURANCE, AN INHERITANCE, OR LAWSUIT PENDING) YES ☐ NO ☐ IF YES, DESCRIBE FULLY IN NARRATIVE.

B.

REAL PROPERTY DESCRIPTION	OWNED BY: APPLICANT (A) SPOUSE (S) CHILD (C)	OWNER OCCUPIED RENTED VACANT	PURCHASE DATE	APPROXIMATE MARKET VALUE
1.				
2.				
3.				

DETAILS OF MORTGAGES OR OTHER ENCUMBRANCES ON ABOVE PROPERTY:

C. ESTATE OF DECEASED SPOUSE

(I) WAS THERE ANY ESTATE? YES ☐ NO ☐

(II) WAS THERE A WILL? YES ☐ NO ☐

(III) WERE THERE LETTERS OF PROBATE OR LETTERS OF ADMINISTRATION CALLED FOR? YES ☐ NO ☐

(IV) PARTICULARS:

D. TRANSFER OF PROPERTY -- REAL OR PERSONAL -- BY APPLICANT, SPOUSE OR DEPENDENT CHILDREN HAVE ANY ASSETS BEEN TRANSFERRED WITHIN PREVIOUS THREE YEARS - BY GIFT, SALE, QUITCLAIM OR FORECLOSURE? YES ☐ NO ☐ IF YES, GIVE PARTICULARS IN NARRATIVE.

E. DEBTS

NAME OF CREDITOR	DETAILS	VERIFIED YES	NO	AMOUNT

7 DISABILITY

DOES THE APPLICANT CONSIDER HIMSELF OR SPOUSE TO BE BLIND, DISABLED, OR PERMANENTLY UNEMPLOYABLE? YES ☐ NO ☐ (IF YES, PLEASE ARRANGE FOR COMPLETION OF FORM 4 OR FORM 5, AS APPLICABLE)

8 TRUSTEE   IS APPLICANT CAPABLE OF HANDLING ALLOWANCE? YES ☐ NO ☐

IF NO, PROVIDE DETAILS AND RECOMMENDATIONS

9 IS APPLICANT OR SPOUSE PAYING PREMIUMS FOR: O.H.S.C. ☐ O.H.S.I.P. ☐

DOES APPLICANT OR SPOUSE WISH TO CONTINUE SEMI-PRIVATE COVERAGE: YES ☐ NO ☐

APPLICANT: OHSIP NO. _____ OHSC NO. _____ SOCIAL INS. NO. _____

SPOUSE: OHSIP NO. _____ OHSC NO. _____ SOCIAL INS. NO. _____

231

10 LIVING EXPENSES

A. BOARDING AND LODGING: _____ WITH: _____

    RELATIONSHIP: _____ RATE (MONTHLY) _____

B. RESIDENT OR PATIENT OF ☐ NURSING HOME ☐ CHARITABLE INSTITUTION ☐ HOME FOR AGED ☐ OTHER

    NAME OF INSTITUTION: _____

    ADDRESS OF INSTITUTION: _____

    DATE ENTERED _____ PER DIEM RATE _____

C. OTHER LIVING ARRANGEMENTS:

    OWN HOME ☐ WHICH IS   ATTACHED ☐ OR DETACHED ☐ AND HAS   ROOMS

    RENTING ACCOMMODATION ☐ WHICH IS   ATTACHED ☐ OR DETACHED ☐ AND HAS _____ ROOMS

    AND   IS HEATED BY APPLICANT ☐   OR HEATED BY OTHER PARTY ☐

    DESCRIBED AS: HOUSE ☐ APARTMENT ☐ FLAT ☐ ROOM(S) ☐

    CONDITION OF PROPERTY: _____

    DETAILS OF EXPENSES: RENT (MONTHLY (M) OR WEEKLY (W)) $

                  MORTGAGE PRINCIPAL AND INTEREST (MONTHLY) $

                  TAXES (MONTHLY) $

                  INSURANCE (MONTHLY) $

                  OTHER (DESCRIBE) $

                  FUEL (ESTIMATE ANNUAL COST) $

    IS PRODUCE DERIVED FROM PROPERTY?   YES ☐   OR   NO ☐

    DETAILS _____

D. SPECIAL DIETS REQUIRED BY BENEFICIARY:

    PREGNANCY SUPPLEMENT (LAST 3 MONTHS) ☐ GASTRIC TYPE ☐ DIABETIC ☐

    OTHER (DESCRIBE AND ATTACH CERTIFICATE OF DULY QUALIFIED MEDICAL PRACTITIONER)

E. LIFE INSURANCE ON LIFE OF APPLICANT (A) OR SPOUSE (S) :

POLICY NUMBER	(A) OR (S)	COMPANY	FACE VALUE	BENEFICIARY	MONTHLY PREMIUMS	PREMIUMS PAID BY

11 INCOME:

A. EARNINGS: IS APPLICANT OR SPOUSE WORKING? YES ☐ NO ☐ GROSS EARNINGS $_____ MO. OR WK.

    IF APPLICANT UNDER SECTION 7 (1) (D) OF THE ACT GIVE NUMBER OF HOURS WORKED PER MONTH _____

    GIVE FULL DETAILS OF TYPE OF EMPLOYMENT, FUTURE PLANS OF APPLICANT AND SPOUSE IN NARRATIVE

B. RENTALS: ROOMERS (R)   BOARDERS (B)   (GIVE AGE IF UNDER 18)

NAME	RELATIONSHIP	(R) OR (B)	AMOUNT	WEEKLY	MONTHLY

WHERE BOARDER UNDER 18 IS CHILD OF APPLICANT OR SPOUSE, GIVE DETAILS OF GROSS INCOME:

C. TYPE OF INCOME

	APPLICANT		SPOUSE	
	DATE COMMENCED	MONTHLY AMOUNT	DATE COMMENCED	MONTHLY AMOUNT
OLD AGE SECURITY				
ANNUITIES, PENSIONS, SUPERANNUATION,				
INSURANCE BENEFIT (PROVIDE DETAILS)				
INCOME FROM FARM OR BUSINESS				
(PROVIDE DETAILS)				
DIVORCE OR SEPARATION ALIMONY				
MAINTENANCE (DESERTING HUSBAND OR				
PUTATIVE FATHER)				
RECEIPTS FROM MORTGAGE, LOAN OR SALES				
AGREEMENT				
TRAINEE ALLOWANCES				
OTHER (PROVIDE DETAILS)				
D. THE PENSION ACT (CANADA)				
UNEMPLOYMENT INSURANCE ACT				
WAR VETERANS ALLOWANCE ACT				
CIVILIAN WAR PENSIONS AND ALLOWANCE ACT				
WORKMEN'S COMPENSATION ACT				
CANADA PENSION PLAN				

E. ANY FUTURE INCOME EXPECTED FROM ANY SOURCE? YES ☐ NO ☐

    IF YES, PROVIDE DETAILS _____

F. MEANS OF SUBSISTENCE OF APPLICANT AND/OR SPOUSE

    PROVIDE DETAILS OF ANY ASSISTANCE PAYMENTS FROM MUNICIPALITIES _____

G. DID APPLICANT OR SPOUSE SERVE IN ALLIED ARMED FORCES? YES ☐ NO ☐

    IF YES, PROVIDE DETAILS _____

PART III - TO BE COMPLETED WHERE APPLICANT HAS A FOSTER CHILD

(12)

A - PARTICULARS OF NATURAL PARENTS

1.

	NAME	MAIDEN NAME	ADDRESS, IF APPLICABLE	MARITAL STATUS	DETAILS OF EMPLOYMENT
MOTHER					
FATHER					

B - PARTICULARS OF FOSTER-MOTHER

2. MARITAL STATUS ☐ SINGLE ☐ MARRIED ☐ WIDOWED ☐ DIVORCED ☐ SEPARATED ☐ DESERTED

3. DATE FOSTER MOTHER ARRIVED IN CANADA _____

4.

DATE CHILDREN TAKEN INTO CARE OF FOSTER-MOTHER:	RELATIONSHIP OF FOSTER-MOTHER TO CHILDREN:	AGE OF FOSTER-MOTHER _____ AGE OF HUSBAND _____
IS FOSTER-MOTHER LIVING IN CHILDREN'S HOME? YES ☐ NO ☐	IF "NO", DESCRIBE ACCOMMODATION:	NO. ROOMS
IS FOSTER-MOTHER EMPLOYED? YES ☐ NO ☐	IF "YES", GIVE HOURS WORK _____ A.M. TO _____ P.M.	IF "YES", WHO CARES FOR CHILDREN IN HER ABSENCE?
HAS PREVIOUS APPLICATION BEEN MADE ON BEHALF OF CHILDREN? YES ☐ NO ☐	IF "YES", BY WHOM?	DATE

DO THESE CHILDREN HAVE ANY BROTHERS OR SISTERS UNDER 18? YES ☐ NO ☐

IF "YES", LIST NAMES AND ADDRESS _____

PART IV

(13) I, _____ DO CERTIFY THAT :

(FULL NAME)

1. I AM THE APPLICANT NAMED IN THE FOREGOING APPLICATION FOR AN ALLOWANCE (OR THE PERSON MAKING APPLICATION ON BEHALF OF THE APPLICANT).

2. ALL THE STATEMENTS IN THE FOREGOING APPLICATION ARE TRUE TO THE BEST OF MY KNOWLEDGE AND BELIEF AND NO INFORMATION REQUIRED TO BE GIVEN HAS BEEN CONCEALED OR OMITTED.

_____
SIGNATURE OF APPLICANT OR AGENT

(14) I CERTIFY THAT I HAVE VISITED THE APPLICANT AND COMPLETED THE APPLICATION IN HIS PRESENCE, THAT THE BENEFITS AND THE APPLICATION FORM HAVE BEEN EXPLAINED TO THE APPLICANT AND THAT I HAVE WITNESSED THE SIGNING OF THIS FORM BY THE APPLICANT OR HIS AGENT.

DATE _____ FIELD WORKER'S SIGNATURE _____ REGIONAL OFFICE NO. _____

(15) SPACE FOR FIELD WORKER TO PROVIDE DETAILS:

(16) THE FOLLOWING FORMS, DOCUMENTS AND CERTIFICATES ARE ATTACHED:

TO FOLLOW _____

80-00-001 (6/71) PAGE 4

233